'Sister, Sister *is the vivid and intimate tale of two person-
able sisters who survive the great European catastrophe.
Anna Rosner Blay interlaces the two accounts—
fascinating, whimsical, robust and horrifying—with her
own remembrance, playing with the unanswerable
question: why were they so grossly imperilled, while I grew
up in safety? In celebrating these two vigorously human
sisters, the author does eloquent honour to all the lost
sisters of history. Many will cherish this book.'*

THOMAS KENEALLY

Sister, Sister

Anna Rosner Blay

Dear Gabi,

All the best,

Anna Rosner Blay

HALE
& IREMONGER

10 9 8 7 6 5 4 3 2 1

Typeset by
Midland Typesetters Pty Ltd,
Maryborough, Victoria 3465

Printed and bound by
Australian Print Group
Maryborough Victoria 3465

For the publisher
Hale & Iremonger Pty Ltd
PO Box 205, Alexandria, NSW 2015

National Library of Australia
Cataloguing-in-Publication entry:

Blay, Anna.
  Sister, sister.

  ISBN 0 86806 647 8.

  1. Rosner, Helena, 1924– . 2. Gross, Joanna, 1914–1994. 3.
  Holocaust, Jewish (1939–1945)–Poland–Biography. 4.
  Holocaust survivors–Australia–Biography. 5. Immigrants
  –Australia–Biography. I. Title.

940.53180922

This project has been assisted by the
Commonwealth Government through the
Australia Council, its art funding and
advisory body.

Foreword

The Holocaust experience has broken the hearts and ravaged the souls of many survivors, and beyond them, those of their children. Today a number of us, the adult children of survivors, are discovering our intimate and unique connections with that tragedy, vaguely sensing the impact of our parents' experiences on our own lives. Obviously, we were not there, we did not have to face first-hand what our parents endured; and yet, in a sense, many of us feel *as if* we were there. How could this be?

Anna Rosner Blay, one of the growing number of second-generation writers, has managed, with an insider's knowledge, to convey the deep continuity of experience linking the generations, from her family's pre-war lives, shattered by the Holocaust, to her own.

In order to make explicit these often subtle undercurrents between the generations, she has had to negotiate a number of barriers. First, she needed to come to terms with her own heart, plumb the depths of her own soul, there to find and mirror her aunt's and her mother's courage, pain and will to survive. Next, she had to retrieve and chronicle that transmitted past, culled from spoken words as well as from her fine attunement to the unspoken signals from the two grieving women. Finally, she had to transform with love and care those collected accounts of fragmented lives into this remarkable book.

Such a feat is itself worthy of praise, but she went further.

Like Eva Hoffman's *Lost in Translation*, Mark Baker's *The Fiftieth Gate* and Anne Karpf's *The War After*, Anna Rosner Blay's *Sister, Sister* is a masterful blend of family history and a deeply personal act of commemoration. By using snippets of autobiography and fleeting, poignant self-references, she has managed to hint at those states of wordless anguish and conflicting emotion that can exist between the generations. One senses the silent inner struggle in her quest for a separate identity, an identity not subdued by and so entangled with the burdened identities of her mother and her aunt. Through all this, Anna Blay has managed to locate and convey her previously unsayable thoughts and experiences; in doing so, she has spoken of feelings shared by so many other members of the second generation.

Against the background of the lottery of life and death endured by her family, Anna Blay makes us subtly but irrefutably aware that the Holocaust is not a thing of the past. In sharing briefly so much of her personal life, she creatively and convincingly charts those elusive links between her aunt's and her mother's past and the different phases in her own life.

She describes feelings and experiences that echo with the past, and daily resonate in her very being: her dread when visiting a doctor, the shivers of anxiety evoked by symbols of war, her nightmares, guilts, her yearnings, her dawning knowledge of what she is not meant to know. Each echo is transported across the barriers of time and space, transmitted from one generation to the next, to the daughter who, with the immediacy and intensity of personal ownership, relives them as if part of her own past.

A gentle, lucid and keenly observant writer, Anna Rosner Blay has brought her deep sense of family commitment and commemorative instinct to add this vital personal dimension to the solemn subject of her family's history. The descriptions are imbued with a deceptive simplicity, yet they yield penetrating insights into the transmission of parents' experiences to the second generation. This process, skilfully captured in her book, located somewhere between literature and psychology, has been described as the phenomenon of transposition.

Professor Judith Kestenberg, the noted authority on the

psychological impact of the Holocaust on child survivors and their children, has used the term to denote this unique form of transmission across the generations. Specifically, it refers to the process by which children of survivors experience aspects of their lives, including some symptoms at clinical levels of intensity, severity or duration, as if they had themselves lived through the Holocaust—a feeling of 'it happened to me'.

Through the pages of this moving book, we observe Anna in the process of gradually untangling her entwined self, almost an act of self-redemption. This hard-earned freedom from the unknowns of her childhood, transformed from fleeting recognitions into words and eventually into the precious sentences which convey the essence of her struggle, fills us with inspiration and hope as she comes to terms with her family's previously unbearable past.

So, out of the despair and blackness there emerges a growing sense of celebration; of a family, having run the gauntlet of the bestiality of Nazism and beyond, sustained by faith, surviving, bearing witness. The aunt and the mother—sister, sister—celebrate the beginning of a new life, the birth of a son and daughter, a daughter whose legacy it will be to chronicle the fragments of a culture, a way of life, and the God-given resilience shown by members of her family who, despite the odds, triumphed over the atrocities that confronted them.

Miraculously, they resumed their lives, rebuilt their homes and, through hard work, secured a future. Such lives are lived by a few, remarkable people. A generation later, the story is retold by a survivor's child who, in telling it with such courage and grace, produces a work that also verges on the miraculous.

Dr George Halasz
Melbourne, 1998

Prologue

I carefully collect the details of the stories, and as I arrange and weave them together the random threads begin to form a design. The cloth is intricately woven, with recurrent patterns emerging. But when I go to spread it out before me, like a delicately crocheted tablecloth, I see it is full of spaces. These are blanks that can never be told, can never be put into words. Or even if words are found they can only be approximate, providing a pale suggestion of what really occurred hour after hour, in the days and years of those born before me.

We, the second generation of Holocaust survivors, can never look directly at the horror but only at the messages reflected in the pain of our parents' eyes. And all we can do is attempt to record, as clearly as possible, what life was like for them as the children and adults we never knew.

This is a very personal and in a sense private book, in that it looks at two sisters' lives from the inside. They lived through an extraordinary period in history, one which has been well documented but usually, it seems to me, by men, from a male point of view. Here is the story of two women, representing countless others who struggled for survival, yet very special to me because of their influence on my formative years and beyond.

In my childhood, when others spoke of grandparents, great-aunts and great-uncles, I was aware that I had none of my own. There was silence, a dark hole, an emptiness that made me ache. The war years were a horrifying and unspeakable period of which I was vaguely aware, but I knew no details. I didn't ask, and they didn't tell. Like so many other children of survivors, I had been protected from horrendous experiences and a treacherous world. Naively, I believed my history started with me.

As I grew older the realisation gradually dawned that I knew almost nothing about my past. A curiosity and hunger grew within me to know more about my roots and my ancestors, and eventually I found myself embarking on this book. As I began to hear certain names repeated, as I made links between different stories, a whole lost world of people started to emerge: vital, real, occupying the spaces that once had seemed so empty. I began to have a sense of who I am and where I came from.

There was another reason why the book was commenced: my aunt, my mother's older sister, wanted to tell me about her past after almost fifty years of silence. Some parents talked incessantly to their children about their experiences; we lived with a wall of secrecy. Soon after my aunt started talking to me I became aware of how many of her experiences were shared with my mother. These two women had been bonded in such a close way throughout their lives that it was impossible to write of one without the other. Each of them spoke to me over many months, sometimes in English, sometimes in Polish. At different times I sat in their kitchens with my tape-recorder going, letting each of them tell fragments of their stories which I then transcribed and rearranged. Or else I would walk with my mother in the park near her house, a small notepad and pen clutched in my hand so I could record what she told me. These notes and tapes became the seeds of my book. I did not intend it to be a historical document, though it speaks of things that really happened. As far as possible I stayed faithful to their accounts and confirmed the details, though at times I had to imaginatively enter realms for which they had no words.

As I listened to the recollections of my mother and my aunt from childhood, from the war and from their early years as migrants in Australia, I was struck not only by the similarities of their stories but also by the curious way memory works in selecting and storing what is personally significant, so that the same event may have quite different interpretations. Some memories may not accord exactly with historical fact, but this is a reflection of how memory works. I was delighted and horrified in turn by the clarity of detail and remembrance of tiny incidents which in themselves might seem trivial but, seen as a whole, create a rich and powerful tapestry.

The third motivation to persevere with the book was the sudden death of my aunt. Although she was nearly eighty and had led a rich and fulfilling life, her loss was nevertheless a shock to all of us and we are still grieving. Thus I felt an increasing urgency to complete the task, to document her life and her stories about the past, for those who come after. This book is not written for those who were there; they don't need to be reminded. It is for their sons and daughters, and their sons and daughters, and their sons and daughters . . .

It is also for my mother, who feels that a part of herself has been cut off with her sister's death. The boundless love between my mother and me is beyond words. I have written this account to comfort and reassure her that neither of them will ever be forgotten.

∽

The scent of the tightly curled buds of daphne in my mother's hands overpowers all the others. I hold her arm as we make our way, slowly, along the gravel paths. Her steps are small, but determined. When we reach the grave she takes the home-grown flowers that she picked this morning, one by one, out of the basket, and inserts them with shaking hands into the earth.

It's been two months since her sister Janka died. A rough wooden sign with her name stencilled on it has been pushed into the dirt. It's not yet time to make a granite headstone; the period of mourning will continue. My mother slowly covers the cold earth with colour, the fresh flowers concealing the faded ones from the week before. The petals are vibrant in the weak rays of the winter sun and the scent of the daphne sprigs lingers over us. My mother gives back to her sister the flowers she loved so much all her life.

The tears keep falling. 'She must be so cold!' she mutters. And then she sobs, 'My life is so empty without her!' I put my arms around my mother and hold her trembling shoulders. There's nothing I can say to make the pain go away.

1

Janka: You know, I do believe in miracles. I am grateful for each new day, for a long warm shower, for a thriving green plant full of buds, for a beautiful sunset. I can find joy in the most unlikely places and still be surprised by the obvious.

Yet I can never take comfort and security for granted. The memories of times when these things were brutally taken from us are always present, trembling just below the surface. I have had many years to lay these memories to rest, but it's not true what they say about time healing all wounds. The years may have allowed the memories to surface less often perhaps, but they haven't blunted the pain. It still shoots through me, intense as ever, in the middle of the night when I can't sleep. It still invades my dreams and keeps reminding me that behind the facade and the illusion of comfort lies the randomness of evil, with the possibility of annihilation at any moment.

And yet, as I start to reminisce, sweet, long-forgotten memories of how good life can be come flooding back. I see the eyes and faces of the members of my family, those gone forever, and those still close to me.

I had one brother, Kuba (Jakob), and one sister, Hela (Helena), both younger than me. My sister and I, despite the difference in our ages (I am ten years older), or maybe because of it, have been very close all our lives. When we were girls Hela was like a flower that had opened too early, its fragile petals still crumpled and sheltered from the ways of the world. But she also had the strength to persist in harsh times, and to continue to flourish even in a storm.

We shared our most intimate moments, our most crushing

griefs, our days of unrelieved terror. We also shared the joys of creating new life, of carving out homes in a strange country, of watching our friends grow old with us. Our stories are intertwined, flowing side by side, to this very day. In an era when so many relatives perished, our sense of loyalty and love for each other triumphed over all attempts to divide us.

Hela: My sister, Janka, was always like a mother to me, from the time that we lost our own mother. I have always turned to her for advice, for approval, or just to cry on her shoulder when things get too hard. Not a day goes by when one of us doesn't ring the other, sometimes two or three times, to share the little trivialities, to check on gossip, to complain about minor annoyances. We discuss grandchildren, or a friend's party, or a film we've just seen. She, more than any friend, more even than a husband, understands how life treats those who are sensitive, and how old memories can bond as nothing else can.

Janka: Our maternal grandmother, Rozalia (Rózia) Weitzenblum, lived on a farm in the countryside. When I was young, she always sent us produce from the farm, like fresh cream and butter. Most of her family lived in the country, near the border of Poland and Czechoslovakia. She had three brothers and five sisters. Our extended family was very large, and they were similar to us, familiar with Polish culture and living a fairly assimilated life. My family kept their own Jewish culture and customs, but also had deep local roots.

Mother's father, Herman (Hersch) Weitzenblum, was a very good person; too good, some said. He was naive. Whenever he had some money, he used to lend it. He came from the Russian–Austrian border, where there were people who were 'financiers'. He would lend them money, without documents or security. When the First World War broke out, they left this border area and took all his money with them. All that remained was a book, and in it were written all the sums that people owed him, but he never recovered his money.

Yet he was a happy person and had a great sense of humour. They had a servant and a boy to look after the cows. Our grandmother Rózia worked hard, but she had a comfortable life. When grandfather Hersch was doing his military service, he refused to eat non-kosher food, but lived on bread and water. His death in 1919 of stomach cancer was attributed to this. After he died, grandmother came to live with us.

There wasn't such blatant anti-Semitism in the countryside as in the cities. The Jews in the country were very much like all the other peasants, and they wore the same clothes. They were not like the Chassidim who lived separately in Kraków, in the Kazimierz district. There they wore black coats and black hats, and kept themselves separate from the others, from the *Polaki*. But our family were country people and they made few distinctions, except that they went three times a year to synagogue. They always performed ritual circumcisions on newborn boys, and kept kosher kitchens: they only bought meat that had been ritually killed by a Jew, and kept their milk separate from their meat. (There was a Jew whose job it was to observe the milking of the cows, to see that it was kosher.) Otherwise, their lives were very similar to the Poles'.

Although she came from peasant stock, mother was a well-educated woman. Her Hebrew name was Chana, but she was known as Andzia Weitzenblum. (It was customary for Jews to be given a Hebrew name at birth, but they were often known by a more commonly used name.) She was born in February 1892, in Modlnica, a village in southern Poland. Before marrying, she boarded with her cousins in nearby Kraków, paid for by her mother, and went to a private *gimnazjum* (secondary school) there. She studied Greek, Latin, German and Polish literature. Later she went to a special school for a year to learn housekeeping and sewing. She was seventeen when she and father met.

I loved him very much. His name was David Leib

Haubenstock (known as Daniel Weiss), and he was born on 28 October 1886 in Kobylany, another village in that part of Poland. Father also went to a *gimnazjum*, and loved learning. He continued studying all of his life. At school he was aware of anti-Semitism. When he was called up to write on the blackboard, the other students used to taunt him, saying that his father bought human flesh and sold it; he was always made aware that he was a Jew.

As a young man, father lived in a country town and came riding in to Kraków on a big white horse. It was love at first sight, or so mother told us; she was a real romantic. They were engaged for quite some time, but continued to address each other by the formal *pani* and *pan*. He wrote her many love letters and verses, always showing her great respect and honour. When they went at last to buy an engagement ring, they walked around Kraków all day, examining the wares in every jeweller's shop. Chana was too embarrassed to admit that she needed to go to the toilet, and held on for so long that eventually she fainted. All through their betrothal, they were very proper; they never met without a chaperone, and Daniel never even held her by the arm until their wedding day.

They were married on 13 January 1914 in Modlnica, and after the wedding night he assured all his friends, as was the custom, that she was a virgin. They rented an apartment in a fairly prosperous district of Kraków.

Father was a merchant, running a big delicatessen shop in Kraków during the 'twenties and 'thirties. It was a family business, with several family members helping to run it. During this time our life was fairly middle-class and comfortable.

Hela: We lived a warm and close family life in pre-war Poland, and were united by many shared experiences. Yet memory has a way of being very individual, and as I scan through the years, the images I pause at or reflect on are not necessarily the same as Janka's. She tries to see the good in everyone, and is much more tolerant than I am.

I was born in Kraków on 31 July 1924. Janka was born ten years before me, on 28 November 1914, and our brother Kuba on 29 January 1916. Janka was beautiful, with dark flowing hair and high sculptured cheekbones. She always enjoyed life, and loved flirting and being sociable. I admired her greatly. Kuba was another story.

Mother didn't plan her third pregnancy, and I was not really wanted. When I was young she confessed to me that when she found she was pregnant she decided to have an abortion. On her way to see the old woman who looked after these things, she met her cousin, a dentist, on the road. When he questioned her she told him where she was going. 'Andzia, don't do it,' he pleaded, and reminded her of the sanctity of life. She realised she couldn't go through with it, so she turned round and went home again.

Janka: Salomon Weiss, our paternal grandfather, was born in a town called Chrzanów, about forty kilometres west of Kraków. Jewish communities had existed in Poland for centuries—although from 1795 to 1918 Poland did not exist as such; it was divided among Prussia, Austria and Russia. I remember Salomon's father, our great-grandfather, as an energetic and lively man. He walked all the way from Chrzanów to Kraków once, when he couldn't find transport. He was full of life, but was also a strict authoritarian. All the children were afraid of him. A cousin of father's happened to be smoking one Saturday, when great-grandfather walked through the door. The cousin panicked and hid the cigarette behind grandmother, which burnt her apron. He got into double trouble! Great-grandfather died at ninety-seven, still full of life.

Grandfather Salomon lived most of his life in Chrzanów and worked as a merchant. He was an educated and cultured man with a white beard, and was interested in reading, especially history and metaphysics. He often wrote articles that were published in Polish newspapers.

Salomon's wife, Ester Jachet Haubenstock (known as Joasia), our paternal grandmother, was two years older than her husband. Father's parents had a religious wedding, but not a civil one, so their marriage wasn't recognised by the Austrian authorities. Thus father was named after his mother's family, Haubenstock, and we, the children, were given the same surname. Originally there were two brothers called Haubenstock, who came from Spain via Germany to Poland and settled in Chrzanów.

Joasia ran the local pub and was a very hard worker. She was small and slim, but if someone was drunk or rude she knew how to slap him and throw him out. She was a very courageous woman. The family were not very religious for those times. They ate kosher food at home because of tradition rather than belief, but occasionally ate ham. They went to synagogue three times a year, when Joasia would wear a beautiful black wig (it was the custom for married women to conceal their hair) and a fine lacy shawl over it. Her husband wore only a small beard, with no sidelocks.

Joasia had a hard life. Once, when she was pregnant, she had to go to the cellar to fetch coal. She bent over to pick up the heavy load and crushed the unborn baby. Another time, when her younger sister Karola caught typhus, Joasia left her family, the youngest of whom was only three months old, and went to nurse her sister. After several weeks she became infected herself and died. She died very young, aged thirty-six, leaving a husband and eight children. Grandfather Salomon was devastated and never remarried. I was named after her in my Hebrew name, Ester Jachet.

I dream I am in a large stadium, surrounded by several levels crowded with people. I'm clutching a handful of coloured balloons and scanning the faces in the crowd. Eventually I recognise a woman not too far away. She has dark wavy hair and solemn eyes. She sees me and waves. I want to give her a balloon, but as I start to move towards her I notice that the floor I'm standing on has a slant to it and I begin to slide. I try to scrabble forward, but the floor is shifting beneath me and I am moving further away from her. I wave the balloons at her and call out 'Goodbye!' as I let them go. But instead of floating towards her, they drift away, higher and higher. I am overcome by grief.

Janka: It was I who decided on my sister's name. Grandfather Salomon had a sister with two daughters, one of whom wasn't talked about much; she was the younger daughter and the black sheep of the family. Her name in Yiddish was Sure Perl, but she was known as Helena.

It was customary at the time to employ a young tutor, a *belfer*, to teach Jewish studies to the children. He would visit all the Jewish homes to teach the children how to read and write in Hebrew. When our grandmother Joasia died from typhus, Helena was sixteen or seventeen. After Joasia's death, Helena's parents went away for a short time to stay with grandfather, and left Helena alone. This *belfer*, who was about eighteen, came to visit and, young people being what they are, she became pregnant. There was a dreadful scandal. In those days it was something terribly shameful.

The two children (for that's all they were) were forced to marry quickly and were sent away to America, to New York, to live with an uncle there. He couldn't look after them for long. They were still very young, with a baby, and life was a struggle. They lived in poverty and hardship. Then a second child was born, but Helena was reluctant to ask for help from father's two brothers who lived there because she was so ashamed of what had happened. She and her husband could not find work and had nowhere to sleep. He died, and not too long after so did Helena.

Afterwards the family always used to warn everyone of the dangers of leaving a young girl alone with a boy. When my sister was born, mother wanted to call her Dora, but I really didn't like that name and wanted her to be named Helena, after grandfather's niece. People said, you can't name a child after a girl who conceived a baby out of wedlock, it's too scandalous; but I won and my sister was named Helena.

Hela: Kraków was a beautiful town, and for centuries it was the capital of Poland. It spanned the river Vistula, at the foot of the Tatra mountains, and was dominated by Wawel Castle, high on a hill overlooking the town. Many Polish kings had lived here. Our home was in Niecała street, but the name was later changed to Zamenhof, after the inventor of Esperanto. We lived on the second floor in a big apartment: two large rooms and a kitchen. It was around the corner from father's grocery shop, on Radziwiłowska street. Our apartment block, like so many others, was a tall brick building around a gloomy paved courtyard, reached by an arched entrance from the street. Every tenant had a part of the attic portioned off, in which to hang clothes, store dishes for *Pesach* (Passover), and keep all sorts of things that were not needed every day. In winter it was so cold up there that the washing would be frozen stiff when the maid went to bring it down. Women had to take it in turns to use the space to hang their washing, as there was not enough room for all of us at once. I loved following my mother up to the attic, when she climbed the stairs on rare occasions to rummage in wooden trunks and cases for a particular dish or an old tablecloth.

The cellar, however, was a different story. I was frightened to go down into its darkness: it always smelled damp and echoed with rustling sounds in the corners. Here were stored coal and wood, as well as potatoes and carrots throughout the winter, as no fresh vegetables could grow when the ground was covered with snow. Down here we also kept large wooden barrels of pickled cabbage that had been prepared by men stamping with bare feet on the cabbage leaves before adding small white Vanetti apples that would give a delicious flavour. Our part of the cellar was divided from other sections by wooden partitions and kept padlocked to prevent one neighbour stealing coal from another, because coal was very expensive.

In the kitchen we had a cast-iron stove fed with coal for cooking, while in the bedrooms there were tall ceramic-tiled stoves, from floor to ceiling, which had to be regularly filled with coal to provide heating. Every morning the cold ashes from the stove had to be removed and a fresh fire lit. Our maid, Hanka, was kept busy all day. She had to scrub the floors regularly with two buckets, one of soapy water and the other filled with clean water. She and mother were occupied in managing the household with the countless tasks that were necessary to keep things running smoothly, and in looking after us children.

We always had a maid and also a woman, Maryna, who came in to help with the laundry once every six weeks. Bed linen was changed only then, and it took three days to soak, boil, starch, dry and iron everything. We used a white starched tablecloth for every meal.

There was no bathroom, so we washed daily in a bowl in the kitchen. But once a week the maid brought up a zinc bathtub from the cellar and filled it with water heated on the stove. This was where all of us were washed in turn, in the same water. Being the youngest, my turn came last. The tub was quite heavy and it was a big job to fill and empty it. The toilet out in the corridor was shared by three families and had a cistern that was emptied by pulling a chain.

Our kitchen was white and very large, and there was a curtained-off alcove with a fold-out bed where Hanka slept. It was always warm in there, with the smells of cooking and steam billowing around the high ceiling. The wooden benches had to be scrubbed clean daily. We kept kosher at home, separating milk and meat, although father worked in the shop on Saturday, the Sabbath. Water had to be fetched in a bowl from the outside pump, and heated to wash the dishes. The kitchen was the centre of activity in the house.

Our pantry was full of food. On the shelves there was chicken fat, melted and solidified into jars, as well as pickled cucumbers and glass bottles of home-made raspberry or blackberry juice. There was also a locked storage cupboard in the corridor outside the door to our apartment. On its shelves were kept jars of preserved fruit such as raspberries and little black *borówki* (bilberries). These grew in the forest, and we collected them in summer when they were ripe. For days the kitchen was fragrant with the heady smell of warm berries. (The juice of the *borówki* was known to be helpful for diarrhoea.) On one occasion my mother was very angry because the cupboard had been broken into and all our supplies for that season stolen.

In a corner of the kitchen, pickled beetroots were kept in a small barrel covered with a cloth, to make borscht. When I was very small I once saw a cat fall into the barrel of beetroots. When the borscht was served at *Pesach*, no one could understand why I didn't want to eat it and kept crying about a pussycat in the soup!

We couldn't buy ready-made produce but had to make it ourselves. Jam was a luxury; often people could not make jam because, even if they had the fruit, they could not afford the sugar they needed. Strawberries were cheap and plentiful but sugar was expensive. Somehow we were not that poor and could afford the sugar for jam. Strawberry jam was made by dipping fragrant strawberries, one by one, into alcohol to dry them. They were then boiled with beet sugar, bought in a tall solid cone from which we broke pieces as we needed them.

Father made his own wine, from grapes fermented with sugar. Nothing tasted as delicious as this sweet wine, which the children were allowed to taste only on *Pesach* or other special occasions. We baked our own *challah* (egg loaf) every Friday, although we did buy bread during the week. There was a bakery nearby that baked fresh bread three times a day. They sold lovely Kaiser rolls and round floured rolls and loaves dusted with caraway seeds. There were also bagels called *obwarzanki* and crescent-shaped *rożki*. I was so spoilt that I refused to eat a roll in the evening if it had been bought that morning; I wanted it to be fresh. But I wasn't always so fussy. I used to go with the maid to the garrison nearby, where we'd attract the attention of one of the soldiers. The arrangement was that we would give him a bag of white rolls through the railing, in return for a loaf of *komiśniak*, a heavy black bread full of grains. I can still feel the taste of it in my mouth, spread thickly with fresh unsalted butter! We baked our own cakes, except when the children were allowed to buy little cakes as a treat.

Our rooms were large but seemed cluttered with various pieces of furniture. The walls had a stencilled design of yellow bananas at eye level, and the floors were bare, except for some small rugs. When I was very little I slept in one of the rooms with our parents in their wide bed, while Janka slept on a sofa in the same room. I was reassured to hear the sounds of quiet breathing in the night. The beds were arranged around the sides of the room, with a large ceramic stove giving off heat in one corner and the large wooden table where we ate all our meals occupying the centre. There was a small crystal radio on a little table in another corner that father liked to listen to. Halinka Roth, who lived on the floor above us, came from a rich family and had a much larger radio than ours. I was always envious of her.

The table and wardrobes were made of pale unpolished birchwood and had to be regularly scrubbed with soap and water. The wrought-iron beds were covered with heavy velvet bedspreads. I was fascinated by the screwed-on brass balls that topped the brass bars on the bedheads. I once swallowed one of these balls, but with no ill effects.

Mother's mother, Rozalia, lived with us. Grandfather Hersch had died before I was born and grandmother was always dressed in black. She was very tidy and very clean. She slept in the second of our two rooms, in a high bed covered in feather quilts and a red plush bedspread. Sometimes I was allowed to climb into her bed, but it was too high and I felt afraid. She had her own candlesticks and lit the candles every Friday night, as did mother.

When I was older I slept with her, while Kuba slept in our parents' room. There was even a short time when mother's younger brother lived with us, and also shared grandmother's room. When she died, at the age of sixty-four, mother was very distressed, walking up and down the corridor, wringing her hands and sobbing. Father tried to comfort her. I was only four years old and was not taken to the funeral. I loved my grandmother, but I didn't really understand what had happened.

∾

I sit in the corner of my cot, which has been pushed to one side of the room. The cramped room serves as kitchen, living area and bedroom for my parents and me. I hear the sounds of the adults talking in whispers. My world is made up of the sense impressions around me. It is cold in the small apartment, and cooking smells linger in the corner. There are loud sounds of traffic coming from the grimy Paris street below the second-floor window, but the voices are still audible, if subdued. The adults don't want me to hear, even though I am too young to understand.

It is two years since the war ended. I look from one face to another, scanning their expressions, watching as the words flow between them. I see my father's furrowed brow and clenched jaw. My mother bites her lips as her fingers clasp and unclasp. My aunt turns from one to the other, her hands making little irresolute movements in the air, then turns to my uncle, who sits very still on a chair near the table. The tension vibrates in the corners of the room and flows down from the ceiling.

My mother's voice begins to quaver and her eyes fill with tears, so she turns to the window to hide from the others. She has to be strong. Showing emotion is a sign of weakness. Displaying weakness is dangerous. Bad feelings also upset other people; better to suppress them.

My father's voice is always the loudest; it has a rich vibrancy that can be mellow and full of laughter, but it can also terrify with its anger. Short, sharp sentences are now erupting from him, filled with explosive emotion. He has no trouble expressing his feelings, and is easily irritated. My mother, still with her back turned, cannot prevent her shoulders from trembling.

My aunt's voice is gentle, cooing like a pigeon's, flowing over the others in a pacifying, soothing way, trying to heal the rift. She

24

has sunshine in her voice. A calm strong bass line underlines the other sounds. My uncle doesn't speak much, but when he does the others stop to listen. His words come clearly and slowly. There are silent pauses of pain.

My aunt now comes close to my mother and places her hand gently on her shoulder. They exchange looks. My aunt lifts a strand of hair from my mother's face and gently strokes her forehead. Weak sunlight filters in through the window and rests on their dark hair, their cheekbones. The men are silent. I feel the emotions, vibrating and pulsing around me. I sense their anxiety and their grief. I feel the weight of their memories pressing in, haunting, tormenting. I observe a look, a gesture, a sigh. I also sense the tremulous efforts to begin a new life, the fragile joys and simple pleasures of daily living that are so precious to them. The two sisters turn back to the room, then continue speaking to each other quietly. They are preoccupied with their own anguish. I construct my own fantasies.

2

Hela: I have mixed memories of my childhood; there were always times of struggle, because we didn't have enough money. Our father wanted the best for us but never managed to be financially secure. Father had wanted me to be a boy, and I had my hair cut short until I was five or six. I think I was a big disappointment to him.

Because we were Jewish I always felt inferior to others, even though there had been Jewish communities in Poland for 850 years. I was much more conscious of being Jewish than Janka was. I knew the Poles looked down on us. We were surrounded by Catholics, and I always heard Catholic prayers and Christmas carols around me. The Church actively promoted anti-Semitism and reinforced primitive beliefs that Jews had killed Christ. The town was full of churches, and many stalls sold golden icons of solemn saints with Byzantine faces, and statuettes of Jesus and Mary. People crossed themselves whenever they passed a church, and even knelt outside the church when it was too crowded inside during a service. There were frequent processions where people in elaborate robes carried a statue down the street, singing and praying. We tried not to be too different, not to attract attention to ourselves. A common ritual greeting was to praise the name of Jesus Christ, and the traditional reply was 'For ever and ever'. If you didn't say these words it was considered very offensive. This was very embarrassing for us Jews. It was the same with the songs and hymns that were sung before Christmas and Easter.

The large church hall is dusty and dim. The light coming in through the narrow windows catches floating specks of dust but doesn't reach the draughty corners. There are old mattresses in one corner, and a box of half-broken toys nearby. We fill in our days by playing with plasticine and learning nursery rhymes. But the highlight of the week is when the local priest comes to visit the kindergarten and to ask if we've been good. He is thin and tall, with bony fingers. He talks in a solemn voice about heaven and hell, but I don't understand most of what he says. I have learnt that he has lollies hidden in his pockets, which he distributes as rewards to those who have been good. The same ritual is followed each week. We sit in rows on the bare wooden floor, our legs crossed in front of us and our hands folded in our laps. Those who call out or wriggle do not get chosen. We must sit very still, with our eyes closed, showing how good we can be, and the tall priest walks between the rows giving out rewards to those he favours.

Week after week I fervently clasp my hands in front of me and sit ever so still, but I never get picked to receive a lolly. I soon learn that justice is random, and being good is not always rewarded.

Hela: We were not extremely observant Jews, but we went as a family to synagogue for the High Holydays. We lit the candles on Friday night, but didn't observe the rules against travelling and working on the Sabbath. Father covered his head only when he prayed. We kept a kosher kitchen, but outside the house I was sometimes given ham to eat, and occasionally the maid secretly brought some ham wrapped in paper into the kitchen via the back door.

Janka: We spoke Polish at home, though sometimes our parents spoke German when they didn't want us to understand, but that was very seldom. Father could write and speak fluently in Yiddish but he didn't use it at home. Mother was born in the Polish countryside and her family never spoke Yiddish at home, so she couldn't speak it.

Our family had very friendly relations with non-Jews. We lived in a Polish suburb and all our neighbours were Poles.

We did not belong to any Jewish cultural or political organisations, as father did not approve of joining such groups. He was very patriotic, and loved Polish literature.

We socialised and mixed well with everyone, just as I did at school. There were about ten Jewish girls in a class of thirty or forty. Our parents did not want us to attend a religious Jewish school so I went to a private secular school nearby. We only had one or two hours of religious study a week. Later I completed my education at the *Wyższa Szkoła Handlowa*, the School of Commerce, and began to work in an accountant's office.

Hela: I always had an awareness that I was different. I was a very protected child and had very little contact with other children. I was shy and sensitive, and didn't go to school until I was seven. Janka and Kuba treated me as a baby. Janka hated it when mother bought the same material for our dresses. She often appeared to have secrets with mother, and seldom included me. I always thought they were whispering about me. When Janka was in high school she had a lot of girlfriends, and mother used to tell her to involve me and take me along with her on their picnics and outings, but she resented it. Her girlfriends were much older than I was, and they would whisper and giggle, excluding me. In fact I felt very lonely. My secret wish was that I could be grown up soon.

Janka: When I was a girl, I had to go to hospital for a small operation and was told not to eat for a day beforehand. That day my menstrual period started. In the bed beside me lay a girl who told me that if my period had started I may as well eat, because they wouldn't be able to operate. So, being hungry, I began to eat. I wrote a letter to my parents, but I didn't want to write the Polish word for 'menstruation' or 'period' because I was afraid the postman would read it. So I wrote the word in German, *Monatliche*, which he wouldn't understand. At that time it was not something you spoke about, it was a big secret when a girl had her period.

When the doctor arrived he was very annoyed because he had planned to do the operation then. I had to lie there in the hospital for three or four more days before I could have the operation. After I returned home and started going to school again, which was about twenty minutes' walk from home, our maid had to carry my books. I was excused from doing gymnastics for the rest of my time at school, which wasn't such a good thing. I was very spoilt.

Hela: When Janka was in hospital to have her appendix out, I wasn't allowed to visit her. Hospitals were terrifying places for me. I used to cross the road to avoid passing next to one.

At seven I started to go to a Catholic school, St Scholastica, where prayers were a part of the everyday routine. Our school building was elegant, and our classroom had wooden panels and a polished floor. Whenever we were indoors we had to wear felt slippers over our shoes, or slippers brought from home, to protect the floors. This was said to be a modern school, as we had tables and chairs instead of long wooden benches.

On the first day of school I saw that the others regularly made special movements with their hands in front of their bodies, and I tried to copy them crossing themselves. When I came home and showed mother what I'd learnt, she forbade me to do it.

My classmates made fun of me, calling me a little Jew-girl. This continued for the whole time I was there and it was always hurtful. We learnt about the Crucifixion and the Resurrection. I had to pray, but was permitted not to cross myself. During catechism the Jewish children went out of the class and had their own religious instruction with a small Jewish man, Dodeles, who used to take little girls on his knee. His lessons consisted of Jewish history and festivals, but there was not much emphasis on religious observance. He spoke to us in Polish not Yiddish.

At school we learn how to read and write Hebrew. I receive colourful postage stamps for my fluent reading, though I don't understand what I read and we never actually speak the language. We also learn Bible stories, looking at large coloured pictures of the garden of Eden, or Noah and his animals, and we hear about God. But my favourite classes are art and craft.

We are allowed to draw for half an hour before lunch and I love using my set of twelve coloured pencils. But I learn quite soon what I may or may not draw. One day I do an elaborate picture of a house surrounded by flowers, birds flying above, and right at the top, encircled by blue sky, God sitting on a chair. My teacher is horrified when she sees it, and patiently explains that we are not allowed to draw God.

'But you told us God is in heaven. Isn't heaven up in the sky?' I ask, puzzled.

'Yes, but we don't know what He looks like, so we're not allowed to draw Him,' she finishes in a patronising tone. 'Just choose something else to draw.'

Hela: At the beginning when I started school, all the girls seemed so strange to me that I found it hard to talk to them. I had never mixed with other children while I lived at home. There were only two other Jewish girls in my class, and maybe fifteen in the whole school. I never really had a close friend. Only later did I make friends with a Catholic girl; sometimes I went to her house, but I always felt a stranger there. At school I continued to feel like an outsider. Once I was asked, along with the other Jewish girls, to join a Zionist youth organisation, but father was cross and refused to consider the idea. He never allowed me to go to any camps or holiday colonies.

We went to school till two o'clock, including Saturdays. When we got home the main meal of the day was eaten—soup, meat and potatoes. We sat at the dining table, covered with a starched white tablecloth, and used silver cutlery. Father would close the shop for an hour and come home to eat. He even found time to stretch out on the sofa and have a sleep, still with his shoes on, before going back to open up the shop for the afternoon.

On very cold days when the ground was covered in ice, mother was afraid I'd catch cold so she would order the maid to wrap me in a warm rug and carry me to school! We wore traditional uniforms: in summer a white blouse with a sailor collar trimmed with a navy-blue stripe and a navy skirt, and in winter a loose navy shirt and woollen skirt. I brought lunch from home, usually a white roll with cheese or occasionally ham. Sometimes I swapped lunches with the poorer girls, who had dark heavy bread and envied my white rolls.

One thing that I hated was the daily line-up at recess. The teacher stood with a large bottle beside her and a metal spoon, and one by one we had to come forward for our dose of cod-liver oil—it was awful! But often I was given 20 groszy to buy a cake or an ice-cream after school.

Although I was a curious child and loved learning, I did not like school. The teachers were all female, with harsh voices and hair tightly pulled back. Discipline was very strict, and there was no calling out—we had to put our hands up with two fingers pointing upward, and often we had to hold them up for ages. I was frightened of being called out to the blackboard and being made fun of. At recess we remained indoors, as there was no outside area to play in. We had to walk along the corridors in pairs, and the only bright spot in the week was our exercise class in the gymnasium. Here there were lots of ropes and wooden horses, and we could let off some steam, do somersaults and generally use up our energy. The rest of the week was very sombre.

Just before Easter all the other children would paint eggs. Mother let me do it too, so that I wouldn't feel left out. Carefully I decorated the eggs in bright colours, put them into a little basket, and went to the church with the other children to bless the eggs. But when they sang songs for Easter about Jesus and the blood from his body, they would all turn to stare at me, and I felt the colour burning in my cheeks. In May there was a parade in which all the townspeople followed a statue of Mary that was held up high, and sang religious songs, so I joined them; I didn't want to be left out and feel sad. On St Nicholas's day, 6 December, we had gifts placed under our pillows, but we also lit the candles for *Chanukah*. At Christmas time I learnt the words to all the carols, and still remember them now, word for word. One year we had a little tree that mother bought for us to decorate. I was excited, and hung baubles and tinsel all over it. But when father came home he became angry and told us to throw the tree out. It didn't happen again. After that I helped one of our neighbours decorate their tree instead.

Janka: There was a big Jewish community in Kraków, and I'm told there were Jewish youth movements in existence at that time, but I was not aware of them. Our family obviously were not Orthodox, though they followed the traditional observances. We went to synagogue only for the Day of Atonement and the Jewish New Year. At Passover we had a traditional *seder*, a ritual dinner with all the special customs. The whole family sat around the table, including mother's brothers, and her mother while she was alive. Father wore a *kittel*, a white garment embroidered with gold, and sat leaning on pillows arranged on his left, as was customary. It was a very exciting time of the year, especially for the children. Being the youngest, Hela was the one who recited the *Ma Nishtanah*, the traditional four questions.

Hela: We had beautiful dishes and silverware that were kept in the attic to be brought out only once a year for *Pesach*. There were crystal glasses and silver trays, which reflected the glowing candles burning in the heavy silver candelabras. Even for meals during the rest of the year, we used silver cutlery and fine glasses in silver holders for tea. Mother's dowry had provided her with wonderful linen and embroidered tablecloths, so we were always surrounded by beautiful things.

Mother was not tall, and tended to be overweight due to her love of cream and cakes. She knew nothing of cholesterol; she was an excellent pastrycook and made rich cheesecakes and fruit tarts and sweet chocolate tortes, using vast amounts of butter and eggs. She loved all sweet things and did not follow a very healthy diet. One of her weaknesses was chocolate, which she relished and consumed in large quantities.

But mother was not a happy woman. She had sad eyes that gazed out from a heart-shaped face, and her thick auburn hair was pulled back loosely in a bun. Although only in her early forties when I was growing up, she saw herself as an old woman. She never took care of herself, had never been to a hairdresser in her life, and used no cosmetics. Her dressing-table was bare except for a lace doily and a silver-backed brush and comb. She was very different from women like Mila Rosner, who used to come into father's shop: she was full of energy and passion, and dressed elegantly. Mother, on the other hand, always dressed in brown or grey. Her dresses were drab and shapeless, never flattering—or maybe they just concealed her lumpy figure. Her jewellery was discreet; just a wedding-band, and occasionally a red coral necklace. She owned other jewellery but it was always hidden.

Janka: But mother loved flowers, especially jonquils and daffodils that she would buy from the market. I remember there were always flowers in the house. She followed the custom of putting a cherry branch in water at Christmas time, so that it would flower for Easter.

Hela: Mother never worked, apart from organising the household, which was a big enough job. I don't know what her pleasures were, or what she did for entertainment. Once in a while there was a wedding in the family, which was an occasion for great preparations and celebration. She read a lot, particularly romances and poetry; she probably escaped her humdrum life through romantic fantasies.

Janka: There were many romances at that time that people used to talk about. One of grandmother Rozalia's brothers, David, had married a woman called Chana, who was not very pretty and had, I remember, a red nose. They were poor and lived in the country in a cottage with a thatched straw roof and a beaten-earth floor. Here they brought up four children: Szymon, Moryc, Andzia and Sala.

Szymon was unusual-looking, with Asiatic features, dark hair and black eyebrows and eyelashes. He married a beautiful blond woman and they had three children, but he also had a son with a country girl. It was quite common that Jews had children with all sorts of country girls, so that many Poles have Jewish blood in them. Szymon's illegitimate son was brought up by his mother, the country girl, and Szymon was very good to her, looking after her in her old age. Everyone called the boy Jasiek Szymek, because they knew his father was Szymon the Jew. When the Germans came, one of the Poles told them that Jasiek Szymek was Jewish and he was killed instantly.

Hela: Mother didn't want me to listen to gossip but I couldn't help overhearing when a scandal was being discussed in whispers. One of grandmother Rozalia's younger sisters, Leonora, lived in the country. There were surrounding forests with tall pine trees sighing in the wind, and wild white strawberries growing. Once a Polish admirer carved into a tree 'Leonora I love you'. I was shown the inscription when I was growing up. Leonora married a man named Birner, who was very tall and strong. But he was unfaithful, and had three children with a Polish woman (with his own wife he had seven). Leonora, greatly troubled by her husband's infidelity, sought advice from the rabbi and complained to him bitterly. He put a curse on the three illegitimate children, and indeed they all died.

Apart from discussing the family, we went occasionally to the theatre in Kraków for the plays that were put on once or twice a year. But generally our evenings were quiet. Mother taught me to sew, and the women would sit near the fire in winter and embroider or darn socks and mend worn-out clothes. Beautiful embroideries and fine intricate lace would be created by her deft fingers. We had cupboards full of fine linen, all hand-embroidered and monogrammed. There were large tablecloths and many serviettes, some hardly used. Mother loved to buy or make things for the house, and spent money on fine glassware and crystal bowls rather than on herself.

She used to take me shopping to a big store called Gross which sparkled with all these lovely things. We also visited the *apteka*, for medicines which were made to order from powders and liquids that were kept in jars and weighed on a pair of scales. Mother often seemed to buy *Kogutki*, a packet of powders that were a remedy for headaches, from which she suffered. She also bought herbs for various ailments, and castor oil was frequently administered.

My favourite memory of her is when she would comb and plait my hair, and sing me songs or recite poems. She loved to recite verses to her children, and my love of poetry came from her. I had a good memory and I learnt long poems by heart at an early age. There was one poem by Mickiewicz about a Polish heroine, a fighter who disguised herself as a male soldier. When she was killed everyone mourned her and honoured her, believing her to be a man, until they re- alised that the soft skin and perfect features belonged to a woman. I also loved Tuwim's verses. Their cadences and rhythms, the romance and excitement of the Polish language, never left me.

My mother and I sit in her bed propped up on pillows. A thick eiderdown quilt covers us. I cuddle into her warm body. Her encir- cling arm holds a red-bound book filled with illustrated children's poems in Polish.

She reads poetry to me from an early age. There are poems about market days, about frogs that are hung up to dry, and one by Julian Tuwim about a forgetful boy whose aunt asks him if he remembered to post a letter. He assures her he did, and goes into a long dis- course about who and what he saw at the post box. Sadly, the aunt

shakes her head: he has been making the whole thing up, because
she never gave him a letter to post in the first place! Every time I
hear the aunt's slow words filled with disappointment, a pang of
guilt shoots through me. I feel so sorry for this boy, who tried so
hard to please her, and never meant to cause pain.

Hela: I loved to read. Father paid for us to belong to a
lending library, on Długa street, and he would take me there
and recommend titles for me to read: books on nature, on
animals, a book by Maeterlinck called *The Life of Bees*, history
books, and fiction stories of war and exploits. I also devoured
love stories and romances about heroes and heroines, by
authors like Sienkiewicz. Both our parents read a lot too.
Mother was annoyed, though, when father went so far as to
bring a book to the table at mealtimes.

I often went walking with mother. The streets around our
home were always filled with pedestrians and horse-drawn
carriages. We went every day to the Planty, a green belt
running around the centre of the city, starting at the Wawel
Castle near the Vistula. I ran along the winding paths, bordered by trees and shrubs. The shadows were cool and
green in summer. There were rolling lawns which you
weren't allowed to walk on. Wooden benches dotted the
edge of the path, but there were also chairs for hire, owned
by the city council, because on a sunny afternoon there were
not enough seats. A man in uniform would come around
to collect the fee for sitting on a chair. My brother and his
friends would sit in the chairs until they saw him coming,
and then would run away, laughing, as they had no inten-
tion of paying. People didn't have their own gardens or
backyards, as we do in Australia, so the Planty was packed,
especially with older people who met there to gossip and
pass the hours observing other people. There was also a
central playground for children, full of delightful swings
and slides which I was half afraid of but couldn't resist
playing on. We would wander down the alleyways, past
many statues and busts of famous people, Polish authors,
poets and statesmen. White swans sailed gracefully on the

lake, looking disdainfully at the children trying to attract their attention.

Sundays were special. The church bells rang from early morning and there was a hum in the air. There were always a lot of soldiers in Kraków, finely dressed in their military uniforms. On Sundays all the maids had a day off, and would make dates with these soldiers. I often went along with our maid, because Janka didn't want to take me and mother was busy, so I looked forward enormously to these outings. We'd go to a play, or go walking in the Planty, or sit and watch the parade of couples and children dressed in their Sunday best. People would often just sit at their windows and observe what was going on; the street was throbbing and alive. There were no cars and few carriages, unless you had to travel a long distance. Everything was close and walking was the main mode of transport. The street was full of people.

We often went for picnics in the countryside surrounding Kraków. Błonje was a favourite destination, as it was within walking distance. For holidays our family didn't travel far. The summer holidays lasted for two whole months, and the whole family, including Hanka the maid, would shift to the country. We loaded our belongings, including bedding, pots and pans, feather eiderdowns and crockery, onto a wooden-sided dray and paid a man to deliver the goods to Zawoja, or to Szyce, little villages where many families spent their summers. We travelled there by train, but father came only on weekends; he still had the shop to run.

The countryside around Zawoja was covered with forests of pine and spruce, with stands of huge oak trees heavy with acorns. Icy streams babbled and flowed swiftly down steep slopes. (We never went to the seaside; it was too far away, so I could barely begin to imagine the sea from the descriptions I read.) We would stay in Zawoja in the family home of Maryna, the small woman who used to come in to do our laundry. Her family were very poor and ate meat only once or twice a year. They lived in a typical peasant hut with a thatched roof and whitewashed walls. There was one cow, two goats, several chickens and geese waddling round the farmyard.

When we arrived they moved out into the barn, while we took over their hut. The barn was large, with ladders leading up to the loft, full of hay. Maryna had a husband, Jantek, and a heavy slow-speaking daughter called Julka. I overheard my parents discussing Maryna in undertones. She had been asked a question relating to her daughter: Who was the father? Was he blond or brown-haired? She replied that she didn't know, he hadn't taken his cap off! I was quite naive and didn't understand the cause of my parents' mirth.

I loved holiday times in the country. We could drink warm foaming milk, straight from the cow. After rain we picked wild mushrooms. I soon learnt about the different kinds that grew nearby, and which ones were edible. I don't remember ever seeing mushrooms sold that were commercially grown; country women would come to town early in the morning, having got up at dawn to forage through the green, moist shadows in the forest undergrowth to find the aromatic delicacies.

We roamed through the surrounding meadows and forests, looking for blueberries, blackberries, or *poziomki*— tiny strawberries that grew wild and had a wonderful strong fragrance. I loved sweets, and while we stayed in Zawoja mother let us go in the afternoons to 'Fiszerówka', the guest house where the richer Jewish families stayed. There we could buy wonderful desserts: thick vanilla slices dusted with icing-sugar, rich creamcakes, and raspberry ice-cream that we ran home with quickly so that we could eat it before it melted. Meanwhile Maryna's family ate a mixture of lard and flour that was baked into hard cakes.

I had few toys when I was young. I had a rag doll that was very precious to me. I played with my cousin Różyczka, whose family were living in Leipzig at the time and were well off. (Różyczka was the daughter of mother's brother Szymon and his wife Itka.) She was younger than me and had a nurse who would take us both for walks on sunny days. Różyczka had a pram, and a doll with eyes that closed.

My doll's eyes didn't close and I was a little bit envious. I also dreamt of having a doll that said 'Mama'. My doll was always a baby, whereas Janka's dolls were much more glamorous. She was good with her hands, and made elaborate clothes and hats for her dolls. She collected scraps from our dressmaker, and imagined her doll was a lady on her way to the theatre or some outing. Meanwhile I changed the nappies on my baby doll and tucked her up in her cradle.

At first she is just like my doll, with eyes that open and shut and tiny fingers spread out. I lay my doll, Shirley, next to my baby sister on the bed, and am gratified to find that my doll is bigger than she is. (My mother chose the name as a typically Australian one. She had seen The Shiralee, *a film set in Australia, and that was the sound she heard.) But soon I find that Frances cries and makes a mess, and I lose interest in her. I have a cradle, which was given to me for my doll to sleep in. It is now removed from my room and taken to my parents' bedroom. I scowl.*

Hela: Our brother Kuba had hundreds of tin soldiers. With father's influence, though it was many years after the First World War, Kuba used to imagine glorious battles with his toy soldiers all lined up—he always dreamed of heroic exploits. He also collected small flags from all around the world; they would come with a little chocolate you could buy, and he was mad about collecting and swapping them with his friends. Stamps, which he collected in an album, were another passion.

Although my childhood was fairly normal, I sensed that it was difficult being Jewish. Father always tried not to be too different or strange. He was very patriotic and had served in the Polish army, whereas many men tried to avoid military service. He had seen action in the First World War. I remember photos of him in his smart uniform and shiny boots, with a serious expression on his face. When he told us stories or sang songs, they were always about exploits of war and heroic battles. He liked to see himself as a bit of a hero, and we of course worshipped him.

He dressed in elegant clothes and carried a cherrywood walking-stick, which was very fashionable at the time. He loved horse-riding and going on picnics. He would stroll around, swinging his stick and puffing on a cigarette. When he could afford them, he smoked Egyptian cigarettes, which he cut in half and placed in a cherrywood holder; otherwise he rolled his own using a little machine into which he inserted cigarette-papers and tobacco. (When I was very little we had a maid called Józka, who was simple-minded. I felt feverish one day and Józka was sent to fetch the thermometer. She returned a few minutes later, carefully cradling father's cigarette-making machine.)

Father was always very interested in nature and animals, and we had a succession of pets. There were two big dogs, a Dobermann and an Alsatian, living in the house, as well as a hedgehog. Janka would squeal when she found it in our bed. There was also a tame blackbird that followed father around when he went outside. He always fed the birds in our courtyard, especially in winter when snow piled up in the corners.

Janka: Jan, a second cousin of ours, shared father's love of birds. He was the son of one of grandmother's brothers, Wicek. Being the only son born after four daughters, he was often spoilt. His family, like all the members of this part of our family, lived in the country. They had a few fields, some horses, two or three cows. They lived just like peasants, except for the fact that they went to synagogue a few times a year. Jan used to visit us in Kraków sometimes, and our parents, who were his godparents, always gave him presents. When he had his Barmitzvah he received from them the customary gift of a watch.

Whenever Jan visited us he would sit for hours in front of our birdcage. Father loved birds and we had ten or fifteen canaries. There was one particular one, a white and yellow canary, that was Jan's favourite, and it sang beautifully. He called it his canary. One day, some time after one of his visits, that canary suddenly died. We found out shortly afterwards that Jan, aged fifteen, had died of a heart attack at the same moment. Who can explain such things? It was a tragedy for the family to lose their only son. This happened about ten years before the war.

∞

I hear the chickens clucking in a gentle, complaining way, because their feet are tied together and they are frightened of the bustle. A rosy-cheeked woman with a red kerchief tied over her head sits on a low stool and calls out in a raucous voice to the passers-by. She holds bunches of purple and white turnips high in the air, and sneers at the well-dressed woman in high heels who disregards her calls. The sounds in the marketplace grow louder as different peasant women compete with each other, and the arrogant rooster in the front crows angrily.

I stare closely at the images on the page, my eyes moving over and around the shapes again and again. Not knowing how to read, I focus on the pictures with intense concentration. It's a market scene in a children's book about daily life in Poland. My mother's words, in her gentle singsong voice, are a background accompaniment giving some order to the jumble of images rushing at me. But it's not her words I remember; I stare intently at the crowded picture, and I keep looking at it long after my mother has left the room.

Several of the women sit with their broad hips comfortably settled on their stools, their knees spread wide beneath striped or plain woollen skirts. One is shelling peas into a tin pot, ignoring the crowds. Another points to a barrel with live fish swimming desperately in circles, the water dark and turbulent. The air is filled with the earthy tang of carrots freshly pulled from the ground and the fragrant scent of herbs picked at dawn, as well as the all-pervasive smell of horse manure wafting by when the wind changes.

Glistening pickled cucumbers are piled next to bunches of beet-roots; a housewife with a large straw basket over her arm and a serious look on her face inspects the goods closely, bargains for several moments, and pulls a few coins out of her pocket.

Everywhere on the bottom half of the picture the colours run riot, clamouring for attention, jostling with each other. The top half, though, is a serene blue: calm, peaceful, undisturbed by the turmoil below. In the top right-hand corner of the page is a clock-face, showing ten o'clock. Despite the clutter and apparent disorder in the picture, things are well arranged on this page.

As my eyes scan the images, the scene gradually resolves itself into one of purposeful design. The goods at the market are plentiful, the women are cheerful, and I feel a warm contentment fill me. This, then, was my mother's world when she was a child. I try to see her as a young girl like me. Her hair is dark like mine, and she is holding her mother's hand as they walk around. I cannot conjure up the image clearly, but I know she is happy. I feel satisfied and reassured every time I gaze at this picture.

The next time my mother sits on the sofa and reads to me from this book, I sit very close to her and put my hand in hers. She holds me gently, protectively. We sit like that for a long time, even after the last page has been turned.

3

Hela: We lived in a building of three storeys, made of brick. Our building was one of several that looked down onto a central courtyard. Of course there were no lifts, only a wooden staircase. From one of our windows that faced the street, we could see the train tracks, almost at the same level as our second storey. We could always hear the steam train passing by with its chugging locomotive. From another window, we looked down onto a Catholic monastery. When I was bored I often looked out that window. I was intrigued by the monks who regularly walked along the paths, reading from their prayer books, but they walked backwards! This was supposed to help their concentration.

The courtyard was the centre of activity and interest for the surrounding tenants. It was shared by about fifty families. Hawkers trundled their trolleys over the cobblestones and shouted out in praise of their wares. There were often travelling musicians or singers who set themselves up and entertained us, waiting for a few coins to be wrapped in a scrap of paper and thrown down from a window. There was even a rather simple man who would come begging into the courtyard, and as soon as his voice was heard singing a ditty, mother would pull me away from the window and block my ears. He sang, 'If you don't give me enough coins, then you can kiss my arse!' and he would bare his buttocks. What a terrible scandal to use such vulgar language!

Into the courtyard there sometimes came an exotic darklooking man with a brightly coloured parrot which perched on his shoulder, and for a fee it would select a piece of rolledup paper that told your fortune. The kitchen maids would run downstairs to find out if true love awaited them. A rag-and-bone man also visited regularly, and his cry echoed from the stone walls, offering kitchen utensils that you could choose in exchange for old rags and shoes.

In Kraków there was a special market called Tandeta, where you would go to sell old clothes and second-hand objects. Many a woman who had to clothe her children took her husband's suit that was getting a bit shabby and had it turned and remade into a boy's suit. Tailors were cheap, whereas fabric was relatively expensive, so it was very common to go to a tailor to reverse the material, hiding the worn spots, and finish up with a suit that looked like new. Our family weren't that poor so we didn't shop at Tandeta, but many people did.

Janka: There was poverty all around us in Kraków, but it was all a matter of degree. I remember Kazimierz very well; it was the poor Jewish neighbourhood where most of father's family lived. It was crossed by narrow streets and alleys which had existed since the fourteenth century. This was where the Jewish cemetery and the synagogue were. The tenements were old and dilapidated, crowded with people. While mother was alive, we went every Sunday to visit father's family in Kazimierz. Father had five brothers and two sisters. A younger brother, Efraim (Kuba), and a sister, Leonora (Lajka), lived near our grandfather. Uncle Kuba (known as Big Kuba to distinguish him from our brother) never married because he had to look after his father, Salomon.

Hela: Grandfather Salomon would sit in his wheelchair, moaning and complaining. He was a jealous and bad-tempered man. My impression was of a very old man with a grey beard (even though he must only have been in his fifties), suffering from rheumatic pains. The children had to kiss his hand as a sign of respect. I found that very difficult to do, as he frightened me. He always asked us to sing a song for him, and gave us money. Mother hated going to

Kazimierz to visit him, because it was depressing and dirty.

There was a Jewish girl who lived upstairs from grandfather, and she started to get friendly with my uncle Kuba. When grandfather heard about this he got very upset and said bad things about the girl. He started to scream and yell, and absolutely forbade his son to see her. He was a difficult man, because he was sick and in pain, but he made everyone else's life a misery. Old people like that can be great egoists, always demanding from their children and ultimately ruining their lives. He insisted on his son looking after his every need, so Kuba could never get married. Grandfather died before war broke out, but the rest of the family all perished during the war.

Janka: Big Kuba wanted very much to marry me. He was thirteen years older, and when I was about sixteen grandfather told mother I should get engaged and marry his boy; that way we would stay close to him and look after him. Being my father's younger brother, Kuba was my uncle— among Jews it was allowed for cousins or uncles and nieces to marry. But although he was a very decent person, physically I was repelled by him; it was as if he were my brother, I'd known him ever since I could remember. All his life Kuba was in love with me, in the true meaning of the word. He said he would not only give his blood for me, but would give his veins too, if I would agree to be his wife. He always paid a lot of attention to me, and this tired me. It was a burden in my youth. Even when I married in the ghetto he became very jealous, and once punched my husband in the mouth. All through my young years his love was difficult for me to deal with.

Hela: Father's sister, Lajka, lived in terrible conditions in Kazimierz. She was an attractive girl and was in love with a cousin, but she had no money for a dowry so she was matched up with a Jew from Odessa, a tailor called Świczarczyk. He could hardly speak Polish and was very primitive. They had two daughters, named Janina and Helena.

45

They were pretty girls, clever and studious. My aunt's family could afford meat only once a week, on the Sabbath. They all lived in one room, which always smelled of urine and beer, as there was a pub opposite and people would urinate outside their door. They lived in this tiny room with their two daughters and a sewing-machine, where the father tried to make a living. My own family was rich in comparison. It was said that despite the conditions they lived in, he was a miser and had money hidden under the floorboards. Later when he ran away to Russia they claimed he spent his time counting his money, but I heard afterwards that he died of hunger there.

Janka: Apart from Big Kuba and the poor sister in Kazimierz, father had four brothers: Nechemiasz (known as Chaim or Hemiu), who married Gusta Pozner and had one son, Jan, a good-looking blond-haired boy; Szymon (or Szymek, later changed to Sam in America); Zygmunt (Saul); and the youngest brother, Mojsze, who was a bright boy, interested in reading and music. He died at a very early age, apparently of a heart attack while playing football.

It was said that our brother Kuba took after Szymek, the one who was sent to America. Szymek was a rascal: he didn't want to go to school and was expelled several times. He was sent from one town to another, from Kraków to Lwów and elsewhere, but was always thrown out of school. He was a troublemaker and a fighter. He used to ride on horseback at top speed through Kraków, and when he saw a policeman in the marketplace, with his tall hat, he would knock the hat off his head and ride away. He would play all sorts of practical jokes. His mother Joasia, of course, had died young, and his father never remarried, so he didn't have a very stable upbringing.

Because he was so wild, it was decided to send him to America. Father escorted him to Germany, to the port in Hamburg. The boy threw himself on father's neck and wept loudly, begging not to be sent away. In America he had a very hard life.

The third brother, Zygmunt, was also sent to America, at the age of eleven, and became a waiter. Later he became a manufacturer of men's hats. He changed his name to Saul and became very successful. These two brothers had no problem having their surname Weiss officially recognised when they went to America.

Hela: Uncle Hemiu and uncle Kuba, the one who remained single to look after his father, ran a fruit business in Kraków. They would rent an orchard for a season, pick the fruit, transport it in horse-drawn carts to a storehouse in Kazimierz, and then sell it in town. It was a risky venture because so much depended on what sort of season it was: if the weather had been kind, it was quite a profitable business. My uncles grew many varieties of apples. There were golden Renata and brown Renata, and Coxes—I remember as a young child the beautiful fragrance of the apples they kept in the dark coolness of the cellar.

There were also heavy, juicy pears that I picked up gently and sniffed, as well as strawberries, raspberries and cherries in season. The different shades of red and pink fascinated me. I was quite small when they took me to the orchard with them while they were loading drays with cherries, piled high. These were in season for only a short while; sweet red cherries, pink ones, little sour cherries and the almost translucent white ones. As they were being harvested and loaded up, I grabbed handfuls of them and started to eat them, with the red juice dribbling down my chin. They were so delicious I gorged myself till I could eat no more. Afterwards I felt so sick I couldn't stand the sight of cherries for years.

Janka: One of the things that made mother unhappy was her son. She always had problems with Kuba, my younger brother. He was born a bad person, if such a thing is possible. From the time he was born he cried so much that mother thought he must be sick and didn't know what to do with him. When he was little he stole chocolates, then later even money. Mother had many worries because of him. Kuba

47

always wanted attention and approval. He was red-haired, which in Poland made him a target for teasing. Red hair was also associated with the devil, so Kuba suffered for it. Another problem was his name: it came from Jakob, from the Bible, which wasn't a very Polish name and identified him as a Jew. He wanted to impress his Polish friends, because we lived in a Polish district, and began to steal money at a young age to buy lollies to give to these friends.

He was also a terrible liar. He spent his youth reading books about heroes, and always fantasised about his exploits. He wanted to make out that he was better than he really was. When he hurt his forehead falling against a table, he went round telling people he had been in a duel. He lived in a fantasy world.

In the twilight moments between waking and sleeping I make an awesome discovery. There are in fact two of me. One, whose name is Anna, is a pretty, clever, dutiful child. She always makes her parents smile and everybody likes her. But there is an exact replica, named Rosner, who is naughty and rude. This child is always getting into trouble, scribbling on walls, picking flowers from neighbours' gardens and shouting at grown-ups. Of course, she has to be punished when she is naughty.

There is a secret room behind a tall partition. Above it I can see strange crane-like objects. Maybe they are the instruments of torture I have seen at the dentist, metal arms and pulleys and sharp probes. From this secret room come terrifying sounds of people screaming. That is where Anna threatens Rosner she will have to go to, if she does not behave.

This secret 'bad' girl doesn't stay with me for long. But while she is around, even while I am scolding her I envy her freedom to be herself, her ability to remove herself from a role I'm locked into.

Janka: Mother used to hide some money, some of the takings from the shop, in the wardrobe. She scrimped to be able to buy small luxuries. Once when the money went missing she thought maybe the maid had stolen it. An uncle of ours accused the girl and slapped her face. She cried and cried, protesting her innocence. All the while Kuba watched silently, not revealing his guilt. Another time it was noticed that some money was missing just when Kuba had gone to the toilet. A little while later the money was found hidden in a pot-plant in the toilet. Imagine what a mother would have suffered, having a child like that.

Later he stole a watch from me, a beautiful gold watch that my father had given me as a present on my birthday. I remember it so clearly: it had a green winder adorned with tiny emeralds. He knew I loved it very much and I was terribly upset when it disappeared. I cried and cried. He had pawned it to get some money, but later, seeing my distress, he brought it back.

Hela: Kuba always wanted to impress. That was a characteristic that stayed with him all his life. The only way he knew how to impress his friends was by buying them little gifts with stolen money, and boasting of his bravado. He was often beaten for his bad behaviour. Mother always had trouble with him and was constantly worried about him, even after he left school and was training to be a dentist.

During these pre-war years it was very hard for Jews to have a career. They could only very rarely take on a profession like doctor or lawyer; it meant enormous hard work and sacrifice by the parents to be able to send a Jewish boy to university. Also there were restrictions on Jews attending. Grandfather had two brothers who had high positions in the railway, but being Jews they were not able to get a promotion so they converted to Christianity. (They remained part of the family and visited regularly, until they left Europe to go to America; I heard later that one had become a bishop and died without any family of his own.) I am sure father could have had a successful career, as he was very intelligent and always read a lot, but he didn't have the opportunity to get an education and had to earn money for his family.

So Jews became shoemakers and tailors, or shopkeepers like father. There were so many of these grocery shops, each one trying to make a meagre living. In father's shop people would buy only very small quantities of tea or coffee or sugar—things like that were a real luxury.

Janka: Father wasn't a good businessman and didn't run the place well—he was too busy reading all the time. He always ordered goods on credit, never going himself to select the goods but only taking what was brought to him at the shop. If he ordered a sack of flour for 150 złoty, it would be delivered to the shop on credit, with a charge of 165 złoty, which meant he made very little profit. On one occasion he was so engrossed in reading that a large sack of flour was stolen without him realising. A friend went to him and said, 'Mr Weiss, you are reading such an interesting book that soon they will steal your whole shop.'

Hela: The shop was poorly lit, with crowded shelves and a dark timber counter polished by years of use. Everything was sold not in packets but by weight—around the shop were sacks of flour, salt and cocoa. The walls were lined with tins of tea and coffee, and on the counter sat large scales with a set of weights. Beet sugar was very expensive and was sold in hard cones. As well as groceries there were fresh vegetables, and in one corner stood a dark wooden barrel of pickled cucumbers. Whenever I came into the shop in the afternoon, the pungent sour smell made me wrinkle my nose, although I soon got used to it. We also sold cheese, a hard white cottage cheese and a yellow Swiss. Mingled with the smells of pickles and coffee and cheese was the warm dusty scent of the wooden floorboards, and the stale odour of countless working people who regularly came in to provide for their families' daily needs. In another corner was a large barrel in which live fish swam, particularly carp. Jewish women bought fish for Friday night, and non-Jews also bought fish for their festivals. I watched their creased faces and clumsy fingers as they counted out their few coins and laid them carefully on the counter. As they turned to leave I saw motes of dust floating in shafts of late-afternoon sunlight, settling silently over everything as father turned back to his book.

In our shop butter was sold by the gram and wrapped in paper, but it could also be bought from the peasant women in the *Rynek*, the marketplace. This was a noisy, bustling area, full of interesting sounds and smells. The *Rynek Główny*, the huge square right in the centre of Kraków, was a meeting-place for many people as well as the focus of activity on market days. This was where the peasant women would come to sell their produce. But Jews would rather go to the *Plac*, a smaller square in Kazimierz where they could get kosher food, freshly killed chickens for Friday evening's meal, and live fish.

The country women came to town in the early morning and wrapped their portions of butter in moist leaves to keep them cool. They brought milk to the market in heavy metal containers, slung with a shawl on their backs. They used a metal cup to measure out a quarter or half litre of fresh unpasteurised milk. We then had to boil and cool it before it was used. I was always afraid that the milk would boil over; it happened so often. I watched and watched, and then suddenly it rose with a gush and spilled over the sides. I hated the smell of burnt milk, and the pot was so hard to clean! After the milk had been boiled, the cream rose to the top, thick and rich. We loved to eat it; it was a real treat to take a spoon and scoop up the cream, and we fought over it. You could also buy a thinner kind of cream, liquid and sweet. The boiled milk stayed in the pot all day, as we had no refrigeration, not even an icebox. Every day we had to buy fresh supplies of whatever was needed.

As well as bringing milk to town, the peasant women brought home-made cheeses tied up in cloths. (You had to be careful because sometimes, when you brought the cheese home, you discovered a stone in the middle of it.) Chickens and geese were sold live at the market and I often went with mother to choose a good fat chicken,

51

which she checked by blowing below its tail-feathers to see if it was nice and fat and yellow. We bought chicken fat or goose fat for cooking. Geese were very popular, much more common than beef.

Clothing was always hand-made by a dressmaker, who sat all day at a treadle sewing-machine. I would go with mother to choose material for the dresses. We went in and out of little shops, and I followed her while she looked and touched and asked the prices of various fabrics. I also felt the lovely silky textures and saw the shimmery bolts of cloth unrolled before us. But usually mother bought something fairly plain and practical, rather than the fancy materials which I thought so beautiful.

Everything was sewn by a dressmaker, even my school uniforms. She was an ugly woman, with a huge goitre that wobbled when she talked. I would have to go for two or three fittings. Once mother chose the same material for both Janka and me, a red foulard silk with white spots, to be made up into dresses for us. Janka was very unhappy: she didn't want to look like her little sister. My shoes were also made to measure by a shoemaker called Jawień, who was very well known in town. Ready-made shoes were available, but father always wanted us to be well-dressed, even though he couldn't afford it. I had a very expensive pair of brown and beige shoes made to measure by the shoemaker. I was unaware of the saving and scrimping our parents had to go through to keep up the facade of being well-to-do.

Janka: That was father's biggest problem—he always owed money. He trusted people and sold them goods on credit, because they were paid their wages monthly. Father had a big ledger in which he wrote down the names of customers and what they owed him. Usually they did pay their debts gradually, in small sums. But father was so naive, he trusted too readily, and the amounts grew and grew over many months till people owed him a lot of money, which they couldn't repay. Father likewise had bills to pay and found it increasingly difficult to meet his commitments. He was forever taking out promissory notes, and couldn't repay them on time. The amount kept increasing because of interest charged. He wanted us to have the best of everything, but he couldn't earn more than a few pennies from the shop.

Hela: There was a period when he had to start pawning some of the family possessions: a silver candelabra, a watch or a piece of jewellery. People were always coming to the door, asking for money that we owed them. I remember mother crying a lot, and worrying over the constant financial pressure.

Then the Depression came in the 'thirties and we could no longer afford to stay in town. We had to shift to Suduł, a village about half an hour's walk beyond the town limits, to try to save money. It was relatively close to Kraków by today's standards, just on the outskirts, but then it seemed very far. Wherever I walked in the village, I would come across a crucifix nailed to a tree-trunk, under a little protective roof, and there the Catholics who passed knelt down and crossed themselves.

We rented a shop and a dwelling nearby of two rooms, a large corridor and a kitchen. We were fairly isolated and mother had no company, so it seemed to me she was always sad.

In Kraków father had owned a delicatessen, and now he opened a business in Suduł selling not only groceries but alcohol as well. Yet he couldn't make it profitable. Because the shop sold alcohol, there were a lot of drunkards who came in; common peasants who shouted and swore in vulgar language. Mother, a delicate and protected woman, was now exposed to all this, and also suffered in trying to shelter her children in such an environment. She became more and more depressed.

I continued to attend the same school in the centre of town, which meant I now had a much longer walk to get there. On the way I had to pass through a dark little wood that used to frighten me. When the wind blew through the pine trees, I heard strange sighing noises and imagined there were footsteps behind me; I was always afraid. Another fear I had was of a group of Polish hooligans who would call out comments and taunt me. I was always over-protected at home and didn't know how to look after myself.

To get to school I also had to pass a very old cemetery that was set aside for cholera victims. I would run as fast as I could past it, and try to control the shivers of fear that went through me. I had heard many stories of ghosts and evil spirits, and, being an imaginative child, the cemetery became a daily torment.

Funerals and cemeteries are not for children, my mother says. I never go to a funeral as a child. Fortunately, no one very close to me has died, but there are family friends whose funerals my parents have to attend. I always know my father will come back from the cemetery in a bad mood. Funerals give him a headache. For the rest of the day he bursts out angrily at any small irritation. Although I have never seen him cry, my mother tries to explain that he is just upset. That's why children shouldn't go to funerals; they would only get upset. Children should be happy.

Hela: To get to school took me about an hour. After passing the cemetery, I had to go along an unmade road, which turned to mud whenever it rained and was covered in snow in winter. By the time I arrived at school I felt ashamed because my shoes were all caked with mud, which I tried to wipe off with a rag. On my way home mother would always try to come to meet me halfway.

Near our home lived a carriage driver. Father sometimes gave him two or three cigarettes so that he would drive me to school in his horse-drawn carriage. I know I was father's favourite, as I was the youngest, and it pained him to see me trudge out into the rain and slush. But he couldn't afford to pay for the ride too often. It was a real struggle, the whole time we lived there.

∾

I am about five. It is spring. The back garden is surging with green growth, mysterious and alive. I wander through the unmown grass and among the flowering fruit trees. The sunlight through the gnarled branches is dappled and the breeze makes patches of light and shade sway on the grass.

I come out of the shaded area to see our little almond tree bathed in sunshine. The air is warm. The bare dark branches are dotted with fragrant white blossoms, looking as if they were glued on, the way we glue cottonwool to sticks to make trees at school. The flowers are almost translucent in the sunlight, and I reach up and cradle my chubby fingers around one. It detaches easily. I stretch out my other palm and carefully lay the blossom there, examining its perfection. I reach up for another one, and another, and soon both hands are full. The thin branches on the lower part of the tree look once more as they did all winter.

The treasures quiver in my hands. Slowly, so they won't spill, I go back up the mossy brick path towards the house. I call out at the back door for someone to open it, to see what beautiful things I have found.

The wire door slams against the wall; steps come heavily down the two back stairs. 'What have you done?' My uncle's voice is filled with unconcealed anger.

I look up into his thunderous eyes, then down at my two hands. I can't speak. He turns abruptly and goes inside. I stand there trembling, then sit down on the step, letting the blossoms fall into my lap.

A few moments later he reappears. He no longer looks so angry. He looks at me solemnly, then sits down beside me. Gently he picks up one of the blossoms. 'Do you know what this is?' he asks. His voice is tight but controlled. 'This is life. This is the birth of an almond, of food. Now that you have picked it, it will die.'

I look up at him but his eyes are downcast. 'All winter we've waited for the almond tree to flower, and then bear fruit. There will be no fruit this season.' The sadness in his voice overwhelms me as I realise the enormity of what I have done. He puts his arm around my shoulders and I turn to sob into the warm rough fabric of his jacket, as the white-petalled flowers fall from my skirt to the ground.

4

Hela: In 1935, while we were living in Suduł, something happened that destroyed my childhood security. I was eleven years old.

Where we lived there were no neighbours nearby; we were quite isolated, and the nights were very dark. There was nowhere to go and no one to talk to except the Polish landlord to whom we paid rent. One day I was alone in the house with mother. Janka, who had completed her studies, was working in Kraków at an accountant's office, and father was at the store. Mother began to feel unwell and went to lie down on the bed. I noticed her pale face and the sheen of sweat on her brow. Of course we had no telephone, so in a panic I ran out to get father.

When I reached the store I gasped out my story, and he swiftly removed his apron and took my hand. Some other Polish women came with him and a doctor was sent for, but by the time he arrived it was too late. Mother was lying there, lifeless. My head began to spin and I was quickly pushed out of the room. I could hear subdued whispering. Never-ending questions began to fill my mind. How could my beloved mother, a healthy woman of forty-three, disappear from my life so suddenly? What could I have done? Was it my fault? I felt dizzy and sick.

I was not allowed to go to the funeral, as it was thought I was too young. A heavy blackness filled my thoughts and I swung between numbness and fear. For one week all the mirrors in the house were covered by sheets, and people came daily, speaking in whispers and gazing at us in sorrow. We had to wear slippers and sit on low stools, as was the custom. Once the week of mourning was over, there was silence. Father didn't talk about mother's death, and walked around the house in a daze. No one mentioned her name and anxious questions continued to fill my mind, but there was nobody I could ask. I became more fearful than ever. I was constantly on edge, looking over my shoulder, expecting someone to appear.

In the deep silence that followed the funeral week, I kept thinking I heard noises, heard someone at the door. I kept going to open it, but no one was there. Again and again I heard the knocking. I was sent to Kraków for a while, to stay with an uncle of father's. They thought I would forget what had happened if I went away. I prayed to God, trying to find some comfort. We had prayer books at home, in Hebrew and in Polish. I recited *Kaddish* (the prayer for the dead) in Polish so often that I knew it by heart and never forgot it.

In his grief, father could not comfort me.

Even two years later, when an aunt brought a wind-up gramophone and put on a song called 'Only One Mother's Heart', father slammed his fist on the table and refused to listen to the music.

Janka: Father was totally distraught. He was still a relatively young man. He always kept a revolver under his pillow, which he had owned since the First World War. It had his initials engraved on it. One evening I saw him take this revolver and put it to his head. I leapt towards him and knocked the revolver out of his hand. I remember him saying that his life was over, not thinking at all about the three children he would be leaving behind.

I know nothing about my grandmother except that I am named after her. I try to imagine my mother as a little girl, with a mother of her own, but the image refuses to materialise. This grandmother Chana is nothing to me, a total stranger, I tell myself.

She is there in my childhood, transmitted through words, but they have no weight. All I know is that her hair was so long that she could sit on it, and her waist was much smaller than mine.

There is nothing I can see or feel, so I dismiss her together with stories about the slaves in Egypt and dinosaurs—a remote past that has nothing to do with me. It is many years before she begins to invade my dreams.

Hela: Shortly after this I began to menstruate. Mother was no longer alive, and no one had ever explained to me what to expect. I was terrified of the blood coming from my body. My sister slapped my face to make my cheeks rosy, following some ancient custom which I didn't understand. From then on I was always fearful of the sight of blood. I hated having to wash out the rags we had to use. Even a blood nose would send me screaming for help.

Some time afterwards father's brother Zygmunt arrived from America, and he was able to help us a bit financially, as we were really struggling. He gave father a ring, which he was able to sell for enough money to rent a new apartment. We could now shift from Suduł back to the centre of town.

The apartment, at 12B Wrocławska street, was on the first floor of a relatively new building, and for the first time we had a bathroom with hot water as well as two large bedrooms and a kitchen. The floor was no longer raw wood but parquetry. Father opened a shop in nearby Śląska street, next door to a smallgoods shop with large windows. Our shop was elegant, and we sold high-quality fruit and confectionery as well as drinks made with soda water, and raspberry or lemon fruit syrups served in tall frosted glasses. There were glass-fronted cupboards and drawers, full of chocolates, nuts and sweets. Kraków had three chocolate factories and they produced quality chocolates that were in great demand. Intricate cakes, layered with fruit or marzipan, were carefully arranged on trays, beside rum babas and cakes in the shape of little pillows or dolls. There was a special glass-fronted case just for creamcakes. All of this sweetness did not lull my feelings of loss. I was glad to be away from the fearful loneliness of Suduł and the ghosts there. Father threw himself into his work and stocked the shelves high with food.

In those days in Poland, vegetables were sold in a separate shop, never together with fruit. Fruit was seen as a luxury, especially items such as bananas, which were imported from overseas. They were weighed individually, and the tops had to be cut close so that they wouldn't weigh too much. There were red and green grapes in heavy bunches, and occasionally fragrant furry peaches. Oranges were another luxury. There were thick-skinned ones from Jaffa and pink-fleshed blood oranges. When the oranges started to get old and the skin began to wrinkle, the fruit was peeled and sold in segments, which was cheaper. The peels themselves were dried and also sold. Fruit was seasonal of course, and often rare. Cherries had a short season and were plentiful for a while. Apples could be kept longer, in the cellar.

But in winter there were no fresh fruit or vegetables at all; everything was covered with snow. I wandered around the shop picking up things and putting them down again. It was very cold and I felt a continual, aching longing for mother.

I had finished primary school by this stage and was of an age to go to secondary school. There wasn't enough money to send me to a private school, and I was not such a brilliant student that I could pass the entrance exam to be accepted into the *gimnazjum*, where you could go without paying. So it was decided that I would leave school. Janka had gone to a private school and it had cost our parents a fortune.

But I wasn't too upset to leave school, as I had always found the work and the environment difficult. I loved reading and poetry, but I was afraid of the teachers and embarrassed whenever I was called out to the blackboard.

My parents take great pride in my achievements at school. My mother looks in wonder at my schoolbooks, filled with neat writing and coloured pictures, and she gently fingers my seventy-two Derwent coloured pencils. She shows my reports to everyone, and will keep them for years in a drawer, beneath her underwear where she hides all her treasures. I love to see her so happy. I feel determined to try even harder the following year. My father asks about my marks but he doesn't read my stories. If I get nine out of ten, he wants to know where I lost the mark. He loves to help me with my homework. He carefully outlines my maps and writes my headings in bold black ink. I feel grateful, having such a capable father. I know I can never be as clever as he, and hand over my tasks uncritically. I am very competitive, and pray that I will do well.

Hela: So I was sent to do a sewing course, and at the same time I helped in the shop. I learnt to wrap little cakes in paper tied with string, and I could do it so quickly and neatly that everyone admired me. The lady who taught me to sew worked hard to make a living, while her Chassidic husband did nothing all day except read books and pray in the synagogue. I remember how he always hovered about when the milk was being boiled, and greedily ate the cream from the top all by himself.

I did a lot of the work in our home after mother died. In fact, I took on the role of the housewife. I learnt how to cook and how to bake, and everyone praised me. I was very good with my hands, quick and well-organised. I scrubbed the floor and did the laundry. I was a strong girl, much stronger physically than Janka; although a bit shorter, I was stouter and had more stamina. I tried hard to be an observant Jew, believing very much in God and the Jewish laws. It was my role to *kasher* the meat by soaking it for half an hour in water and half an hour in coarse salt, then rinsing it. I knew how to split open a chicken in the correct way, removing the stomach, and how to scald it with boiling water so the skin would peel and come away together with the dirt. I had to trim the claws off the feet, otherwise it wouldn't have been kosher. Everything that needed to be done to run a kosher kitchen I knew how to do. On Friday mornings the kitchen was filled with the warm yeasty smell of the *challah* I baked. I knew how to plait the strands of dough, not just three but six, evenly woven together, under and over; the *challah* was then sprinkled with poppyseeds and baked till it was golden on top.

We also made our own noodles for the chicken soup. The pastry was kneaded and pulled, then laid out to dry on a cloth on one of the high, wide beds. When it was ready I rolled the sheets carefully and sliced thin, even slices to make the fine noodles that father liked so much. If the dough had been too dry it would crumble; if it wasn't dry enough it would be sticky and impossible to slice evenly. I lit the candles on Friday nights and recited the prayers. In synagogue during the High Holydays I followed the service, reading all the prayers in Polish.

I was very concerned about observing all the rules. If anyone took a milk knife and used it mistakenly for meat, I would have to bury it in the earth to make it usable again. I got very upset if milk and meat dishes were mixed up, but no one else seemed to care much after mother died. (On the other hand, as before, we would sometimes eat non-kosher food outside the house.) I wasn't familiar with the ultra-Orthodox form of our religion, and only occasionally saw very religious Jews in Kazimierz. But I thought of myself as religious and prayed regularly to God. I believed in God all through my life, right up to the present day.

Of course, like everyone else we had a non-Jewish maid to help with household chores, but father never remarried, although he was only in his forties. His younger brother Kuba remained single as well because of the demands of his father, our grandfather.

Gradually things began to improve for us. The shop was running well and we had a very nice apartment with two rooms, a kitchen and a bathroom with running water. This was considered relatively comfortable for those days.

Janka: Although things were going well for us in the last two or three years before the war, anti-Semitism, of which I was only rarely aware as a young girl, became more evident. People were told not to buy from Jews—then we felt it, because fewer customers came into our shop. But it was not something personally against us, not something we felt as individuals, although it became very hard for Jews generally. On the trams a rope was used to segregate Jews from others; shops now carried signs declaring that they were pure Aryan.

We began to encounter people who had been born in Poland but had lived in Germany till that time. Now they were being expelled and sent back to Poland, and we realised that things were getting very bad in Germany. The expulsion was reported in the newspapers too. A special camp was set up for them in Zbąszyń, and we knew that some of our relatives were there.

We were shocked to hear bad news from our family in the country. The Germans had come to uncle Szymon's house and wanted to take away his two horses and a cart, which were his only means of transport and the only way he could make money. He had become stubborn and refused to give up the horses, so one of the Germans had pulled out a revolver and shot him on the spot.

∽

I am a young girl living in Melbourne. My world is fairly small—my house, my street, the local shops, and occasionally a trip to the city. I am loved and protected; the world around me is safe. Death and destruction are far away and children are not supposed to think about such things. Yet the symbols are everywhere around me, evil and menacing. I observe my surroundings very carefully wherever I go.

For some reason, I take particular note of where cannon are situated. They are hard and cold and metallic. They threaten me. They don't move and don't breathe, but I imagine they are holding their breath waiting for the right moment to release their destructive power. I feel a small heavy stone under my ribs whenever I pass them.

There are two of them in Hopetoun Park in Glenhuntly Road, the street we live on. They face out onto the road and are aimed at any passers-by. They are surrounded by flower beds and innocent green grass. When we walk by a shiver of anxiety passes through me and I hold my mother's hand more tightly. Even though the long metal nose of each cannon is plugged up, I am not reassured.

There are two other cannon in front of a long grey ivy-covered building close to the city. The monsters squat menacingly by the roadside, waiting silently. I watch for them each time we ride in the tram and I am aware of their presence many moments before I catch sight of them. As the tram rumbles on I keep looking out the window in their direction even after they have slid by. I have no idea why they are there, but I am conscious of their grim presence.

I am also aware of where skull and crossbones are. They are painted on a wooden box beside the railway crossing near our home; they are displayed on a sign above a café called 'The Jolly Roger' near my school; they are even on a bottle under our sink in the kitchen; I know what they mean.

I fear the sounds of planes roaring overhead. As the noise gets louder and louder and the vibrations fill my body, I clench my fists and stand very still, waiting for the threat to subside. I know there is nowhere to run to. And the penetrating wail of ambulance sirens fills me with dread, echoing in my ears long after the vehicle has passed. Unaccountably, I feel close to tears. The world is a dangerous place.

5

Hela: In September 1939 the war broke out. I was fifteen. At the beginning I didn't realise what was going on. War was something exciting. We were used to hearing tales from our father about the First World War, which sounded like an adventure full of heroism and glory. We thought war meant that soldiers would go to fight in their shining uniforms, somewhere on distant battlefields. Kuba's eyes glittered with excitement, and father, patriot that he was, was sure that Jews like us wouldn't be affected.

Janka: I remember very well the day that Poland was invaded. It was the beginning of September 1939. We lived near an industrial area, where the bombs started to fall. All our windows were shattered and it was a terrifying time. A factory next door to us was hit and destroyed. When the bombs began to fall Hela became hysterical—she was very young. She still panics whenever she hears thunder or loud noises. We ran to the cellar, which was used as a bomb shelter. Other people also used the cellar to hide in, but I was curious, wanting to see where the bombs were landing, so I used to creep up to the street to watch. I never seemed to feel the same terror as others.

The sky has been dark and ominous all afternoon. As the end of the school day approaches, lightning starts to flicker and gash the sky. A few seconds later we hear the first crashes of thunder. The lesson is over and I grab my bag, wondering if I'll get drenched waiting for the bus. As I come out through the school gate I hear an insistent car horn. I turn, and there I see my mother behind the wheel of the family Holden sedan. She never picks me up from school! Gratefully I run across the road through the pelting rain and slide in beside her. She eases the car into the line of traffic. Her knuckles are white as she clutches the steering-wheel. The rain continues unabated. With each flash of lightning I see her wince in anticipation. As the thunderclap hits, she shudders, and the car lurches slightly, but she doesn't lose control. 'I thought you might be afraid of the thunderstorm,' she tells me.

Hela: Slowly the decrees began to come in. It was soon announced that all Jews in Kraków had to wear a distinctive identifying mark. A white armband displaying a blue Star of David was to be worn on the right sleeve of clothing and outer-wear. Whoever failed to comply would face severe punishment. Whenever I met one of my Catholic school friends in the street, we were both embarrassed by the armband. Some Jews would take it off and put it in their pocket when they went out in the street or to a restaurant. In the beginning it wasn't so strict but slowly the penalties became harsher. Then restrictions were announced on the hours when we could go out; there was a curfew of nine o'clock for Jews.

Janka: We were out one day, father, Hela and I, on our way to visit someone. Hela was unwashed and uncombed; she looked a real mess. She was afraid of everything. Then the bombs started falling and we had to turn back. Hela was screaming hysterically.

The other thing we were afraid of was gas. Rumours were flying that gas bombs were being dropped and we would all die of gas poisoning. We didn't know what to do. We had home-made gasmasks which we would put over our faces when the bombs were falling—not that they would have helped one bit if there really had been poison gas. The Germans weren't actually using gas at that time, but would spread rumours about it to cause panic. Indeed everyone did panic.

A lot of people decided to leave Kraków, as it wasn't safe

66

to stay there, and we too decided to run away to the East. Father, Hela and I hurriedly packed a few belongings (my brother Kuba was in the Polish army doing his military service) and joined the crowds on the roads. We started to walk, hour after hour, part of a steady stream of people bowed down with possessions, pushing wagons or carts laden with pots and bundles. But after we had been on the road for a few days, the Germans overtook us. They came in tanks, rows and rows of them. Terrified, we hid in ditches. We dug holes to shelter in at night, and passed burning fields and corpses by the side of the road during the day.

Father had served in the French and Austrian armies, and he decided to volunteer to the Polish army to help to fight the Germans. There was a lot of encouragement for able-bodied men to join up. He believed his family would be better off, and that we would be well looked after. He thought, naively, that he would be given a gun and be able to fight the enemy. He assured us he would be back soon, and he left us girls and went on ahead. I decided that Hela and I should go back to Kraków. We were totally unprotected on the open road; at least in Kraków we had an apartment. So we returned, walking for days, hiding when the planes flew past, and occasionally getting a lift in the back of a small truck or wagon.

When we got back to the apartment it was difficult for us of course. All the glass in the windows had been shattered when the bombs fell. Without our father to protect us, we covered the holes as best we could with cardboard and rags. Fortunately it was still quite warm and we could sleep at night.

The first real shock, a foretaste of what was to come, occurred at this time. It was just a small thing, you might think, but it really affected me. We were given coupons to buy bread with, and every family was entitled to half a loaf of bread. I went to the bakery, where the man had always been friendly to me, but he looked at me for a moment and then said, 'I am sorry, miss, but the Jews get only a quarter of a loaf.' This was the first time it really hit me, that I was different from others. He felt sorry for me, but he had his orders. Later, Jews were thrown out of queues and couldn't buy anything. Luckily we still had enough money at that time to be able to buy some bread from the peasants who sold on the black market. If you had the money, they didn't care to whom they sold.

Where we lived there was a woman named Mrs Święchowa who looked after our building. Her husband had gone to the army, and for the half-year that we continued to live in Kraków we fed her and looked after her. She was very good to me. We lived on the first floor, and opposite us was an apartment belonging to father's cousin, Haubenstock, who had run away to Russia. It was quite large, and vacant at the time.

One day three Germans in uniform came to our apartment. They walked around and peered into different rooms while we stood frozen. One of them, of higher rank, told us he liked our apartment. He was giving us three hours to get out, so that he and his companions could set up their offices there. We were only to take clothing with us, nothing else. All our other things would be put into storage, and nothing would be damaged, he assured us. A list would be drawn up, and I would get a copy of it with an official stamp. I started to tremble, but also felt a cold rage beginning to rise. I told him that I lived here alone with my sister and there was no way we could shift out in three hours. I felt desperate, so I said to the Germans that I was not going to move, that it was too difficult for two young girls. One of the German soldiers took out his revolver and put it to my head. 'Are you going to do it or not?' he asked.

The Polish caretaker, Mrs Święchowa, had come to see what the commotion was about and was standing next to me. She stepped forward, addressing herself to the first German. 'Why are you doing this? Don't you know there is an apartment opposite which is empty? It would be much easier to shift into there.' The German looked at her, then at me. He could see I was desperate, and he was probably surprised that I had defied him and had not been afraid.

At last he said, 'All right,' turned on his heel and left with the others. We stood still for many minutes, listening to their footsteps fade away. That was how we were able to stay where we were for another six months.

A few weeks after this incident the Germans gave the order that all weapons had to be handed over. If they discovered that anyone was concealing a weapon, that person would be shot on the spot. Father owned a beautiful revolver with his initials on it, the one he'd nearly shot himself with. I knew it was hidden somewhere in the house, but where? I was very frightened and started to look for it. All day a troop of Germans was going from house to house, searching for weapons. I didn't want to leave the apartment, because I knew that if you left your home it could be requisitioned by the Germans and taken away from you. It was getting late by this time, so I thought, why should they kill both Hela and me? I told her to go to sleep at a friend's house, so that if the Germans came they would shoot only me.

I stayed home alone and throughout the night continued to search every room. I turned out the contents of drawers and cupboards, I rummaged in the pantry, I hunted in the cellar, the attic, every hiding-place I could think of, but I couldn't find the revolver. Many hours passed as the Germans searched methodically, one house after another, and as the sun rose higher in the sky I knew they were getting closer. But by the time they got really close—one building before ours—it was lunchtime, and the search was called off. After lunch they started in a building further down the street and never returned to us. This was the first miracle.

Father in the meantime had reached Lublin, but the Germans had overtaken him and he was unable to join the Polish army, so he decided to return home. (Kuba was also sent home from military service.) Father walked in through the door, tired and worn out, thin and dirty. As soon as I saw him I threw myself at him, and my first words were, 'Father, father, where did you hide the revolver?' He looked at me in a puzzled way, then took me down to the cellar.

There, just behind the door, lay the revolver, quite exposed. All those hours I had spent searching through the coal, it had been there, unobserved. On hearing my story, father took the revolver and buried it. What a lot I had suffered because of it!

Hela: Daily there were edicts announced which made our lives more difficult. But we believed that if we could just follow the regulations, all this would soon be over. The beginning of 1940 was very cold, but we had to save coal and couldn't afford to heat the apartment. There was no longer any sugar in the shops, and we began to use saccharine. There were no lemons for our tea, so we had to make do with artificial essence. Fortunately we still had many jars of jam: strawberry, raspberry and cherry. They were the last remnants of our days of plenty.

Janka: We had to have a *Kennkarte*, a work permit, in order to stay in Kraków. Sometimes we were ordered to sweep the streets of snow or wash the footpaths, as a form of degradation, with the Poles looking on. The Germans would catch Jewish people in the street at any time, and force them to work for many hours. We lived in great fear of not being able to return home. Bad news was coming thick and fast.

Next the order came expelling all Jews from Kraków to neighbouring towns and villages. We were forced to abandon our home and went with several other families to a little village in the country called Tonie, not far from Kraków. Father thought it was safer to stay close, but some of mother's family went to Lwów, and further east into Russia. We left home in a horse-drawn cart, with all our pots and pans, our feather pillows and eiderdowns, and everything else we could fit onto the cart that would be useful. We lived in Tonie for about a year, renting a farmhouse from a peasant woman. She was a thin woman with wrinkled cheeks who always wore a kerchief over her head. She was not very friendly to us and eyed us with suspicion. We didn't have to work there; we had a little money to pay for our food and board, but things were not easy. Some of the other families staying in Tonie had no money or income at all.

It was organised that six or seven families who had a bit of money would take turns to help the others. Hela and I cooked once a week to provide a meal for them. Our diet was mostly based on soup, made with a bit of garlic for taste, potatoes and bread. There was no coal for heat or cooking and we had to prepare our meals on a wood-fired stove. The room we lived in had a low ceiling and a beaten-earth floor. We slept on straw-filled mattresses that were hard and prickly. Our conditions were crowded, with all of us—father, we three children, father's sister Lajka with her two girls, and my uncle Kuba—all living in one room in the peasant woman's home. We were shocked, in June 1940, to hear that Paris had fallen to the Germans. I lived with the feeling of a dark cloud coming closer and was afraid. For me it was a period of poverty, anxiety and arguments.

Not that my sister remembers it that way. She was a good-looking girl, with thick dark hair and eyes that gleamed with passion. She was not overweight, but had a buxom figure. There were always lots of boys after her.

Hela: My memories of Tonie are always bathed in sunlight, like precious crystals as beautiful as they were fragile. Tonie was set among fields of wheat and meadows of rye and oats. It was the beginning of summer, with insects lazily droning in the still air. For me our move to Tonie was like a big adventure, a repetition of our summer holidays in the mountains, where we would take over a peasant woman's hut while the owners moved to the stables for the summer. Like many typical peasant huts, this one was painted bright blue, with white window and door frames. Indoors the walls were whitewashed.

The fields surrounded our hut, and there were sparkling streams babbling nearby. We would pick the ears of wheat when the farmer wasn't looking, and eat the berries raw. Rye was more prickly, and you could choke if you got a husk caught in your throat. There was nothing to match the taste

71

of carrots or radishes pulled straight from the earth, fresh and crunchy. The days were hot, with flies buzzing around our heads, and on balmy nights father would put our mattresses outside and let us sleep under the stars.

The sun rose early, and while the rest of the family was asleep I stole away in bare feet, eager to meet the new day and rejoicing in the myriad warblings and whistles of the birds.

I began to walk through the farmyard, towards the field of rye that was gently ruffled by the morning breeze. I found a narrow path weaving its way through the green spikes. It was moist and cool under my toes, squelching slightly in parts where the soil was mostly clay. As I stepped along this path through the waving rye, I could see vibrant red poppies, purple bell-like flowers called *kąkole*, and blue cornflowers that drank in the colour of the sky. I began to pick them from the right and the left of the path. Soon I had a large pile in the crook of my arm. I had to be careful, though, of the thistles and nettles that also grew in profusion.

As I wandered along, reaching out to the flowers, I didn't notice the old peasant waving his fist at me, until his shouts broke my delightful peace. He was angry at me for trampling the young rye stems, as he would have trouble harvesting them later with his scythe. I scurried away from him and hid among the stems, laughing.

We were surrounded by friends and members of our family. Father didn't work and life in the country was leisurely. The sky was blue, and feathery clouds drifted in the gentle breeze. I was part of a group of young people who went on outings and picnics, singing joyful songs, never realising what was going on elsewhere. Maybe the adults talked about war in whispers, remembering the horrors of the First World War, but to me it was all very distant and didn't concern me. It was an idyllic existence.

I had begun to be interested in boys and I knew how to turn their heads. I was fifteen. Janka had several admirers, boys who wanted her to notice them, and I was thrilled to find that they were nice to me as well. I also started to meet boys of my own age. When the warm evening breezes blew we played at romance and discovered the thrill of lingering glances and secret kisses.

There was a Polish boy, Tadeusz Pokusa, who was in love with me, as was Romek Rusinowicz, a Jewish boy living there at the same time. Romek was the oldest of five boys, a handsome youth with fiery dark eyes, while Tadeusz had typical Polish features, with fair hair and intense blue eyes the colour of the cornflowers that dotted the fields. *Pokusa* means 'temptation' in Polish, so my friends made fun of me and played on the word. It was Tadeusz who taught me how to swim in the icy waters of a little river nearby, encouraging me to put my head underwater and laughing when I splashed him.

Romek had smooth dark hair, slicked down above his broad forehead. His eyes twinkled as he paid me compliments. I told him I loved him, conveniently forgetting that I had given the same assurances to Tadeusz the night before. One of my girlfriends, Dorka Rath, shrewdly observed the goings-on, and casually began to sing a popular song of the time: 'Him or me, you have to choose . . .' She made fun of me and, being older, could see the folly of my behaviour. She was a very clever girl from a rich family that sold stationery in Kraków, but they had shifted, like us, to Tonie because of the new regulations. She had a lovely voice and taught me many songs, including 'The Alphabet Song', which had the first line innocently saying what 'A' stood for, but the second and every alternate line were quite vulgar. When my father heard me singing this song he was shocked, and terribly angry at me. He couldn't understand what was happening to his little girl.

The two boys fought over me, and I of course was delighted. My dark hair was long and thick, and I would braid it and wear it in different styles to impress them. I swept it up and arranged it in three locks on the top, or wound the braids around my head. When it was my sixteenth birthday in July, both of the boys brought me huge bunches of flowers, competing with each other for my affection.

It was a time in my life of burgeoning romance and innocent happiness, of fragile joy and confusing emotions. This
joy was short-lived, however, because dark days lay ahead.

∽

*My mother is full of mysteries. We sit together near the window
late one warm afternoon, with the soft drone of insects carried in
on the breeze. She lets herself sit still for once, and with her hands
folded in her lap she starts to recite poems for me, poems from her
childhood. I am mesmerised by the melody of her voice, even though
I don't understand many of the words, for they are not part of the
everyday vocabulary needed between a parent and a child. They
are mysterious words of longing, of faraway places, of strange pas-
sions and unfulfilled desires. My mother's face is dreamy at first,
with eyes half-closed, as she lovingly forms the vowel sounds and
the rhymes flow in a gentle tide. But as she gets caught up in the
drama of her recitation, her face becomes more animated, with two
pink spots appearing on her cheeks. The words begin to tumble
over each other and I have difficulty in even following the gist of
the poem. Her gaze is no longer on me, on my curls glowing in
the last rays of the sun and my dimpled cheeks; she stares into the
distance, caught in a time and place I know nothing about. Her
hands have started to tremble in her lap, the fingers touch each
other, cautiously at first, then more urgently, clutching, kneading,
clenching and unclenching. I watch in fascination, knowing I am
no longer being observed, and listen more intently to her words.
There is a strength and control in the rhythms of her voice that I
have not heard before, and she is bathed in energy that drives her
on and on.*

*At last the end is approaching; I can tell, because her voice is
slowing down, the intonation more singsong, the expected con-
cluding rhyme just around the corner. Her eyes are small and
bright, and as I keep my focus on her face I realise with a shock
that there are many things I don't know about this woman. The
muscles of her face relax as she finishes, and her gaze once again
rests on me, a wistful smile playing about her mouth.*

6

Janka: After about a year, another order was issued. All Jews had to go either to a place in the country called Skała, sixty kilometres from Kraków, or into the Kraków ghetto, the Jewish quarter which had just been closed off with bricked-up walls and barbed wire. I didn't like country life much and I wanted to stay among Jews, so I preferred to go to the ghetto. I felt that here at least we could settle with our own people. My sister Hela started to cry; she had enjoyed the country and didn't want to be closed in by the ghetto walls, but a decision had to be made. Some people ran away to Lwów in the east, towards Russia, but most had no choice.

The streets leading to the ghetto were full of carts piled with wardrobes, clothes and kitchen utensils belonging to the Jews moving towards it. Streams of people like us were arriving from all directions, loaded down with their belongings. Some carried suitcases, others pushed small wagons stacked high with packages, chairs, pots and pans, anything useful that would fit. It was a lovely sunny day but no one was smiling or appreciating the weather. Everyone looked grey and depressed. At the same time the Poles were leaving, going in the other direction. What chaos!

Father had borrowed a horse-drawn wagon to load on all our things to take to the ghetto. We bought some sacks of potatoes and corn to take with us and packed them on with our belongings. I also took a flowering oleander in a pot, which I couldn't bear to part with; I had watched it grow through the seasons and I thought it would brighten up our life. I was sure the war would finish some time soon and things would return to normal. After all, the Germans were a civilised nation.

The ghetto was situated in Podgórze, a suburb of Kraków near the Vistula river. It had been closed off by bricking-up certain streets, although a tram still ran without stopping across the centre of it, through an arched gateway and down Limanowskiego street. We arrived on 20 February 1941. By March, all the Jews in the district had been rounded up and herded into the ghetto. It was very difficult to shift into the ghetto itself. Because there were so many people crammed into every room, it was hard to find a place to live. I had a friend, old Mrs Penner, who told me about half a room that might be available, but I had to go to the *Judenrat*. This was the Jewish council that was set up in each community to carry out the Germans' orders and control the Jews. They had to supply labour squads and organise housing. The elected members had to cooperate with the Germans in order to avoid a worse fate, and to keep some sort of order in the midst of chaos. We didn't feel resentful of them because we knew they were forced to do the things they did; if not they, others would do them. Perhaps they even made life a bit easier, because they stood between us and the Germans.

So I went to the *Judenrat*, where another friend worked, and she arranged a room for us. When we found the place, in Józefińska street, we lugged our cases and bags up the stairs. We discovered that we had to share the room with another family, a couple named Opoczyński, who had two little girls. The husband made little boiled sweets in the ghetto and sold them to make a living. We looked around at the room and wondered how we would manage. We had to share this half-room between us: my sister, my brother, our father and me. The first thing I did, before I unpacked anything else, was to put the oleander bush out on the balcony.

There is a strange misshapen cactus that grows in Auntie's garden. It has flattened, fleshy stems with wavy edges, and it seems to put up with a lot of neglect and mistreatment. You can transplant it

easily, just by breaking a leaf off at its base and planting it else-
where. It is a very slow grower and not very attractive to look at,
except when it comes into flower. Auntie has told me it flowers
only once a year, on November 28th, her birthday. Nine times out
of ten she is right. Each year in spring I watch the tiny pink buds
elongate and swell with every passing day. Towards evening in
late November the first flower opens. It is large and spectacular,
with creamy white petals and a powerful fragrance. I am amazed
by this clever cactus, and the gifts it brings. I know more than
ever what a special person my Auntie is.

Hela: After living in the country, I hated having to come to
the ghetto. I felt resentful and deprived of my short-lived
happiness. All the light and the colour had gone from my
life. We had to live in cramped conditions that we shared
with another family. I found this really difficult and missed
my friends. I heard that Romek had also shifted into the
ghetto with his family but I rarely got to see him.

Janka: An old wardrobe was used to divide the room in half.
Hela was terribly unhappy and used to cry, 'I'm suffocating
here, I can't stand living in the ghetto any more. Let's go
back to the country.'

I replied, 'All right, go back to the country, but I won't go
with you.' Mother had died in the country, and I always
believed that if she had been in the city and could have had
medical attention, maybe she would have stayed alive. In
those times you had to take a horse and ride miles to the
city to fetch a doctor. Hela kept pleading for us to leave the
ghetto, to go to Skała. Father didn't know what to do and
felt very frustrated. Despite Hela's entreaties we decided to
stay in the ghetto, and she resigned herself to our narrow
existence.

After a few weeks came the news that the thousands of
Jews who had gone to Skała, the country town, had been
shot, every single one of them. Among them were many
members of mother's family: her uncle David and his wife
Andzia, their son Moryc and his wife, her uncle Wicek with

his four daughters, Adela, Mania, Stefa and Rózia (whose son Jan had died at the same time as our canary), uncle Janek . . . aunts, uncles, cousins—some forty members of our family perished.

For me, this was really the second miracle: that I had chosen to go to the ghetto and insisted on staying there. Thankfully, Aunt Lajka and her daughters had come with us as well.

Hela: Every day was a real struggle. Our room was dark, the rays of the sun never reached it. It smelt of dampness, clogged plumbing and poverty. Everyone lived in over-crowded conditions and people's worst characteristics became obvious. Depending on where they came from and what sort of upbringing they had had, they responded in different ways to the constant suffering. They argued over drying space on the clothes line, or about the shared cooking space. At night when everyone came back from work, all the available space was taken up by folding beds and you couldn't move. In the morning everything had to be folded up again. People complained, swore in vulgar language, became stubborn and stupid. Nevertheless we had to get on together; we had no choice.

Janka: In the ghetto we were issued with a new *Kennkarte*, a yellow work card, with name, age, profession and other essential information, and a sepia photo attached. There were frequent checks, and if we didn't have our card with us we could be arrested and sent away in cattle trucks.

One day the Germans set up tables and sat in rows to check our cards. If we were lucky they would stamp them with a large blue 'J', which entitled us to work and remain in the ghetto; if they didn't stamp the card, we would be taken away. Hela and I lined up in different queues. Slowly the line moved forward and I kept glancing across to Hela. I clutched my card tightly. I had written 'embroiderer' as my profession. Before the war I had worked in an accounting firm called Raber's, but I knew there was no point in writing

78

'office worker', as they had no need of office workers here. At last I reached the table. The German looked at my card, then brusquely told me they didn't need an embroiderer and refused to stamp my card. 'Move on!' he yelled. I turned to leave, then suddenly caught the look in my sister's eyes. Her profession was written down as 'dressmaker', *Schneiderin*, and she had succeeded in getting her card stamped. She had been observing me from the corner of her eye and was terribly frightened. She motioned to me with her head, indicating that I should move to a different line.

So I went to stand in another queue, in front of a different German. When my turn came he looked at the card, then looked at me for a few moments. He looked down at the card again, at my surname Haubenstock, and said, 'Oh, I know someone called Haubenstock, he was a very good worker in my stable. He was wonderful with my horses.' (This was the cousin of father's who had left the flat empty in Kraków!) A smile formed around his mouth and without a second thought he stamped my card. And that's how it was that I could stay in the ghetto with Hela and had permission to work.

We began to work in a clothing factory, located on the site of an old chocolate factory, 'Optima', in Węgierska street. It was run by a man called Wagner. Here he supervised the production of military uniforms and work clothes. Our job was to sew embroidered eagles onto the pockets of the uniforms, or *Wehrmacht* braid onto the epaulettes. Sometimes we sewed on gold buttons. There were ten girls working at each table. We were with Rózia Kornhauser, Lutka Goldberg, Andzia Reich, Rutka Szmulewicz and Emilia Braw, a pretty girl with dark curly hair who was only fourteen and a half. I had a calm, placid temperament so I got on well with all of them, and I was particularly fond of Emilia, or Mila as they called her. I was happy to have a job to do.

Our other main concern was food. We had to try to buy something to eat, and to cook it. We were fortunate that we had managed to bring potatoes, corn and a bit of wheat with us to the ghetto. We borrowed a small mill and used it to grind the grain painstakingly by hand. Hela and I used the oven that we shared with our neighbours to bake this meal into a kind of bread; it was terribly dark and heavy, but at least we had something to eat.

Many people from the surrounding areas continued to flood into the ghetto. They often arrived beaten and very hungry. We could no longer go to the market on the *Plac*, but we still had enough to eat because those who worked outside the ghetto, marching out in columns every morning, were able to smuggle food in, which we could buy. With this, and the potatoes we still had, father made us cook a big pot of soup every day, to feed these newcomers. Hela and I protested and just wanted to give them some raw potatoes, but father insisted we cook for them. He was a very kind and generous man.

He also got me to help him when he carried pots of soup to the hospital, for those who were sick. The hospital was overcrowded, with groaning people lying on the floor in the corridors and a terrible smell hanging over everything. I hated having to go there.

Hela: Conditions in the ghetto were fairly primitive; in our room there was a basin to wash in, but no bath or shower. The toilet was outside somewhere. We were restricted as to the times we could use electricity, and our room was often dark. At night we would burn a carbide lamp, which gave off a little bit of light but smelt terrible. When the weather became warmer, there was a sickly sweetish smell of dirt and garbage in the air. There were people everywhere, crowding the rooms and the streets. It was impossible to find a cool quiet place to sit; even the cellars were crowded. I sat in the cellar, in a corner, feeling hot and miserable. I recalled the cool dimness and spaciousness of the huge Mariacki church (Church of the Virgin Mary) in Kraków where our maid had often taken me when I was little. I had also often gone there with father; he was a very tolerant man, and a great admirer of church architecture. I tried very hard to block out the present and to imagine I was there.

I could see it before me, the Mariacki, standing with its two uneven towers in the main square of Kraków, the *Rynek Główny*, which had existed since the thirteenth century. Sunlight streamed through a beautiful stained-glass window made in 1370, and I felt the hushed atmosphere surrounding us as we admired the magnificent altar by Wit Stwosz, built in the fifteenth century. Suddenly the silence was broken by the sound of a loud trumpet. Every hour was marked by this trumpet call, commemorating an ancient story about a trumpeter who tried to save the city from an attacking army. Kraków was Poland's third-largest city and was full of churches. I knew nearly all of them, and started to name them to myself. My school was near St Mark's, and also near the Church of All Saints, which had large plaster statues of many saints around the outside walls.

As well as all the churches, there were little statues and shrines on almost every corner, and Catholics who passed crossed themselves or knelt for a moment. Nuns and priests were a common sight in the streets of Kraków. I also remembered the Grand Synagogue, on Szpitalna street, where we would go with our parents on *Rosh Hashanah*, the New Year, to hear the *shofar*, or ram's horn, being blown. The men sat separately from the women, but it was a place to meet people and socialise, as well as pray. I tried to hold on to the pictures in my mind, and to hear the words of the Jewish prayers. Instead I became aware of a man and a woman quarrelling near me as I sat in the hot cellar. I was dragged back to the present. My attempt to escape faded away and once again I felt miserable.

Janka: The *Judenrat* started to ask young men to volunteer for civil service, to form a group that would keep order in the long queues, watch the gate, and be responsible for the formation and counting of the labour groups, which had to be delivered to certain points of assembly. Those who volunteered could in some way protect their elderly parents and family, and they had a bit more freedom to move around. Their job was to keep order and make sure things ran smoothly. The young volunteers received a cap and an armband, so as to be visible in the crowds. All seemed well. But the moment they received a uniform—and a stick—they became the police. They were viewed with suspicion by many of us and were sometimes accused of being collaborators, but their survival and that of their families depended on their cooperation with the SS. Refusal to carry out orders meant not only that they would be shot but that other innocent people would suffer also.

When the war broke out, Kuba had been in the Polish army doing his military service. He was impressed by uniforms, and with his past history of feeling discriminated against, he wanted to be important. So he volunteered for civil service to become an *Odeman*, or OD (*Ordnungsdienst*).

Other people we knew became ODs as well. At first they were identified only by the cap and armband; later they wore a smart uniform with high polished boots. They came with lists from the SS for the transports, and went about their tasks with self-importance. Although the ODs were Jewish, they were the police and had orders to carry out. Some of them would try to help, or warn people to hide on a particular day, as they had seen the latest list. But their job was to fill the quotas, and push the lamenting victims out onto the street. People like Symche Spira, who had been little more than a messenger boy before the war, now strutted around and dealt directly with the Germans. He was the Commandant of the ghetto, although he was almost illiterate. He spoke Polish very badly, like a lot of the Orthodox people from Kazimierz, and couldn't speak any language properly.

An OD could make your life a bit easier. Kuba could get us extra bread or find out things for us. I was told that he would sometimes beat his own people. But he explained to me that if a worker was not working hard enough, and an SS man was watching, he had to beat the worker to avoid the alternative: the SS man would have shot the worker on the spot. I didn't envy Kuba's role.

Kuba thought that becoming an OD would give him power and would impress people. He never really had friends. When you are weak and are given power, it is very bad for your character. I didn't want anything from him, I didn't want any favours. In the ghetto our diet consisted mainly of bread with margarine or sometimes marmalade. Meanwhile Kuba, who had a job at the airport, would get chocolates and all sorts of delicacies, which he would give to his comrades and his girlfriends (he was a real ladies' man). I didn't want any of that. I never loved him, and always felt that mother had died because of him. He tried to get me to accept his gifts but I refused.

I'm convinced mother had a heart attack because of Kuba. Maybe she suffered unknowingly from angina as well, but I'm sure his behaviour and the worries he caused her were a contributing factor to her death. Even after mother died there were problems. I couldn't find her wedding-ring and suspected that he must have stolen it. I suffered a lot because of him. He was a womaniser and a compulsive liar, always trying to make out that he was more important than he was. People in the ghetto would point at him, and I felt bad because he was my brother. All through my growing-up years I had worries because of him, but even more so when he became an OD.

Despite everything he was very clever, and probably that's what helped him to survive. I know that he once rescued a small child from the ghetto by hiding it under a blanket and taking it out in his rucksack; he was able to help a lot of people because of his position. Also, I know that when the atrocities started, many ODs tried to withdraw from their jobs. Their commander made them understand that there would be retaliations directed against their families. Even if they considered committing suicide, their families would be the victims. So what could he have done? Maybe he joined up to help us; maybe he was cowardly and needs to be pitied. I don't want to judge him.

We still had our own clothes in the ghetto, and that helped us a lot because it meant we still had something to sell. I had two or three good-quality suits that I had brought with me from home. One was a beautiful brown check, made of

English wool. I gave it to a Polish tailor who worked with us in the factory, and asked him to look after it for me. I also asked him to keep some dresses and a new pair of long brown leather boots. He assured me he would take good care of them.

Some Poles were helpful in that they could sell some of our things for us and bring us the money. We sold a few of our good suits and jumpers for food. We even sold our sheets and tablecloths to the Poles. I still had a wedding gift that had been given to mother—a box of silver spoons. It was worth a lot of money, but it was so precious to me that I didn't want to sell it, even when we needed the money. I also had some beautiful porcelain cups that we drank tea out of, and crystal dishes. All these things we had brought to the ghetto, and we used them daily despite the oddness of this touch of luxury amid the squalor.

I had also brought with me all the jewellery that had once belonged to mother and grandmother. I sewed a square of material onto the front of each of my underpants and always kept the jewellery secure against my tummy. Luckily I was so slim that it wasn't noticeable. Sometimes the weather was very hot, but I always kept the jewellery on me. There were two chains; one was a big heavy chain of grandmother's with a watch, and the other, which had belonged to mother, had a diamond clasp. I also had her diamond rings, and a ring of father's that he had worn on his little finger. There were earrings as well, and a ring that uncle Zygmunt from America had given me. All of this I wore against my body the whole time I was in the ghetto. Of course it was not easy. When I had to wash my underwear, I had to switch the jewellery into another pair of underpants without anyone noticing. I didn't want to sell any of it, as I was very sentimental. Later on, of course, it was all taken from me, in Płaszów.

I am walking with a lot of other people. We have a journey to make and I know it's important. It seems a long way to travel, and as I keep walking, the path is becoming narrower and steeper. The ground, I notice, is strewn with round glass pebbles.

I pick up and hold one of these pebbles, but it is now a glass egg with translucent layers, very precious and fragile. I keep climbing, taking great care with the egg, holding it close to my body, but suddenly it slips from my hands and rolls away, the outside layers breaking off. I pick it up, horrified, but I keep walking on, clinging to the damaged egg. I look around and see a table spread with food, including a bowl of these transparent glass eggs. I start to look for an unbroken one to replace mine but find they are all cracked or damaged. I search desperately for a whole egg, but can't find one. In the end I take one of the damaged eggs and wrap it in foil, so that no one will know. I am aware of great sorrow and regret at not having been able to mend what was broken.

Janka: We were never sure what would happen next. Lists were being drawn up daily of people who were to be deported, a hundred names or more at a time. We never knew where they went. Every night we slept in fear; every morning we would wake wondering who was on the list this time. One of the first to go was my friend Kuba Stempel. He had always been very fond of me and now he was gone, we had no idea where. His parents were in the ghetto with us, and a younger sister, Hela. Later, when his parents were being taken away, Hela insisted on going with them, saying they were old and needed someone to look after them. I begged her to stay with us, as no one knew where they'd finish up, but she went with her parents and they all perished.

Hela: Nevertheless life went on fairly normally in the beginning. Tadeusz, my Polish boyfriend from the country, came secretly to see me several times in the ghetto, and, knowing we were hungry, he brought bread and sausage for us, or other supplies. On one occasion he couldn't get out because he wasn't supposed to have been inside the ghetto in the first place, and he was challenged at the gate. We had to bribe an OD, giving him 5 złoty to let Tadeusz out. I never thought I'd see him again, but time has strange ways of bringing people back together . . .

So life continued with some sort of normality. The ghetto was like a small town with shops, a bakery, a post office, a ghetto newspaper, a bank, a butcher, a hairdresser, and even a café where musicians would play and people danced in the evenings. Slowly we became accustomed to our conditions, thinking that if we could only be patient, things would surely improve. But we were crowded and restricted in our movements and couldn't go outside the ghetto. Life was controlled by the Germans, but there were not many of them within the ghetto walls. They gave authority to the Jewish council to carry out their orders and do all the paperwork. There was no work available individually; you had to be allocated to a work team that was marched daily out of the ghetto to its place of labour, then returned in the evening. I never went outside the ghetto.

Janka: Father brought books with him to the ghetto; he was a great reader. He loved botany and had many illustrated books on the subject. I used to spend hours as a child looking at the delicately drawn pictures of flowers and leaves. It was from him that I got my love of flowers.

Once, I was complaining to him about how bleak our existence was, and how much I missed having flowers. He gazed at me for a moment, then suddenly ripped off his blue-and-white armband with the Star of David. Father didn't look typically Jewish and he was very proud of his Polish background. Somehow he sneaked out of the ghetto and went to the market in the nearby district of Podgórze. He bought me a big bunch of white orchid-like flowers, called *storczyki*. They grew in the forest near Kraków and smelt beautiful. I buried my face in their fragrance and wept, both for the lost life that still continued outside the ghetto walls and for the love I felt for father, who had risked his life to buy flowers for his daughter. If he had been caught outside the ghetto, he would have been shot!

Auntie carefully winds the fern frond around the woody green stems to make a pleasing arrangement with the full-petalled yellow

*and pink roses from her garden. What a fragrance they have! With
her head tilted a little to one side, she steps back and examines her
handiwork. Her hands are still deft, even though the veins show
like cords beneath the wrinkled skin. She moves towards the tall
vase on the glass-topped table and adjusts another flower. The sun
streams in through the half-opened curtains. Maybe her friends
who are coming to visit won't notice the care she has taken to make
everything look right, but then again she is doing it more for her
own pleasure than anyone else's. Flowers have always been important for her; little symbols of beauty that exist for themselves,
conscious only of their needs, living purely for the pleasure of it.
Flowers mean life, growth, survival.*

Hela: One of our greatest fears was that we would be
grabbed from the streets by the Germans. We could be taken
at any time, loaded onto the back of a truck with kicks and
yells, and made to spend the whole day doing hard physical
work. We heard that they were building barracks on the site
of the Jewish cemetery, outside Kraków, to transfer the
ghetto there. People would be grabbed to help with the
building, which was being carried out at a fast rate. Often
they didn't return from there.

One grey and drizzly day I was seized in this way, and
forced to work on the railway track all day long collecting
human waste and putting it into buckets. Mud and filth were
everywhere. Another time I was sent with other girls to
sweep snow from the streets. People sometimes spent the
whole night clearing the city of snow. If you paused for a
moment to rest or catch your breath, the German in charge
would kick you or hit you. Some of the bystanders seemed
to feel sorry for us, but others thought it was a big joke.

On other occasions Jews were taken not to work but to
give blood. It always surprised me that they treated us like
scum, yet our blood was good enough for German soldiers.
I stayed indoors a lot and tried to avoid being caught.

There was also the constant fear of being taken from your
home. Often we heard the heavy march of boots, screams
and shouts above or below us, as people were brutally

roused from their beds and marched away. I always slept in fear, jumping at the slightest noise.

∞

The cold water of the Ovens River flows swiftly over shimmering pebbles on the river bed. It is a hot day, with the sun warming the fragrant pine needles lying in layers beneath the dark pines near the water. I play on the edge, picking up and arranging the pebbles, disappointed that the vibrant colours fade when they dry. Close to me, there is the ceaseless movement of the current, deep and dangerous. My mother warns me to stay away from the edge, but I am tired of sitting on the blanket where they play cards and tell jokes with their friends who once lived in the same home town.

One of these friends, Ignac Borkowski, has strong brown arms, and he swims effortlessly through the cold water, calling out to the others to join him. He has heavy eyebrows and twinkling blue eyes. As I gaze in admiration he moves towards me, sweeps me up in his arms and carries me into the water. I squeal with the shock of the cold and the unexpected force of the current flowing around me. He pretends to let me go for an instant, then catches hold of me again. I am breathless with fear, but also exhilaration at being there with him, in this dangerous river. I feel the thrill of danger, of the unknown. Ignac laughs out loud, and I laugh too. With his strong arms holding me close, I sense the possibilities of adventure, beyond the boundaries.

But stronger than all these is the fear in my mother's voice, calling from the edge. 'It's dangerous! Come back!' She wades a little way into the water, a bit unsteady because of the shifting pebbles, her arms outstretched.

As soon as we're near enough she grabs me from him and clutches me close to her body, so close that I feel her heart beating, pounding out the rhythm of her love for me. Waves of love encircle me, protecting me from harm. The world is a dangerous place; I could be snatched away at any moment. Her relief turns to anger at Ignac. 'Idiota,' she spits out. 'She could have drowned!' But he only laughs uproariously, the water streaming off his dark hairy body.

Holding my hand tightly, she leads me back to where the rug is spread under the shade of the pine trees' hot stillness. The cushioning pine needles crackle as we walk, and all we can hear is the occasional fly buzzing past and the murmuring of the water. I look back longingly at the cool river, but it is forbidden. I watch the river for a long time, trying to follow the swift current with my eyes, but unable to picture its long journey, beyond my sight, beyond the safety of here and now. Ignac is still smiling broadly, and when no one is looking he gives me a big wink.

Long after everyone has gone back to their card game, she clings to me, holding me on her lap and drying me with a towel. She gently rubs my cool skin, enveloping me in her concern. As the sun beats down I begin to feel stifled and my eyes turn to the sparkling water, a million diamonds dancing on the surface. My mother's eyes sparkle too, and her eyelashes are moist. There are little furrows between her brows as she croons quietly to me.

Forever after, the scent of pine needles brings flooding memories of hot silence, broken by the rippling sound of water, deep and cold, flowing to somewhere else, somewhere full of possibilities but charged with danger. It swirls and tugs at me, but stronger than the river is the message from behind me, holding me back.

I often dream of water, surging around me, the ground shifting beneath my feet. I see the dark smiling face of a man, taunting, cajoling, tempting me to go further—but I can't, because of the softness of my mother's arms and the moist sparkle in her eyes.

7

Janka: There were frequent searches, confiscations and deportations. We lived in constant dread of the sound of heavy footsteps, the knock at the door. Sometimes it was an *Odeman* checking papers. Other times they would come for jewellery, or order us out for roll-call. Often people were grabbed from their beds, in their nightshirts. Lists continued to be drawn up by the Gestapo, but for what reason? They took people with or without *Kennkarten*; they took children without parents, and parents without children. People often disappeared without a trace. When there were rumours of another transport being organised, people would sleep at each other's houses, trying to avoid being caught. We heard shouts and cries from the floor above. I tried to sleep. Later I heard they'd taken a mother but left the rest of the family.

My earliest nightmare is of a narrow cobblestoned lane. Fences on both sides crowd me in. As I walk along, alone, I realise I am being followed. An old man comes behind me with a sack, and grabs me. I struggle and scream. Although he is old he is much stronger than I, and he puts me in the sack and carries me away. I wake in panic. The dream returns many times but I don't tell anyone about it. Sometimes he takes me to a bare brick room, where there are large metal hooks in the walls. He hangs me up on one of these and leaves me there, helpless. Other times he throws the sack into a river, or into a deep pit. I struggle, unable to escape.

Hela: Early in June 1942 there was an *Aussiedlung*, a deportation of Jews out of the ghetto. It was a hot and stifling day.

We were told we had to go inside and stay in our homes until given the signal. We were not to go near the windows, on pain of death. Soldiers guarded every corner and laneway, so that not even a mouse could escape. We could hear snarling Dobermann dogs and shootings, as the SS began systematically taking all the people over fifty-five years of age and all the young children. Screams and shots became louder as they came closer. We huddled in a small group with our family, almost too frightened to breathe.

With their heavy boots they burst through the door, threatening us with their guns. Amidst the savagery and noise they called out father's name and grabbed him roughly. I began to scream and tried to hold on to him, but it was all over in a few seconds. He was gone.

Father had turned fifty-five the previous October. He was still a relatively young man, full of energy and quite fit. He had never been sick in his life, never needed to go to the doctor, and, since his years in the French army, had learnt to do gymnastics and wash daily in cold water. He called out to me as they took him away, 'Don't worry, I'm going to fight!' Then he was marched out through the gates of the ghetto with all the rest of the older Jews. Always the soldier, he never believed he was going to die. We knew nothing then about Auschwitz or gas ovens. I persuaded myself he was going somewhere to work, or to join the army. He had always been so patriotic towards Poland, and was convinced he was going to fight for his country.

Janka: After the SS had taken our father, I stood there, terrified and shocked, but eventually I roused myself. My only thought was to rescue him. As I was about to race out into the street, an OD collided with me in the doorway. He had found father's *Kennkarte* lying on the ground just a moment before and was bringing it to me. Clutching it in my hand, I ran downstairs and into the street. Although I was very afraid, I went from one German to another to beg them to let father stay in the ghetto. There was a young boy in Sienkiewicz's book, *W Pustyni i w Puszczy* (*In Desert and*

Wilderness) who said, 'I am afraid, but nevertheless I will go.' That's how I felt. These words echoed in my mind as I ran through the streets. Despite the fear, I had to try. It wasn't even courage, just an overpowering need to try to do something to save father. But it didn't help.

For several days I couldn't eat anything and developed a stomach ulcer. I was to suffer from this continually in the following months. We did receive one letter from father, which said, 'Don't worry about me, I will be all right.' He thought they were going to the east, to a labour camp.

Maybe he went to Auschwitz, or maybe to another concentration camp; we never found out. I never saw him again.

I close my eyes and focus on my grandfather's image. At first he is indistinct, blurred. But gradually I can see his neatly brushed moustache and his deep brown eyes, crinkled at the corners. He is sitting at a polished wooden table opposite me, slightly sideways, with one knee carefully crossed over the other. His fingers, long and neatly manicured, play with a silver teaspoon which he turns over and over as the thoughts flow through his mind and he considers my questions. I watch carefully, for he seems about to speak; I desperately want to hear his words.

But as his mouth opens the image is frozen. There is only silence. Hard as I try, I can never hear his voice, his words. I look at his half-opened mouth, his immobile hand still clutching the spoon, and realise that I will never know the answers. I feel angry at his naivety, his inability to see into the future. I feel angry at him for denying me the right to have grandparents like other children at school did, grandmas who baked cakes and cuddled you into their soft bosoms, grandpas who showed you how to play card tricks or sat in comfortable armchairs and told you stories from the past.

I heard no stories from the past. The past was a sealed and silent box that sat in a corner, just behind me; a box that no one around me would open.

Hela: The 'Actions' continued. Again and again we were assembled in the town square, *Plac Zgody* (Place of Agreement), and they read out lists of names of the people who were to be taken away. We stood for hours and hours, called up day or night, while the shouting of names went on. By June they had already taken all the elderly people. Sometimes they took anyone who looked a bit unhealthy or feeble. Sometimes it was sheer chance; I'd be standing in a line and they would decide they had enough people, so they halted just before my turn. It didn't seem to depend on anything, only luck. We never knew what would happen, what was the right thing to do in order to survive, and could take no precautions. This uncertainty tormented us.

Janka: We were waiting in lines as names were being read out. There was a young dark-haired woman in front of me who had a knapsack on her back. A German soldier was walking slowly along the line of people, casually glancing at us every now and then. He paused near us. He came closer to the young woman and peered at her. Suddenly, detecting some slight movement in her knapsack, he began to hit her with his truncheon. She screamed out and pleaded with him, trying to avoid his blows and begging him not to kill her baby. Again and again, I heard the sickening thud of his truncheon amid her shrieks. But all her pleas were useless. I will never forget the gloating look of satisfaction on his face as he killed that child. His grinning face has haunted me all my life.

The only way to get out of this misery was on false Aryan papers. But then you lived in constant fear of discovery. I had a girlfriend on Aryan papers, with a five-year-old daughter. She was denounced by someone who knew her, and was arrested. She was taken to a clearing in the forest and forced to dig a grave. She then had to watch as they shot her daughter, before shooting her.

Hela: One hot day in summer, they rounded up all the children that were still left in the ghetto. Heavy transport trucks pulled up outside the kindergarten, and little children, some clutching rag dolls, were led into the trucks. With their large eyes and serious faces, they were taken away. The mothers howled and pleaded but were brutally driven back. Every child that was not hidden that day was taken away and murdered.

Janka: Again there was an *Aussiedlung* that all of us had to go through. We had to assemble in the square, and were marched in single file past the Germans who were sitting calmly at tables. Without any fuss, they raised a finger and pointed, selecting us to go to the left or the right, for life or for death. Before me were two of my second cousins, a girl and a boy with the surname of Zales. What I remember most about the girl was her thick golden hair, plaited in two strands, gleaming in the sun. She was sixteen, and with her blond hair and blue eyes she did not look typically Jewish. The boy was seventeen, tall and good-looking. The Germans looked at the girl and said to her, 'You are too beautiful, too fair,' and she was chosen for death, as was her brother. I was right behind her and was told to go into the other column. I will never forget the beseeching look in her eyes as she moved away. (Only her older brother, Józek Zales, who had gone earlier to Canada, survived from that family.)

Father's older brother, Hemiu (the one who ran the fruit business in Kraków), had a wife, Gusta, who was also a blonde; though no longer young, she was an attractive woman. During this *Aussiedlung* she tried to join a young people's group, hoping that this group would survive and the Germans might believe her to be younger than her forty years. But she was pulled out of the group and sent to her death too, in Bełżec. It was heartbreaking to see my uncle Hemiu come home from work looking for his wife, only to find her gone.

Hela and I now had no parents and we were very lonely. The bitter winter had given way to spring. The evenings became warmer and, despite everything, there was a feeling of romance in the air. The greyness of our surroundings was invaded by the fragrance of jasmine wafting across from beyond the walls. We went regularly at dusk to wait for milk, because sometimes peasant women would come to the ghetto at the end of the day to sell their milk. One mild evening I stood with a tin can, waiting, and started chatting to a man who was also waiting for milk.

We met several times after this, and felt attracted to each other. He was two years older than me, and very handsome, with dark-blond hair and green eyes. I worked in the clothing factory with some other women and I told them about this man, Salek Immergluck, that I had met. They were pleased for me, and were not surprised when, within a very short time, I announced we were getting married. He had been lonely too, and told me he loved me, so we decided to marry. I had not been able to marry before the war, as father couldn't provide a big enough dowry.

I thought a lot about Salek. I don't know whether I loved him, but I didn't want to die a single woman; if I had to die I would rather be married. I didn't know what would happen and my mind was in turmoil, filled with conflicting emotions. I thought about mother and wondered what she would have advised. I missed her presence and longed for her wise words.

On a sudden impulse, I removed my armband, bribed someone so that I could illegally get out of the ghetto, and went to visit mother's grave in the Kraków cemetery. I felt I had to share my feelings with her at this important step in my life.

I sat by her grave and poured out to her all of my longings, fears and hopes. After sitting for a time by the cold stone, I felt in some way comforted. I returned to the ghetto in a defiant mood. Come what may, I would continue to live my life for however long it lasted. Salek managed to get a ring from somewhere, and we made preparations. There was a rabbi in the ghetto who could also perform the civil ceremony of marriage.

On 18 October 1942, I fasted all day. It was a mild autumn day and the wedding was held outside, with a lot of my friends around. I was married in a lovely navy suit that I had brought with me from home, and a beautiful pair of navy crocodile-skin shoes. I borrowed an off-white hat from a friend. Some of my friends whispered to me, 'Janka, are you not afraid to marry him? He has had so many girlfriends before you!' But I was not afraid. In fact he knew that I was a flirt, and he was so busy watching me that he didn't have time to look at other girls.

During the ceremony we both had to hold candles, but a sudden gust of wind blew out my husband's candle. I was superstitious and felt this to be an omen. But Salek's sister had prepared a big pot of chicken soup for after the ceremony, because they said that if you ate golden chicken soup you would have a golden life. I ate it with relish.

Hela: We had been living in the ghetto for about two years now. Life went on with a kind of normality, despite my constant fear and sense of loss. Although things were pretty bleak and sad at this time, people still tried to keep their spirits up. In spite of the squalor and overcrowding, the fear and the disputes, people shared the same beliefs, desires and memories. They knew the same songs. Sometimes a concert was organised to entertain us and raise funds for the increasing number of orphans. This would cause a bit of excitement and noise in the small streets for a few days. Even on the days of deportations, the young people would arrange to meet together in the evenings in tiny rooms, to sing and dance and forget their misery for a while. It was as if we were driven by a need to confirm the value of life, to prove that we could survive in spite of everything that was going on around us. In the coffee-houses musicians would play, and people would sing all the old songs, trying to recall past days of joy. We were still young and didn't know what the future held. As people around us were being taken, those who were left clung all the more fiercely to life. Apart from the coffee-houses, there were public baths we could go to, which were another meeting-place for us. Otherwise young people met in doorways, in corners and in hidden lanes in the evenings.

My sister was married and I was lonely. There was a young man I had noticed some time back, with piercing blue

Chana and David Leib Haubenstock, Hela and Janka's parents.

Family Weiss (Haubenstock). *From left:* 'Big' Kuba, David Leib, Szymon (later Sam), Zygmunt (later Saul), Lajka *(at rear)*, Mojsze, Salomon.

David Leib in military uniform, World War I.

The Kraków Salon Orchestra in the 1930s, led by Poldek's father *(front row, third from left)* and including Poldek's brother, Herman *(back row, fourth from left)*.

KRAKOWSKA
ORKIESTRA SALONOWA
pod DYR. H. ROSNERA.

Lajka and her husband, Świczarczyk, 1922.

Lajka with her two daughters, Janina and Helena, who died in the 'Action' in October 1942.

Days of innocent happiness for Janka, Kuba and Hela in Tonie, 1940.

Dorka Rath, Hela and Janka in Tonie, 1940. The village was 'set among fields of wheat and meadows of rye'.

'Playing at romance' in Tonie. The two middle couples are Hela with Romek Rusinowicz, and Janka with Tadeusz Pokusa.

Janka and her friend Kuba Stempel, with armbands. He was one of the first to be sent to Auschwitz from the ghetto.

'Big' Kuba and Hela in 1940, enjoying the peace of the countryside.

Hela drawing water at the well in Tonie, 1940.

David Leib, just before going to the ghetto, early 1941.

Lfd. Nr.	H.Art. u. Nat.	H.Nr.	Name und Vorname.	Geburts- datum.	Beruf.
361	Ju.Po.	69208	Hahn Dawid.	20.10.97	Werkzeugschlosserm.
362	"	9	Immergluck Zygmunt.	13. 6.24	Stanzer.
363	"	69210	Katz Isak Josef.	3.12.08	Klempnergehilfe.
364	"	1	Wiener Samuel.	11. 5.07	Tischlergehilfe.
365	"	2	Rosner Leopold.	26. 6.18	Maler.
366	"	3	Gewelbe Jakob.	22.9. 97	Photographmeister.
367	"	4	Korn Edmund.	7. 4.12	Metallarbeiter.
368	"	5	Penner Jonas.	2. 2.15	Stanzer.
369	"	6	Wachtel Roman.	5.11.05	Industrieciamunten.
370	"	7	Immergluck Mendel.	24. 9.03	Eisendreherges.
371	"	8	Wichter Feiwel.	2. 7.26	and. Metallverarb.
372	"	9	Landschaft Aron.	7. 7.09	anf. Metallverarb.
373	"	69220	Wandersmann Markus.	14. 9.06	Stanzer.
374	"	1	Rosenthal Israel.	24.10.09	Schreibkraft.
375	"	2	Silberschlag Hersch.	7. 4.12	ang. Metallverarb.
376	"	3	Liban Jan	29. 4.24	Wasserinst. Gehilfe.
377	"	4	Kohane Chiel.	15. 9.25	Zimmerer.
378	"	5	Senftmann Dawid.	6. 9.03	anf. Metallvorarb.
379	"	6	Kupferberg Israel.	4. 9.98	Schlossermeister.
380	"	7	Buhfiner Norbert.	12. 6.22	Lackierer Geselle.
381	"	8	Horowitz Schabhne	31.12.88	Schriftsetzmeister.
382	"	9	Segel Richard.	9.11.23	Steinbruchmineur.
383	"	69230	Jakubowicz Dawid.	15. 4.26	Steinbruchmineur.
384	"	1	Sommer Josef.	21.12.14	ang. Metallverarb.
385	"	2	Smolarz Szymon.	15. 5.04	ang. Metallverarb.
386	"	3	Rechen Ryszard	30.5.21	Automechanikerges.
387	"	4	Szlamowicz Chaim.	16. 5.24	Stanzer.
388	"	5	Kleinberg Szaja.	1. 4.20	Steinbruchmineur.
389	"	6	Miedsiuch. Michal.	3.11.16	Fleischergeselle.
390	"	7	Hillman Bernard.	24.12.15	Stanzer.
391	"	8	Konigl Marek.	2.11.11	and. Metallverarb.
392	"	9	Jakubowicz Chaim.	1o. 1.19	Steinbruchmineur.
393	"	69240	Domb Izrael.	23. 1.08	Schreibkraft.
394	"	1	Klinburt Abram.	1.11.13	Koch.
395	"	2	Visnizk Abram.	30	Behrling.
396	"	3	Schreiber Leopold	15.10.25	Schlossergeselle.
397	"	4	Silberstein Jakob.	1. 1.00	Galvaniseurmeister.
398	"	5	Eidner Pinkus.	20.12.14	Dampfkesselmeister.
399	"	6	Goldberg Berisch.	17. 5.13	ang. Metallverarb.
400	"	7	Feiner Josef.	16. 5.15	Automechaniker.
401	"	8	Feiner Wilhelm.	21.10.17	Stanzer.
402	"	9	Low Zyeze	28. 8.97	Kesselschmied-Meister.
403	"	69250	Low Jakob.	3. 3.00	Kesselschmied-Meister.
404	"	1	Pozniak Szloma.	15. 9.16	Backer.
405	"	2	Ratz Wolf.	20. 6.09	Metallverarb.
406	"	3	Lewkowicz Ferdynand.	12. 3.09	Arzt Chirurg.
407	"	4	Lax Ryszard.	8. 7.24	Automechaniker Ges.
408	"	5	Samuel Berek.	5. 1.05	Tischler Gehilfe.
409	"	6	Horowitz Izydor.	25. 9.98	ang. Instdlateur.
410	"	7	Meizels Mlema.	2. 2.16	Fleischergeselle.
411	"	8	Korman Abraham.	15. 1.19	Buchalter.
412	"	9	Joachimsmann Abraham.	19.12.95	Stanzer.
413	"	69260	Sawicki Samuel.	9. 4.17	Koch.
414	"	1	Rosner Wilhelm.	14. 9.25	Schlossergenilfe.
415	"	2	Hirschberg Szymon.	23. 7.08	Stanzer.
416	"	3	Goldberg Bernard.	1o.1o.16	Koch.
417	"	4	Gerstner Leib.	16.10.12	Glaser.
418	"	5	Hudes Naftali.	1o. 7.99	Bilanzbuchhalter.
419	"	6	Pufeles Maurycy.	5.10.12	Bilanzbuchhalter.
420	"	7	Wulkan Markus	30.10.10	Bronz-Silberschmied.

A page of men's names from Schindler's list, including Leopold Rosner and his younger brother Wilek.

CENTRAL COMMITTEE OF LIBERATED JEWS
IN THE AMERICAN OCCUPIED ZONE IN GERMANY

Tel. No. 480378, 480379.

Departement juridique.

MUNICH, 17.9.46.
Siebertstraße 3

Ref.: 225/46

Certificat.

Selon les declarations des temoins nous
certifions par la présente que la photo ci-jointe
représente Mme Rosner Helena, née Haubenstock, née le
31 juillet 1924, à Kracovie, Pologne, fille de Dawid et
d'Anna, née Weitzenblum, résidence Munich, Aussere
Prinzregentenstr. 67.
Ce certificat doit servir pour être remis au Consulat
general de France.

Pour le chef du Departement   Comité Central

Le visa de transit ci-contre apposé
a été délivré sur le vu d'un certi-
cat attestant que le porteur recevra
dès qu'il se présentera au Consulat
su Vénézuéla à Bordeaux un visa d'entr
et un passage pour le Vénézuéla.

VISA DE TRANSIT SANS ARRET
Nom et prénom ROSNER Helene
VISA DE TRANSIT SANS ARRET N° 13.41.
Pouvant être utilisé jusqu'au........
15 Octobre 1946........
Valable pour un seul voyage.
Motif du voyage transit pour Venez

Munich, le

LE VICE-CONSUL

2 SEP 1946 E
6 STRASBOURG

A transit visa allowing Hela to travel to the USA via Venezuela. She chose
instead to follow her sister to Australia.

Munich, 22 September 1946: wedding of Poldek's younger brother Wilek and Erna Cukierman *(centre, with flowers)*. The tall man at left is Oskar Schindler; next to Wilek is Schindler's girlfriend Giza Schein, then Hela and Poldek.

Wedding of cousin Różycka and Moniek Apelowicz, at Feldafing, near Munich, 1946. Józek and Hela are at left, Janka and Poldek at right, with Różycka's aunt (sister of her mother Itka) at the front.

eyes. He lived in our apartment building but on a different floor and I didn't know him. Everything was very close together; there was a coffee-house called 'Polonia', run by Förster, in the basement of the building we lived in. People would come here to forget their worries, to drink and to dance to the music. They didn't know what would happen to them from one day to the next, and lost themselves in a forced gaiety.

This man I had observed was working as a musician in the coffee-house, playing a piano-accordion. (Father had taken my sister and me to the coffee-house once or twice to listen to the orchestra. I still had girlish plaits down my back, and had felt very grown up being taken out like this. I had found the smoky atmosphere and loud laughter exciting.) I now watched this musician, gaily playing popular tunes from before the war, and everyone joined in singing. His music was full of passion and I couldn't take my eyes off him, but he took no notice of me. I saw him walking around, asking people for requests. When eventually he approached me, my heart began to pound, but in a brave voice I asked for a tune called 'Nobody is Longing for Me'. His eyes twinkled as he struck up this popular melody.

Smoky nightclubs, noisy strangers, women dressed in purple sequins and feathers. I sit at a white-covered table, strewn with wine glasses and ashtrays, but my gaze is on the musicians. My father is there, swaying with his accordion in time to the music, and various other men playing drums, piano or trumpet. My father always smiles when he plays and his eyes crinkle up; the joy of the music flows through him and into his nimble fingers flying over the keys. The audience is appreciative and their applause makes him happy. But I quickly learn that other musicians are not so happy. Drummers, in particular, tend to squint, frown and grimace, their jaws working in time to their rhythm. Some of the piano-players hum or sing in an undertone, heedless of the extra accompaniment they are adding. Trumpeters' cheeks are blown in and out like a balloon and sweat flows freely down their faces. But the music flows on, regardless of individuals and their quirks. It

sweeps me up in its insistent beat and I sit forward to hear the
harmonies as they move apart and resolve. Sometimes people dance
to the music, close together, dappled by smoky spotlights. I lean
against my mother, my feet too short to reach the floor, but I can
feel the rhythm vibrate through my chair and through her body as
she encircles me with her arm. My eyes start to close.

Hela: I found out that his name was Leopold Rosner, but he
was known as Poldek and came from a large and well-
known family of musicians. His parents had been taken
away in the same deportation as our father, leaving seven of
their nine children in the ghetto. (One daughter, Bronia, had
died before the war, at the age of eight or nine, from a terrible accident when she fell into boiling water; an older
brother, Jerzyk, or George, had gone to America.)

At first I started to go out with one of Poldek's younger
brothers, Samek, a violinist, because he appeared more available and interested. He came to visit me and took me for
walks. But it was Poldek who had caught my eye that first
day. I thought of him constantly. Poldek was slim with wavy
black hair and penetrating blue eyes. He had a lovely smile,
and smoked a long-stemmed pipe. I used to ask Samek lots
of questions about him. Samek got upset at all the questions
and my lack of interest in him; but he eventually agreed to
introduce me formally to his brother, and our romance
began.

I went more and more often to the coffee-house to watch
Poldek. There I met one of his sisters, Marysia, who used to
tell entertaining stories and sing old songs. She played piano
beautifully and could speak five languages. I also met
another sister, Mela, who could play the piano-accordion just
as well as Poldek. She was thin and small, but very pretty.
She was married to Szymek Zanger and they had a little
boy of about three, named Józiu. I was also introduced to
Poldek's oldest brother, Herman, who looked a lot like him
and played the violin. Poldek lived with Herman and his
wife, a pretty Austrian girl called Manci. Upstairs from the
'Polonia', on the top floor, lived Ignac Schreiber, a dentist

who was a bachelor. There were often parties at his place, full of noise and smoke, and as the vodka flowed the crowd became more and more raucous. The couple of times Poldek took me there, I was shocked by the uninhibited behaviour of the guests and felt uncomfortable.

Though on stage Poldek was full of confidence and knew how to entertain an audience, he was quite shy around girls. When I visited him at Herman and Manci's they were very polite to me, but Poldek always put on a record for me to listen to, when all I wanted to do was talk to him. I think this was his way of avoiding having to speak. We used to go out on the balcony at night and kiss under the stars. That was the only place we could meet in private. I was a naive young girl, overwhelmed by strong emotions that subdued my loneliness. I knew nothing about contraception, and lived only from moment to moment.

Janka: On 28 October 1942, there was another *Aktion*. We heard rumours that this time they were clearing everyone out of the ghetto who didn't have permits to work for the Germans. We were safe because Hela and I had a job. But father's younger sister Lajka, the one from Kazimierz, was in the ghetto with her two teenage girls, Janina and Helena (whose father had escaped earlier to Russia); they worked in the kitchens but didn't have a *Kennkarte*. At this time one of the daughters, Helena, was sick with typhoid and had been placed in the ghetto hospital. That's where she was on the day of the *Aktion*. Janina, fearful of being taken, begged us to hide her.

In the kitchens where she worked there were many shelves. One of these was very high up and quite wide. On this shelf were kept canisters and large saucepans. Janina was about eighteen but quite slight for her age, so we told her to hide behind the canisters. She climbed up to the top shelf, and we covered her with a flour sack and placed the canisters in front of her so she couldn't be seen. All day she lay still.

We returned from our work that evening, full of dread. Most of the streets were empty and there was an ominous silence, broken only by the sounds of people wailing. We asked someone what had happened. We were told that the hospital had been liquidated and everyone in it massacred. We also found out that they had taken everyone from the kitchens. I felt terror sweep over me, but at least, I thought, my cousin must be safe in her hiding-place.

Desperately we ran to the kitchens and looked up on the high shelf, but it was empty. The floor was strewn with pots and canisters and spilled flour. We learnt that the SS had come looking for all the workers and had discovered Janina's hiding-place without difficulty.

It was such a terrible feeling to realise that she had been taken from us, together with her mother and her sister. During the first *Aktion*, at least those who were hidden had survived; but this time hiding hadn't helped.

Hela: Earlier on, during one of the frequent searches, Poldek's younger sister Mela had begged us to hide her little son Józiu in our room, in our wardrobe among our dresses, before we went to work. That way he had escaped detection. But shortly after, there had been another selection, in which women who did not look physically strong were separated to one side, along with any children that were found. They were assembled on Józefińska street, next to the *Arbeitsamt*, the Work Office where they stamped your permits. Poldek had been standing with a group of men, having to watch the proceedings. Mela stood clutching Józiu to her, her eyes wide with fear. She refused to put the child down when ordered to, and begged them for mercy.

A moment later a burly Nazi, ignoring Mela's pleas, wrenched the child from her arms. He held him by his feet and swung him against the brick wall, smashing his skull. Calmly he pulled out his revolver and, as Mela was shrieking and clawing at him, shot her through the head. The deafening sound echoed on and on.

Janka: The SS were meticulous in their searching. They found everyone, loaded them onto trucks and took them away.

Father's youngest brother Kuba, the unmarried one who had courted me, had also worked in the kitchens. He was a very strong man. When he was taken away to be loaded onto the trucks, he wanted desperately to escape. He climbed up with the driver to have a better chance but the driver was afraid and pushed him out, so he perished too.

I found out that in this same *Aktion* they had taken away Opoczyński, the lolly man we shared our room with, and his whole family. A day later Polish people who worked for the Germans arrived and took all their furniture and possessions. They also stole a beautiful handbag of mine that I'd managed to keep, made of ostrich skin. In this bag was my stamped *Kennkarte*, the precious document I needed to enable me to work and to stay alive. Later, after they had gone, I found it on the stairs among some papers and photos they had emptied from the bag; they had only been looking for money.

Everyone who had stayed in the ghetto that day without a *Kennkarte* was taken away. Only those who had permits to work were safe. That evening we roamed the streets of the ghetto, looking for anyone we knew, but there was a ghostly silence broken only by our footsteps and people crying. We went from one home to another, searching for a relative, a cousin, a familiar face; but they were all gone.

There is a road running right through the middle of our house where the corridor used to be. The walls are translucent and have no substance. As traffic moves slowly in one direction I keep looking into the cars to find a familiar face. At last I see a man I know and move forward to speak to him, but he is unresponsive and stares past me. I pound the car door to get his attention. Distressed, I try to tell him he shouldn't go away with so many people, it will be too crowded. The car keeps moving forward slowly. At last it stops and he replies in a flat voice, without looking at me. He tells me that he has to go to the airport to meet his father. Everyone has to go there. I am consumed by panic: I can't get to the airport, it's too far away. I don't want him to leave but the car is starting to move. I call out goodbye as he draws away from me, but I don't think he can hear. The line of traffic continues slowly into the distance.

Janka: During this period there were many rumours of resettlement and work camps in the Ukraine. We never knew whether what we heard was truth or lies, desperate dreams or falsehoods calculated to keep us in a state of fear. After the bloody *Aktion* in October 1942, someone employed a Polish railway worker to follow the trains that left Kraków station filled with Jews. He observed that the train reached a hardly-known station, the Jews entered an enclosure, and disappeared. He went to a pub and a local resident told him over a mug of beer that the SS men were burning Jews over there. When news of this filtered through to the ghetto, the reaction was predictable. 'A good *goy*,' some people said, 'is still an anti-Semite, and would invent anything to frighten the Jews.'

We wanted to believe the fantasies. We tried to convince ourselves that the Jews were being sent to the East to work in labour camps. Indeed some people, sent away with the transport, even managed to send back postcards. Who could have guessed that these were dictated to the victims an hour before their death in the gas chambers?

By this time the population of the ghetto had been reduced by half, and large sections of it had been emptied and closed down. New brick walls were built and the people who were left were shifting into already crowded rooms. Salek was living with us, but space was not a problem now that the other family had been taken away. Shortly after, we had to move to a room in Lwowska street.

Salek worked for a while in the ghetto, then was transferred to live and work in a glass factory near Kraków. He would write me letters, which were still permitted, and I'd write back to him. The end of the year was approaching and it became cold, with mud and greyness everywhere. We had lived together for only a short time. My heart was heavy with longing and I missed having him near me.

Hela: Romek, my boyfriend from Tonie, was trapped in the ghetto with his five brothers. His parents, like most of our parents, had been taken away to an unknown destiny. One of Romek's younger brothers, Mendel, was fed up with the way we were being treated and, with the bravado of youth, decided to run away. As he was attempting to escape he was shot several times by a German soldier. He was carried back to the hospital in Józefińska street, where he lay groaning from his terrible injuries when we came to see him. The doctor who was treating him, unable to procure the necessary medication, could only suggest that he needed some red wine to fortify him. Poldek rushed out and organised some wine from somewhere, and carried it carefully back to the hospital, but Mendel died shortly after. Life was so fragile, and each new day held the possibility of more horror.

When Poldek and I decided to get married we asked Poldek's older sister, Regina, for permission, as his parents and my parents were dead by this time. She said we must be crazy to be thinking of marriage when we didn't know what we would eat the next day; but we were in love and were very determined. So Regina made a beautiful little hat for me, with a white veil, and someone lent me a navy suit and a blouse. It was 17 January 1943. I was eighteen. A rabbi came, and Poldek's aunt and uncle (who I discovered were the parents of Mila Rosner, the elegantly dressed lady who used to come into father's shop), as well as Janka and her husband, and a few other people. After the ceremony we had a celebration meal which Regina had prepared with what was available.

But our joy was short-lived. The very next day Poldek was taken away to Płaszów, the labour camp three kilometres from Kraków. We never had a honeymoon. I didn't know what was going on outside the ghetto. But Poldek was sent out to work every day from Płaszów, and through the barbed wires around the ghetto I could catch sight of him, marching in a group. I waved to him every day, with tears in my eyes, in the morning when he went to work and at night when he was marched back to the camp. He was so close, but so out of reach! Occasionally we could kiss through the wires, and I would pass him some soup that I had cooked. But I had to be very careful, because if a German had seen me I would have been beaten or shot. It was forbidden to speak or have any contact with the camp inmates.

I found I was pregnant. Abortions were illegal and I was terrified, but I knew I didn't want to have a baby now. We knew a male nurse, Felek Nelken, a tall thin man, who arranged the abortion. Janka took me to the small ghetto hospital and told them I had appendicitis, so that if any doctor came the records would be clear. She had organised an injection, a drug called Evipan, that would put me to sleep so I wouldn't feel too much pain. It cost a lot of money and had to be obtained outside the ghetto. Janka sold a good woollen suit of hers to pay for it.

Later I found out it would have been a boy.

∽

I have just finished reading The Secret Garden *and am eager to find a little plot of garden for myself. I choose a bare patch in the backyard beneath my bedroom window, and I turn over the earth with an old green gardening fork, pulling out weeds and feeling grains of earth under my nails. I am not too sure if I enjoy this, but I set off one Saturday morning to the nearby shops to buy some seeds. After much contemplation of gaudy packets of flowers, each more showy and colourful than the last, I choose one—that's all I can afford with my pocket-money. It is a packet of Sweet Alice, which I am assured is simple to grow and fragrant.*

When I return home and open the bag of seeds, crouching down beside the bare earth, I am disappointed that they are so few, and so tiny. Dutifully I plant them as suggested and water them, then continue to sit on my haunches, looking at the earth. My friend who lives over the road and is a year older laughs at me, and tells me I've wasted my money on a weed, but I defend myself fiercely and am determined to prove her wrong.

After several days of running home after school, only to find that nothing has yet started to grow, I tell my mother about my efforts. She smiles gently and talks about the need to be patient. But the next day she has something for me wrapped in newspaper: a little stem with hairy roots and a few furry leaves. This, she tells me, is a forget-me-not plant, which a neighbour has given her. There is a faraway look in her eyes and the lines around her mouth soften as she describes what forget-me-nots are like.

I carry my treasure into the back garden and plant it, carefully avoiding the parts where the reluctant seeds lie buried in the dark earth. Again I water gently, but this time I have something to look at. Besides that, I have been told about patience and am keen to hold out for something worth waiting for. Day after day the little green leaves stay green and appear to be healthy. The plant even seems to be growing.

One afternoon, to my joy, I notice a greenish tinge to the soil and, looking closer, I can see tiny shoots coming through the earth where I had scattered the seeds. Suddenly I can understand Mary's emotions in the book. I begin to visualise the beauty of this little patch as it develops, and I'm determined to care for it. I start to see my mother's happy face when I can pick some flowers and give them to her as a present.

I walk in the door after school as usual, have a drink of chocolate milk and go out into the backyard. There, to my horror, I see my garden patch bare, with turned earth neatly piled away from the edges. The gardener has been today, and no one thought to tell him about my garden. I search frantically for a tiny stem, a leaf, but there is nothing. I am furious at the gardener and storm into the house. My mother, however, tells me not to cry, it was only a plant after all. She will never know how much I wanted to make her happy, to see that dreamy look in her eyes again.

I give up trying to plant a garden. Maybe I am not yet old enough to understand about patience.

8

Hela: I lived out the days waiting for the occasional glimpse of my husband to ease my loneliness. I was alone for two months, while different sections of the ghetto were being cleared and closed down. Our living area was reduced again and again.

Janka: The ghetto was becoming more crowded as Jews from little towns in the surrounding areas were brought in. Often several families were now living in one room. We didn't know anything about other ghettos at the time. We heard rumours about beatings, shootings and murders, but they were hard to believe. We still clung to the idea that the ghetto was a crowded but permanent way of life for us. When people arrived from Borysław, or from other camps, we asked them what the 'labour' camps were like—we couldn't believe that people were sent there to perish.

There was some resistance organised in the ghetto. For many years after the war we were asked, 'Why did you Jews go to your death like sheep to the slaughter?' This generalisation wasn't true, as history has revealed. The Jewish Combat Organisation (ZOB), which had been strong in Kraków, was made up mainly of youth-club members. They had their own underground newspaper and were helped by the small Polish communist resistance movement known as the People's Guard. The major Polish resistance movement, the Home Army or AK, was unfriendly to Jews, and in any case was weak in the Kraków region. The ZOB derailed a military train in August 1942, not by blowing it up but simply by unbolting the rails. Then in December 1942 they bombed a coffee-house, 'Cyganerja', frequented by German officers, and killed eleven of them as well as severely injuring many more. They launched this attack anonymously, so as not to endanger the population of the ghetto. (After the war, the proud Poles placed a commemorative plaque on this building, stating that the attack had been carried out by the Polish underground.)

The Jewish resistance was active for about eight months in 1942–43. A man I knew, an electrician called Scheinwitz, had a hidden radio that he listened to. I also had a handsome friend who ran away from the ghetto and joined up with the resistance forces. Some news reached us but it was generally bad. I never heard from him again.

In February 1943, *Untersturmführer* Amon Goeth received orders to bring about the liquidation of the Kraków ghetto and to take command of the forced-labour camp (*Arbeitslager*) at Płaszów. There were still about 12,000 people living in the ghetto at this time. Everyone had to leave: men, women and any children that were left. Most children and old people were rounded up and murdered on the spot, although about three hundred children were smuggled in to Płaszów. Some people left earlier than others, so the whole process took more than a month. It was completed on the morning of 13 March 1943.

We were taken from Kraków to Płaszów in overcrowded trucks. It was terrible to leave all our possessions behind, meagre as they were. We were allowed to take only one suitcase with us, but they stole it later and left us with almost nothing.

On the way home from school I regularly stop at a second-hand shop, knowing I mustn't dawdle for too long but fascinated by its dark interior and mysterious contents. I spend ages gazing at intricately carved wood, or handling porcelain with cracked glazing. I touch gently as I pass or hold carefully in my hand, turning and feeling ... what? A sense of age, of past, of history. Where did such objects live before finding their way to these dusty shelves? Who loved them and dusted them, all those years ago?

I pick up an egg-cup, delicately coloured and slightly chipped. As I hold its translucency in my hand, I see a dark-haired child sitting at a wooden table, swinging her legs to and fro under the chair. She is trying to eat her egg, making a bit of a mess. Her mother, a white apron covering her long dark skirt, bustles around the steamy kitchen. The egg-cup falls over; the child is scolded. The steam grows thicker and I can no longer see clearly. I hold the egg-cup thoughtfully. It has a history, but, like a dream, it is just out of reach, fading as I try to invoke it. I put it down gently. It does not belong to me. It can give me no answers.

Hela: Vicious dogs barking, men screaming, barbed wire, and rows and rows of buildings—these were my first impressions of Płaszów. It was a huge place, surrounded by barbed wire in all directions. There were wooden barracks as far as the eye could see, separated by straight roads. On the horizon were watchtowers with huge reflector lights to survey the whole camp.

Janka: Płaszów was not initially an extermination camp but a forced-labour camp, built on the site of the Jewish cemetery. Gravestones had been used for paving the streets. When we first arrived we didn't know where to go; there was no one to tell us what to do, whether we had to work, or where we could live. Eventually Hela and I were allocated to barracks and we were given some food: a piece of bread and a bit of coffee.

Hela: Three-tiered bunks filled the barracks, sleeping about two hundred people in each barrack. They were built from old wood infested with bedbugs, which soon tormented us all. Initially men and women were not separated. I shared a bunk with Poldek, who had arrived in Płaszów before me; Janka was next to me with her husband Salek, then Heniek Penner, who had been injured by gunshots, then another man and his son.

Very soon, however, our barracks were segregated, and men and women were not allowed to mix. But at night the

Germans confined themselves mainly to the watchtowers that overlooked the camp, so only the ODs were supervising us. People would try to sneak into each other's quarters under the cover of darkness. Once when I was trying to get to see my husband, an *Aufseherin* (a female guard) caught me, a big masculine woman named Orłowska. She began to beat me with a truncheon across my legs until they were swollen and bleeding. She beat me mercilessly, swearing and yelling. I had to crawl back to my barracks alone, and was black and blue for weeks.

Janka: My husband, Salek, came with me to Płaszów and always tried to look after me. When I was terribly sick with my ulcer, he took one of the two shirts he owned and sold it to buy me some milk from someone who worked in the kitchens. Another time, when he had a fever from malaria, I was able to sell some item of clothing to get a piece of white bread for him.

The bunks were built close to each other, on three levels. One day I noticed a young girl who had come from Rabka. Her name, I later found out, was Marysia Sperling. She arrived with only the clothes she wore. Our family had been lucky to leave the ghetto with a few of our things. Marysia lay naked in the bunk at night because she didn't have any night-dresses. I had two, so before I went to work I left one of them on her bed, since we worked in different shifts. The next day I found on my bed a flower made from a scrap of material.

Marysia recalls our meeting a little differently. This is what she wrote to my son on his Barmitzvah fifteen years after the end of the war:

We lived in the concentration camp in the same dwellings, and Janka's bed was in front of mine. On the day my story begins your mother changed her bed linen with a great effort (everything was an effort and a struggle in the concentration camp). She then washed her hair and sat on her bunk like a beautiful flower in the prime of her youth. As it happened, a bad neighbour from the bunk above spilled a can full of urine on Janka's bed, so clean and white, on her fine hair and all her person. These were things that happened sometimes in our barracks, and anybody else in such circumstances would scream and yell and call her names and maybe even scratch the face of the careless idiot. Not your mother. She opened her velvety eyes full of tears and said in a low voice: 'How could you do this to me?'

This unusual reaction was so startling for me, that I felt instantly attracted to your mother. I felt so full of respect and deep sympathy that on the very next day, when we did not meet because of different shifts, I left a bunch of tiny concentration-camp flowers on her cot.

This is merely a little tale picturing for you the start of this enduring friendship, that will last as long as we live, and cannot pale in spite of the immense distance and all this time that has elapsed.

From that first meeting we became best friends.

Soon after we arrived, the Germans asked for five stenographers who were able to write in German. I had studied German at school for seven years and would have been qualified, but I didn't want to leave my friends and my sister so I refused to register myself. The five women who were taken had to deal with important documents and orders. After a couple of months they were all shot.

I was set to work instead in a factory, the *Gross-Schneiderei*, which repaired the uniforms of German soldiers who had come back from the front. They were torn and full of blood and lice; our job was to clean and mend them. Every day we had to march in rows from the camp to the nearby factory. If we had one of the sadistic Germans supervising us, we had to run. For me it was all right because I was young, but for the older women it was really terrible.

On our way back to the camp from work, the Germans often gave us two or three heavy bricks to carry, just for the sake of it, to punish and torment us. Sometimes it was four or five bricks. After having worked all day, this was very hard. Occasionally my brother-in-law, Poldek, would appear as we were coming back from work, and he would take the bricks from me and carry them. Now and then he would arrange to get more soup for me, because he was a musician who played (together with his brother Herman) for the Commandant, Goeth. He could be called at any time to provide music for the loud, drunken parties Goeth held, and being among so many Nazis filled him with fear. But he was given certain privileges, and sometimes leftovers from the table. He always shared anything extra he received with my sister and with me.

Hela: For the first few weeks in Płaszów I was put to work in an office, sorting and filing papers. Later I joined Janka in the warehouse for recycling used, damaged or stained *Wehrmacht* uniforms from the Russian front. There was a big hall with many sewing-machines in rows. We had to repair these stinking uniforms that were stained with mud and blood and were crawling with lice. When I worked in the factory at the machine, my head would keep dropping from tiredness; I'd try to rouse myself a bit and get back to work, and then I'd find I had fallen asleep again.

Janka: There were times at work when we were unbearably sleepy, because we never could get enough sleep. The repaired uniforms were hung in rows in one section of the factory, and if you were lucky you could be hidden for a while among them and catch a few moments' respite, while the other women working there covered for you.

Hela: There was a great feeling of camaraderie among the girls. While some of them kept watch, others would sleep a little bit, sitting at the machine. They would warn us if someone was coming. At other times, I could hide among the pile of filthy, bloodstained uniforms waiting to be repaired, and catch half an hour's sleep.

Sometimes the *kapos* would storm in, arms full of another

pile of uniforms, and start abusing one of us, kicking her or beating her about the head. (*Kapos* were prisoners appointed as heads of work groups; they were placed in charge of their fellow inmates and had to carry out the orders of the SS and ensure absolute obedience.) The violence was accompanied by swearing, calling us Jewish dirt not worthy of touching the saintly garments of the German soldiers. These *kapos* were usually drunk, often continually. They didn't have much of a life either. We took this abuse stoically and hoped they would soon leave. I took a perverse satisfaction in working on army jackets that were stiff with dried blood; I wondered idly whether the wound would have been enough to kill this particular soldier, and tried to imagine how many of them would no longer be around to harm us.

Janka: There was a man, Markus Gross, who was a tailor by profession. (He was, I later found out, the brother of the man who was to be my second husband.) He had a group of girls working for him, and he was told he could take them with him to a German clothing factory in Kraków. The proprietor of this factory was called Madritsch. He was a native of Vienna who ran his factory with cheap labour for profit, but he was known to be humane and not brutal. Prisoners working there were treated reasonably well and, by being employed, were safe. He was one of the 'good' Germans, who bought extra rations of bread for his workers and didn't beat them. We knew that those who went out of the camp to work for Madritsch had slightly better working conditions, as did those who worked at the airport and the enamel-ware factory.

I knew that Markus had already organised his group of girls, but I asked him whether I could be included in the group. He said it was too dangerous. He had been told he could take only two hundred girls; if they counted and there were more than that, they would shoot him. I looked at Markus pleadingly. After a few moments he relented and, with a smile, said, 'All right, you can come.' With these few words he saved my life. This was another miracle.

I was put to work then in this factory, where we made new uniforms for the Germans. Hela stayed working in the *Gross-Schneiderei*, repairing the old uniforms. When I began in Madritsch's factory, it quickly became clear to Markus that I couldn't sew very well. He saw within a few moments that I didn't even know how to hold a needle properly, so he gave me the job of taking sections of fabric from the cutters and distributing them to the machinists. My new job was much easier than dealing with the stench and filth of those old uniforms. With his own money Madritsch bought bread for us, so every week each of us was given a loaf of bread. This was a very big help, as I was able to share it with my sister. I was luckier than many others.

Hela: Once Janka began to work for Madritsch, I was envious of her working conditions. She and I could see each other only occasionally, from a distance. We were no longer in the same barracks, as we had been shifted several times since our arrival, but we could meet sometimes at the latrines. We were only allowed to go the latrines in fives, when the *kapo* called us, and that wasn't too often. We'd step out into the mud to walk along the little alley leading to the latrines. They were a disgusting place, but a good source of information and gossip.

There were long wooden boards to sit on, the length of the barrack, with a stinking hole beneath. It was absolutely freezing in winter. There were no doors, so there was no privacy at all. There wasn't one moment alone, even for the most intimate functions a woman had to perform. Most of the women had by this time stopped menstruating, whether from stress, hunger or something they put in our coffee, I don't know. But whoever still had her period suffered terribly, as there was nothing sanitary to help her. The latrine was the worst thing for me. The communal wash-house was here as well. We showered together, a whole group of women crowding to get a little bit of icy water to wash with.

Hunger of course was a constant torment. Three times a day we heard the trumpet sound, blown by Wilek, Poldek's youngest brother. Everyone in the camp knew him and his trumpet. At lunchtime the soup they gave us was like dishwater. We had to stand in a queue with a tin bowl, waiting for the watery soup and the small lump of hard bread we were given, together with a bit of disgusting ersatz coffee tasting of acorns. When it happened that I couldn't hold on until we were called to go to the latrine, I had to use my enamel dish to wee in, and later use it for the coffee. The humiliation of this never left me.

Janka: Sometimes we had a bit of margarine or marmalade, and sometimes soup made with a few bits of carrots, beets and sago substitute, but that was quite rare. If you knew someone who worked in the kitchen you could get an extra serve of coffee. We were frequently hungry.

Hela: Prisoners were marched out every day to work on various projects. As long as people in Płaszów had permits to work outside the camp, some communication was possible between the men's and women's camps. But there was a death penalty for carrying letters or supplies, for lighting a cigarette, for hiding money or jewellery, or for wearing a brassiere.

Janka: Soon after we arrived the Ukrainian guards came to take all our jewellery away and all the valuables we had left. I was told they were coming, and felt desperate not to lose the few pieces of my own and mother's jewellery that I had managed to conceal till now. I quickly buried them in a jar of marmalade I had hidden. But Hela was terrified that we would be found out and would all get shot. She began to cry and started to retrieve the jewellery and wash the sticky marmalade off. It was very risky to try to conceal anything, because they would have shot not only us but all the other inmates of the barrack. The Ukrainians always did the dirty work for the Germans.

When they arrived, they threatened us with their revolvers and several people were shot in front of our eyes. We had to hand over all the jewellery that had been so precious to us, the gold chains, mother's rings, and even my watch with the emerald winder that Kuba had once stolen. Hela was trembling as they grabbed it all.

Auntie keeps things. All sorts of things. She keeps every letter she has ever received from friends and distant relatives overseas. She keeps every birthday card given to her by her family since her arrival in Australia. She has boxes full of theatre and concert programs that are starting to go mouldy. Newspaper articles, faded and yellowing, clutter up the drawers. Auntie's handbag is always full. Whatever you might need, you'll find she has brought it along: a band-aid, a nail-file, a clean handkerchief, a mirror and comb, three different shades of lipstick, a tube of ointment for mosquito bites, headache tablets, money, keys, a red notebook and a pen, sunglasses, a packet of mint lollies, a small bar of chocolate, and some caramel toffees. She never leaves the house without food in her bag. There is a sense that only through accumulation can she hold on to the memories, and stock up against the risk of scarcity.

From the age of about thirteen I keep a diary, trying to preserve the past, hold on to and explain what's happening in my life. I have my exercise books from primary school; I can't bring myself to throw them out. I cut out newspaper articles and store them. There are also notebooks full of sayings, poems (mine and others'), lines copied out from books I have read. I will reread them all one day.

Hela: All gold or silver jewellery and valuables had to be given up. What I remember most were the little forget-me-not earrings with yellow centres that father had given me for a birthday present when I was a girl. I clutched them tightly in my hand until the last moment. I could see father's smile, and feel his bristly cheek as he kissed me. When I handed over the earrings I was heartbroken.

Janka: Of course they took my gold wedding-ring too. But soon after, a jeweller friend of mine, Pilcer, made me another ring from copper. One day I was sick and I didn't go to work.

I needed to go to the latrine, so I put a scarf over my head against the cold and made my way outside. As I clutched my scarf, the copper of the ring on my hand must have gleamed, and a German who saw me called me over and ordered me to hand over the ring. With some satisfaction I gave him the ring, knowing by his greedy grin that he believed it was gold.

Hela: We were allowed to have only two sets of underwear and one set of clothes. At first we kept our own clothes, which they painted with yellow or red stripes. There was a large Star of David painted on our chest, with black numbers. They stamped our underwear with a star and the label *Arbeitslager Płaszów*. Later they took away our civilian clothes and gave us striped outfits, black-and-white for the men, with a black beret, and navy-and-white for the women, with a white rag to cover the head. Some women, like my sister-in-law Manci (Herman's wife), were angry at having to wear such shapeless garments, and they used what resources they had to make them more presentable, turning them into skirts or waisted dresses. However, this sign of rebellion was soon discovered and they were all punished. The outfits, when new, were stiff and prickly on the inside like thistles. The rough material absorbed heat in the sun, so that we sweltered, but gave no protection from the freezing winds in winter. It also absorbed water like a sponge when it rained, and was damp and smelly for days. But we cheered each other up, saying that if we were given uniforms, it must mean we were going to stay here; they were not going to shoot us. It was a tiny fragment of security to hang on to.

Apart from the anguish of being separated from my beloved, and the hunger, the worst thing I suffered was lack of sleep. There were continual calls which would wake us at night to assemble on the parade ground, the *Appellplatz*. We would stand for hours while they took roll-calls, again and again. When at last I got to bed, exhausted, I couldn't sleep because of the bedbugs. They were terrible; they would bite you till blood came, and you had to scratch continuously.

The itching drove me crazy. So during the day I was perpetually tired.

Amon Goeth, the sadistic and brutal Commandant of Płaszów, had a massive physique and a terrifying presence. He would come by on his horse with his gun and his smile, and would shoot people indiscriminately, as if he were swatting flies. Everyone was afraid when he rode by, for if he felt you were not standing properly, or you looked the wrong way, or sometimes for no reason at all, you could be shot. He had two vicious black dogs, Alsatians, that could rip a person apart. There was a lot of killing in the camp.

Janka: It was very dangerous in the latrines, because at any time Goeth could be there with his big savage dogs, Ralf and Rolf. He would set the dogs on to some poor victim, who was torn apart just for his fun. Once, Goeth's dogs attacked my husband's brother and he was injured terribly, with great hunks torn out of his knee and his hand. All this was done for no reason and without provocation.

Hela: Goeth's presence filled me with terror at any time, but this time I was sure I was going to die. He caught me smoking a cigarette for which I had traded a piece of bread. He pulled out his revolver and held it against my head. I was too petrified to do anything, but someone whispered to him that I was the wife of Rosner, the accordionist. He pushed me to the ground with a grunt and put his revolver back in its holster. I was left trembling—and trying to come to terms with the randomness of life and death, the trivial details that allowed me to survive another day.

∞

Each year I am invited to my second cousin's birthday party. Sol and I are about the same age. His father and my father are cousins but I see that side of the family only rarely. The main thing that makes Sol so different from me is that he has a grandfather. Each year this grandfather writes a poem for his grandson's birthday and he recites it solemnly as we all listen. I don't understand a word because it is all in German, but I watch this old man with reverence. He is always dressed in a heavy woollen suit and a neat tie. He enunciates his words with care, pausing often for effect and looking at his audience from under heavy eyebrows. Is this what a grandfather is like, I wonder. I feel a pang of envy.

Later I wander around the house while other children are eating party pies and jellybeans. I push open the door of the parents' bedroom and feel a chill in the air. The bedhead and wardrobe are of dark wood, as are the bedside tables covered by neat doilies. A heavy satin spread covers the bed. There are no ornaments or objects lying around, but instead the whole room is dominated by two large photographs hanging on the wall behind the bed. Plain oval frames of polished wood surround these two portraits. The woman on the left looks severe with her hair pulled back, a high-necked white blouse with ruffles and a protruding bust. The man on the right has a hat on and his piercing eyes gaze out under heavy eyebrows. They are ancestors, I am told, who perished in Russia. Perished, died, passed away. I look into their eyes and try to understand. Here, in this room, they live on. They are a presence in the house, exerting their influence on the family that lives here and on the little girl who gazes at them. They disapprove of frivolity—there's work to do and no time to waste, they seem to be saying. Life is a serious matter.

In this ordinary suburban house, with a few straggling rose-bushes lining the path to the front door, where children run noisily from room to room and play party games, I feel only sadness. I want to understand more about these ancestors, and about those whose faces I can't see. But no one ever speaks to me about the past.

9

Hela: People arrived all the time; transports from other camps and ghettos. Most of the inmates of the camp were Polish Jews, but there were also some who had just arrived from Budapest, in Hungary, after days of travelling. They had their heads shaved because of the fear of lice. They were very unhappy girls: they didn't understand a word of Polish and none of us could communicate with them in their own language. Some of them became sick, and I saw the frustration of the Polish woman doctor who wanted to help them but couldn't understand Hungarian.

Janka: In Płaszów there were constant beatings and executions for the most minor transgressions. Between March 1943 and May 1944 there were mass executions, and there was a hill, vulgarly known as *Hujowa Górka* (Cock Hill), where single executions were performed. We became used to seeing dead bodies, if such a thing is possible. Soon the whole concentration camp was pocketed with mass graves, but Jews were not transported from here to other camps, for the time being.

Hela: While we were working on the uniforms, rumours reached us of an uprising in Warsaw, in the ghetto there. I tried to imagine how it would feel to fight back, to kill the Germans who were killing us so mercilessly. But I knew of no resistance group where we were. Our lives were filled with the sheer struggle to survive.

Janka: There were frequent selections and roll-calls. Often there would be an *Aktion*, a selection of people to be taken away and killed. These selections were carried out by Blanke, a doctor who, instead of being involved in healing the sick, was responsible for sending people to their deaths.

From May onwards there were lists being drawn up all the time, and people were sent away never to be heard of again. Salek was taken away in one of the transports and I had no way of knowing what had happened to him.

One day, when a transport was being organised, we were called to assemble and stand in rows for another selection. The girls from the Madritsch factory were towards the front, as the factory was situated not far from the rail terminus. We were the first to be marched out and lined up. The sun was shining strongly and it was a very hot day. We saw the wagons lined up, waiting to be filled. Hela and I were being herded towards them. The Germans were shouting and pushing at us with their bayonets. Poldek's older sister, Marysia, the one who sang songs in the ghetto, was with us too. She was a pretty, blond girl and she was very much like her brother: impatient, doing everything in a hurry. She wanted to push to the front, to get on the train quickly, whereas we hung back a bit. They took her with the first group.

Marysia found a spot near the window and was calling out to us. Meanwhile Hela was standing there and crying. I grabbed her hand, shouting, 'Get back, get back!' By this time the Germans were trying to get everyone onto the train, screaming and beating us with sticks, but I kept trying to move back. I thought that if we could avoid getting on the train, maybe our brother Kuba, an OD, or Poldek, who played music for the Germans, could help us to gain some time and prevent us from being taken away. As we were moving off I called out to Marysia, 'Come back, come back! Get off the train!'

She replied, 'No, no, I have such a good position near the window, I'm going to stay here. Come and join me.'

'But you don't know where they're taking you. Get out!' I begged. But she refused. The Germans were hitting us even more furiously now, raining blows on us, trying to make us get in. I kept a tight hold on Hela's hand, pulling her back and saying, 'It doesn't matter, from being beaten you don't die.' And as they continued hitting us we slowly kept moving back through the surge of people around us being herded into the train. At last no more people could be crammed in and the train started moving. The rest of us, bruised and beaten, were taken back to the camp.

Later we found out that the train had gone to Szczecin, a port near the mouth of the Oder River. All the passengers were loaded onto an old ship, the ship was taken out into the middle of the sea, and sunk, with everyone on board drowning except for one person, who was able to swim to safety and tell the story. So I had saved my sister's life and my own. That was a miracle too, that I had the instinct to stay out of that train; of course I had no way of knowing where the train was going, nor that they wouldn't kill us just the same in Płaszów.

Hela: As the camp became more crowded, there were frequent sorting-out procedures, which they named 'Health Actions'. We had to strip and, clutching our clothes, run back and forth in front of a group of doctors who sat dispassionately at tables, shouting orders and selecting us into rows to the right or left, according to how healthy and useful we looked. Before each of these procedures we would pinch our cheeks to redden them, and we tried to move a little quicker without stooping our shoulders, in the hope that we would get into the right row.

We are going to visit another doctor. My mother holds my hand tightly as we march along grey footpaths, and my little legs try to keep up. We go in through a heavy glass door, then enter a dark lift smelling of stale food and antiseptic. We walk along endless corridors, following parallel lines on the walls of square white tiles with black grouting.

This doctor looks pretty much like the others, with grey receding hair and glasses perched on the tip of his nose. My mother patiently

121

repeats the problem to him: that I don't eat enough, that I am too thin.

Everything depends on what he says. My mother's face is anxious. I study all the shiny metallic instruments laid out within reach of his hand, and terror engulfs me.

Janka: One terrible day stays in my memory. We were called to assemble on the *Appellplatz*. It was 7 May 1944, a Sunday. We were told to strip, a barrack at a time, and line up naked in front of the doctors. We were made to run back and forth, to show whether we still had some strength. Even those of us who were not healthy tried to put all our energy into giving the illusion of health, running faster, breathing more deeply. The whole time this operation was taking place, music was blaring from the loudspeakers.

Only the following week did we find out the verdict of the doctors. Assembled once again with music playing, we heard them start calling out names, and watched as they gathered together on one side all the emaciated prisoners and the last remaining children (those who were not hiding). In this selection they took children away from their mothers, and any people who were sick or elderly, or who merely didn't look fit enough—they were all taken away, amidst screeching and crying.

Hela: Music once again formed a backdrop to the most devastating events. While all the children were being rounded up and taken away in trucks, with mothers howling and throwing themselves at the Germans, a German children's song, 'Mummy, Buy me a Pony', could be heard throughout the camp. The music was played over and over again through the loudspeakers, in agonising repetition, to try to drown out the sounds of the women shrieking and wailing.

Janka: We later heard that they were taken to Auschwitz, and few of us could retain any illusions about their fate. This happened several times. Still, some people claimed to have seen personal greetings from beloved ones, scribbled on some planks sent from Auschwitz. The *kapo* of the kitchen received such greetings, allegedly, from his wife and children.

Hela: Our daily life was endless misery. We felt tired and helpless, able to deal only with the daily round of chores, eating, sleeping and avoiding death. I didn't think about the future; only about surviving another day. My only thoughts were whether we would get something to eat, or whether I would be beaten. When I asked once why someone had been shot, the reply was a grim laugh, surprised at the question. There was no reason; the Germans just wanted it so.

In my early years at school I occasionally hear the other children talking about someone called Hitler. It is only a name to me, but bolder, wiser boys discuss him in knowing terms and try to outdo each other in imagined insults. I learn that he was very, very bad, and that Jewish people hate him, but I have only a vague idea of why.

The boys talk about tearing up his picture, stamping on it, burning it. One tough little boy folds his arms and declares that if he had a picture of Hitler he would use it as toilet paper. The rest of them laugh raucously and slap him on the back. I hover on the edge of the group, uncertain, shocked by their crudity. I sense some enormity here whirling around us, and am unable to join in the laughter they indulge in to relieve the tension. I look on silently, store away another little piece of the puzzle.

Janka: Sometimes I dreamed of escape, but I knew it was impossible. If one Jew were to escape, ten Jews would be executed in reprisal. Later the same policy was applied to the working groups that returned to the camp from an outside job. If one person was missing, the group's *kapo* and ten members, picked at random, would be executed. Many people perished after one of their group escaped.

I heard about resistance in other places and wondered what it would be like. How was it possible to imagine the potential liberation of a whole concentration camp? What if the leaders of such an uprising overpowered the guards (including those on the watchtowers), cut off the current, cut the barbed wires—and set free ten thousand Jews? The question was, where would we turn to, or for that matter where would a thousand, or a hundred, or even ten Jews find refuge? Who would shelter us? How many Polish gentiles would risk their necks and those of their whole family to hide a Jewish fugitive? If discovered, their fate would be certain death. But we were not sheep being led to the slaughter; we didn't, and couldn't, believe that eventually everybody would be killed by the Germans. Hope is an amazing thing. We *hoped* to survive, and refused to 'die with dignity' in our thousands. How could other people know of our high hopes, nourished daily by fantastic and optimistic rumours? We had a wild instinct for survival and knew we had to play for time. We were ignorant and lived on hope.

Not one week passed without some stupendous good news. The Jews became brilliant war-strategists; before the southern European front became a reality, some 'Napoleons' knew already that soon a great offensive would be launched from Greece and Yugoslavia, and would shoot like an arrow straight to Poland. The Russian Bear was sure to move and strike a decisive blow from the east. There was even talk of a top-secret lethal weapon which, with one stroke, was going to devastate all of Germany and wipe it from the map of the world. Maybe all this hope was detrimental to the morale of our people. It seemed that the higher the hopes, the deeper the fall into depression. That is why it was so difficult for us to speak of our experiences for so many years.

But all this idle wondering about resistance was overshadowed by a far greater problem: our physical and mental condition. How could we even think of resistance, when we were heartbroken, depressed and grieving? We didn't know where our next meal was coming from, or whether we'd see the next sunrise. We suffered from diarrhoea, and had no toilet paper, no shred of newspaper, not even a leaf. Such trivialities could break a giant.

Hela: The German women who guarded us were brutal. One of them, Orłowska, I can never forget. She was the one who had beaten me so badly for trying to see my husband. She was built like a man, with short blond hair, and she had a deep masculine voice. There was usually a cigarette hanging from her lips, and she often drank the contents of a small bottle of spirits in one go. She was typical of the worst type of German woman guard, one who would happily take children to the ovens. Like the others, she wore a uniform and carried a short leather truncheon and a gun. Some of them were good with their fists; others knew the effectiveness of a knee in the soft part of the stomach. Often men would try to find their girlfriends or wives, and would hide in a bunk with a blanket or sheet hung up for a bit of privacy. All the women guards slept with SS men; nevertheless Orłowska had no sense of pity if she found a couple who had come together for a few brief stolen moments, and would beat them mercilessly.

The ODs seemed to have the possibility of arranging more privacy than the rest of us. They drank a lot, as alcohol was provided to them in abundance as a reward for their duties, and in an atmosphere of desperation they carried on affairs and sought physical contact whenever they could.

Commandant Goeth would often parade around with the Jewish chief of camp police, Wilek Chilowicz, a small Jew who was in charge of the other ODs. His wife Marysia was also an officer; she wore beautiful uniforms that were specially made for her, and high shiny boots. She was small but wielded her truncheon unrelentingly. Both of them were very full of their own importance, and felt as if they owned the whole world.

We called Marysia 'The Commandant' and people made up coarse songs about her. There was one song which labelled her the 'guardian of our virginity'. She would come marching along the rows of bunks, looking for hidden couples. When she found a couple hiding, she would rip down the sheet that concealed them and chase the man away, beating him with her truncheon and using the most vulgar language.

However, not all the women in charge were equally bad. There was one German SS woman who was small, with a crooked mouth. She was known to be a lesbian. She would often come to the bunks to sit with someone and caress her. The other German women were scared of being seen with us, because of *Rassenschade*, racial shame, which didn't permit different races to mix.

Janka: A friend of mine who shared our barracks was married, but when she was separated from her husband she sobbed and cried all day and night. Whenever her husband managed to come to her she would calm down and go to sleep, and we would be able to have some peace and quiet. So we used to beg him to come for a secret visit, because she kept us awake otherwise. Life was so crazy at the time, that behaviour one normally considered private and intimate became a topic for discussion and sharing.

Another woman who had a bunk on the third tier near me had an uncle who would come to her. She fell pregnant, and whenever there was a selection she would try to hide her growing belly with the clothes she was holding in front of her. But she was found out eventually and taken away to be killed.

I was always sick each month when I had my period and it was very difficult for me to go to work. Sometimes I would sneak out of the factory and head for the men's barracks. I knew that Poldek, being a musician, was allowed to sleep during the day, because he played all night for Goeth at his drunken parties. So I would crawl in beside my brother-in-law and innocently spend the day in bed with him!

At that time after my husband had been taken away I was very lonely again. I didn't see my sister much, and felt a great emptiness. One day I met a man, Mundek, who started to talk to me. He was good-looking and was known to be a flirt. But I liked him, and found him witty and intelligent.

126

He was a building engineer, with false Aryan papers, for he was a Jew. He used to work around the camp and had a certain freedom to move about.

Not long afterwards he was denounced by some Poles, who recognised Jews much more easily than Germans did, having lived with them so closely. Mundek was caught and arrested. He was taken with a group of others to stand beside a deep ditch, ready to be shot. Goeth, revolver in hand, asked him who he was. When Mundek told him he was an engineer, building roads and bridges for the Germans, Goeth let him go, thus saving his life. He continued to work for Goeth and was even able to earn some money. I tried to be friendly to him whenever I could see him, and we used to get into long discussions about books and philosophy. The sight of him would brighten up my day.

On one occasion Mundek brought me a beautiful bottle of Chanel No. 5 eau-de-Cologne, which he had purchased on the black market. It was an amazing gift to receive in concentration camp. I kept it tucked away on a shelf next to my bunk. Mundek was very attentive to me and soon became my lover. He would visit me in my bunk in secret, and our relationship developed. We had to be very careful not to be discovered by Marysia, 'The Commandant', so I was glad I had a top bunk. Mundek was well-spoken and cultured, and was very good to me. He had been married before but his wife had perished. He knew how to flatter me and was full of sweet words, like any womaniser. I longed for his secret visits, to snatch a moment of pleasure and escape from our grey existence.

One day I went to see a woman I knew three or four barracks away. I came to her bunk and started talking to her. As we talked I noticed something out of the corner of my eye near her bed. There on her shelf stood a bottle of Chanel perfume just like mine! My mind started racing and I realised how foolish I'd been. When Mundek came to see me that evening I turned him away and told him it was over. He begged me, swearing that she didn't mean anything to him, but I refused to have him back.

Women in Płaszów had a lot of lovers at that time, as we all lived for the moment; we didn't know whether we would be alive the next day so we seized any fleeting pleasures we could. Sex became one of the few brief comforts in our bleak existence. But I promised myself that I would not let myself be used any more. It wasn't that I didn't love him, but I felt cheated and didn't want to continue the relationship. After that I refused offers from other men to sleep with them; they couldn't understand, if everybody else was sleeping with someone, why I didn't want to. I was told that I was a bit strange, but I really didn't want to start another relationship and be hurt again.

Hela: As Płaszów was turned from a work camp into a concentration camp (*Konzentrationslager*) it became more crowded, for other camps were being liquidated. Sometimes there was a population of 20,000. Fences around the perimeter of the camp were electrified, as were those between the men's and women's prisons, so that there was no longer the possibility of contact except on the *Appellplatz* before roll-call. This was when many people devised a personal familiar whistle, a code tune that they could recognise to identify members of their family. Poldek had a particular whistle of four notes, with the last one descending, which all my life I could recognise anywhere, any time. This brief sound and glimpse were the only contact we had.

∽

Linda is tall and graceful and I admire everything about her. She lives across the road from us in a cream-brick house, and although she is only a few years older she epitomises wisdom and experience. Her figure is shapely, while mine is still flat and thin. Having migrated from England some years back with her mother and elder sister, she has a lilting, refined accent, and I feel privileged and happy whenever she notices me in the street and waves with a smile.

I'm particularly thrilled when Linda stops me one day and invites me in for 'a cup of tea'. This sounds so ladylike and civilised that I'm afraid I'll be clumsy. Still, I am so flattered that I say yes, though I have to ask my mother.

After I have nervously shared tea in fine porcelain cups with her family, she asks if I'd like to look at her 'treasures'. We slip off to her bedroom at the back of the house, a dark place crowded with furniture and floral wallpaper. Her dainty fingers search in a small walnut cupboard and pull out an oblong tin, the kind that biscuits come in. Carefully she opens the lid and begins to spread the contents on the bed, explaining what each item is. I sit fascinated at one end of the bed, hypnotised by her fingers and her voice, but more than that, by the objects.

There is a war medal that belonged to her father; she speaks of him in hushed tones but I don't dare to ask what happened to him. There is a necklace of threaded crystal beads given to her by her grandmother. Her treasures tumble out: a pearl-and-gold brooch; a cut-glass stopper separated years ago from its decanter; a greeting-card, pastel and faded, sprinkled with pale glitter, that her grandfather once gave to her grandmother; a coil of pale hair that belonged to her brother who died when he was a baby; several old coins; a tarnished stopwatch that a great-grandfather had passed down. And the photos! She withdraws them one at a time from the box, looks closely at them, and recites a list of unfamiliar names, pointing with her delicate fore-finger. Some are of groups, carefully posed, while others show a severe-looking man or woman looking straight and unsmiling at the camera.

As I gaze at the photos I feel a strange tightness at the bottom of my ribs. I look at the faces, trying to find some shred of recog-nition, knowing at the same time how futile it is. I touch the pearl brooch, let the crystal beads run through my fingers. I feel a tin-gling, a vibration, and I long to clutch the items tightly, to hold them for a little longer, but I know she is watching me closely, a little smile playing about her lips. She asks if I like the treasures; I nod, unable to speak. The tightness grows to a hollowness, an empty feeling that can't be filled. The threads that link Linda to her past are strong, glowing. They are made manifest by the treasures before me, and I sense that it is not the objects themselves that have so taken my breath away. It is not their beauty or value that tugs at me, but the world of significant connections that surrounds them.

My mother doesn't have such a box. I realise with a pang that we have no family heirlooms, no pieces of old jewellery, no book or candlestick, not even a tiny brooch or coin that comes from the past. I thank Linda politely for the tea and tell her I must go, as my mother will be worried.

10

Janka: I think my past has made me more tolerant. I have this belief that the people who tormented us were psychotic, because normal people could not behave in that way. This belief sustained me throughout the dark years.

Auntie always tries to be optimistic. She keeps a little red notebook which she fills with quotes and wise sayings. Whenever doubts or moods of depression creep in she finds solace in rereading them. One of her favourites is the words of Mahatma Gandhi: 'You must not lose faith in humanity. Humanity is an ocean. If a few drops of the ocean are dirty, the ocean itself does not become dirty.'

Janka: When I had terrible stomach pains in concentration camp because of my ulcer, Hela, who lived in another barrack, went in the evening, when no one could see, to bring me a bit of hot water in a cup. As she was bringing the water back to me, one of the guards, Orłowska, saw her and began to beat her terribly. Her face, arms and body were all swollen. Surely that sort of behaviour was not normal.

Even going to the latrines was risky in Płaszów, because we knew Goeth could be there with his big Alsatian dogs that might attack us at any time. This was an aberration; I refuse to believe that human beings normally behave like that.

Another time I saw a very religious woman, a *rebbetzin*, who had a daughter with her. This daughter was very pregnant and the two women prayed continually and comforted each other. The older woman told me that the war would finish before the baby was born, because she believed so much in God and He would save her. Her faith and strength shone in her eyes. But it didn't help. They killed both her and her pregnant daughter.

One incident I can never forget concerns my cousin. My father's oldest brother Nechemiasz, the one we called Uncle Hemiu, was married to Gusta Pozner, who had perished in the early years of the war in the ghetto. They had only one son, Jan Haubenstock. This cousin was very good-looking; he was tall and blond with blue eyes. Before the war, when we lived in the country, Jan had often been sent by his mother to stay with us, so we were very close to him.

In Płaszów I sometimes saw him and his father. Jan worked for a German officer, who seemed to like him. He was given certain privileges and had a wonderful smile that captivated everybody. He was sixteen or seventeen at the time. I heard, but I don't know if it was true, that the son of this German for whom he worked had been killed, and that's why the German was angry. Another version was that Jan had been heard whistling a Russian national song, which was forbidden. Whatever the reason, he was condemned to be hanged, together with another man, Krautwirt. When I heard this I was distraught. The woman *kapo* in charge of me knew he was my first cousin and, with some feelings of humanity, allowed me to stay away from the hanging. All the other Jews in Płaszów had to witness the execution.

I stayed in the barracks and I prayed, for I believed very much in God. I prayed and prayed, begging for Jan's life to be spared, for the ordeal to be over. After what seemed like hours, people started coming in slowly to the barracks, with their heads down and their eyes averted. I began to question them and eventually found out that he had almost been saved. Apparently when the hangman strung him up and kicked away the chair, the rope broke. A gasp went up from the assembled crowd. It's an unwritten law all over the world that if the rope breaks during an execution, the prisoner is entitled to live. But not for Goeth. He ordered Jan to be strung up again, and this time he died, in all-too-familiar agony. My heart broke when I heard this, and I cried out

132

against this God that allowed such things to happen.

Jan's father, Uncle Hemiu, was devastated. He went back to the barracks, saying there was nothing left to live for, and he tried to hang himself too. The other inmates didn't let him so he didn't succeed, but when I saw him again his eyes were sunken and he moved like one asleep. He died later in Płaszów, one of the thousands who had lost hope.

From this time on my faith was badly shaken. Where was God, if He allowed innocent young people to die so horribly? It was very hard to keep believing in a God of love and mercy in the face of all we were going through. And yet I continued to pray to Him. I questioned angrily and cried bitter tears, but I believed that He existed, hiding somewhere.

There were three lines I later saw scratched into the wall at Auschwitz:

I believe in the sun even when it's not shining;
I believe in love even when I don't feel it;
I believe in God even when He is silent.

That's how I felt too. Despite the suffering and pain, the deprivation and torment, I somehow managed to maintain a positive attitude.

Our family is strolling through the Botanical Gardens. It is early afternoon in autumn, with a soft hazy light coming through the trees. Suddenly I see another family ahead of us: a father, a mother and a boy of about my age. But instead of walking along the gravel paths like everyone else, the boy darts in and out of the garden beds, crushing plants as he goes, unheeded by his parents who are deep in conversation. I watch him running around in front of us. Then, as if in a fit of rage, he begins to tear the leaves off a nearby tree. He grabs great fistfuls of dark-green leaves, uttering low guttural sounds. He picks up a crooked branch and starts to slash at bushes and trees as he runs. Torn leaves and crushed flowers are left in his path.

No one else seems to notice this senseless rampage. I feel a growing sense of unease, of horror, that a child close to my age could be so destructive of living things and not be reprimanded. But more than that, I try to understand what drives him to create ugliness where there has been beauty, disorder where there has been serenity. I feel a violence and cruelty in this boy that shock me. I speak of it to no one, but the image of the boy slashing and destroying stays with me for a long time.

Janka: All around me in Płaszów there was constant violence and death. Yet somehow I built a wall around myself and didn't let the violence touch me. One evening we were surrounded by guards with revolvers and other weapons, yelling and pushing us. Women were getting beaten and were screaming. In the midst of the panic I looked up at the sky and saw immense peace and beauty there. The noise around me receded, and all I was aware of was an overwhelming sense of calm. I called out, 'Oh, look, there's a perfect moon tonight, and see how beautiful the stars are!'

People later said to me, 'Are you crazy? How can you look at the moon and the stars when they are shooting us, and beating us, and we're all so hungry?' But the sky and the seasons and the events of nature were important to me. The eternal cycles, in the midst of a world gone mad, were signs that somewhere, albeit far away, some things were still normal. They gave me a shred of hope to hang on to.

From Płaszów there were regular transports going, as we later found out, to Auschwitz. We still didn't know for sure about the existence of gas chambers and crematoria. After the war we were often asked, 'How come you didn't realise that people from Płaszów were being taken to Auschwitz, to be exterminated?' It was because we were lied to continually; the SS officers told us the Jews were going to another work camp in the Ukraine, where they were needed to unload trainloads of supplies for the German army behind the Russian front. We were told the children would be looked after, they were to be used to prepare first-aid kits, to pack rations of food, to make up parcels for a field-kitchen, and so on. While the children prepared packets of biscuits, a can of corned beef, some tea and some sugar, the mother would check and pack the supplies. It sounded plausible. Anyway, we wanted to believe it. They lied to us all the time, but we were so desperate to believe that what they told us sounded reasonable. We even thought that, since large-scale executions took place openly in our camp every day, why would they need to transport additional thousands to some imaginary gas chambers? Only later we heard about the cakes of soap they produced in Kraków, stamped with the letters RYF—*Rein Jüdische Fett* (clean Jewish fat). And how they used to make mattresses from hair, and lampshades from skin. We learnt of documents, such as a receipted account for a grinder used in the camps for grinding human bones. But till then we continued to be naive.

Hela: On 13 August 1944 they called up all the most important ODs, including Chilowicz, the head of the Jewish police, and his well-dressed wife Marysia. These two had power over all the prisoners and were like aristocracy within the system, but apparently they knew too much about Goeth and his black-market dealings. Goeth was becoming afraid, and had all the ODs assembled before him.

We were called out to stand in lines by our barracks, and watch as all the chief ODs were shot, one by one. We then had to walk slowly past Goeth, astride his horse. As we got closer I could see all of them lying there, lifeless. I vividly recalled how Marysia Chilowicz used to be dressed so neatly, with her uniform and truncheon. She used to be brutal and would call us Jewish whores, as if she wasn't one of us. She thought she was so smart. But on this day, there she was, lying dead among the small group of bodies of the ODs, neatly lined up. Many people had hated Chilowicz, but even though he'd run around shouting a lot and waving his truncheon, he had not been too brutal to us. Our life with them was still better than under people like Simche Spira. Another important OD was Mietek Penner, but they spared him, I don't know why.

As I continued to walk past the bodies I dug my nails into

my palms. The SS were checking that everyone looked; we were not allowed to avert our heads or close our eyes, or we would have been shot. I forced myself to look: I saw the flies crawl in their mouths and nostrils, and couldn't believe they had finished up like this. If this was what happened to the important, protected people, what hope was there for us?

That wasn't the end of it. Goeth and some of his henchmen began to move towards the gallows. From one side some *kapos* hauled in the body of a man, still alive but terribly tortured; from the other side they led in, walking backwards, a man with his hands tied behind his back. I closed my eyes for a moment. It wasn't possible. The young man they were leading in was Adam, a tall handsome boy who looked after Goeth's dogs. They were terrible dogs, trained to tear a man apart, but Adam had a way with them and controlled them with gentleness. Now he stood by the gallows. Once, I had noticed from the corner of my eye that Goeth hadn't liked something Adam did, and had been about to set his dogs onto him. Majola, Goeth's girlfriend, had intervened and Adam was saved. Now he stood there, his head down. I looked away. Why were they going to hang him?

Suddenly I felt a painful, stinging blow to the side of my head. The woman guard watched me coldly. No, I wasn't going to lift my hand to my face; that would have meant another blow. I opened my eyes wide. There was Adam hanging from the gallows, and the other man was beside him. Goeth was giving some speech about punishment for any protesters or troublemakers. I wanted to be sick and felt myself trembling. I couldn't wait to get back to the barracks.

Janka: All these bodies were later buried in deep pits and covered with dirt by earth-moving machines. The machines were in constant use these days. Alternatively, bodies were often piled up and burnt. We had to haul wood to stack up around the bodies. For days the acrid smell would hang in the air and fill our nostrils, and a thick black cloud would hover over us. Seventeen train wagons loaded with ash were taken out from the camp. Those who assisted with the executions and the burials received bigger rations of vodka. They laughed and told jokes about the dying. They were drunk a lot of the time.

Hela: The remarkable thing was that people kept their sense of humour, albeit grotesque, amidst the most appalling and unspeakable atrocities. We were always singing and telling vulgar jokes about our predicament. Macabre humour about death and bodies cropped up everywhere. There was a dreadful song about *Hujowa Górka*, the hill where the executions took place, and what went on between the bodies there after dark. Another song which the whole camp knew was sung to the tune of the trumpet call played by Wilek, Poldek's brother, every evening:

Już dziewiąta jest godzina
Cały lagier idzie spać
Już zamknięta jest latryna
Już niewolno więcej srać.

(It's already nine o'clock
All the camp is going to sleep
The latrines are locked up now
You're no longer allowed to shit.)

Even more vulgar were the words to Wilek's wake-up call:

Pobudka wstać
Kurwa wasza mać
Ja już trąbie od godziny
A wy śpicie skurwysyny
Kurwa wasza mać.

(Time to get up
Your mother was a whore
I've been blowing for an hour
But you whoresons just keep sleeping
Your mother was a whore.)

Towards the end, friends used to farewell each other saying, 'Soon we shall meet on a shelf as two cakes of soap.' It was as if only by confronting the worst horrors imaginable, and then making jokes about them, could we survive the daily threats to our existence.

The public beatings and hangings continued on the *Appell-platz*, where all of us would be assembled. We had to stand there in silence for hours and watch the proceedings. Often tables were set up, ten tables at a time, and they selected a hundred people from the thousands there, for public beating. These people, women and men, had to take down their pants, lie on the table and suffer twenty-five strokes of the whip, while counting aloud. If someone fainted, they called for water to revive the victim, because if you were unconscious you couldn't feel the beating. Once revived, the counting had to begin all over again.

Beatings like this were often performed in the evenings, if a certain group of prisoners hadn't reached their quota for digging in the hard earth or shifting stones. The SS congregated on Goeth's balcony to watch for their amusement. Goeth must have been a sexual pervert, enjoying the sight of young girls being beaten on the bare buttocks. Afterwards there were shootings. We all had to witness this, again and again.

Commandant Goeth enjoyed celebrating these deaths with feasting and music, and he would call on the Rosner brothers to provide the entertainment. Poldek and his older brother, Herman, had to take off their striped prison uniforms and put on dinner-suits. They took their instruments to Goeth's villa and played till the early hours of the morning. Sometimes I spoke to Manci, Herman's wife, although we weren't in the same barracks. She and I were always very frightened when the two brothers were called to play, as nobody knew whether they would come back alive. But if things went well they could return with a piece of sausage or some bread from the kitchens.

My mother often tells me that the one thing she prayed for when she was pregnant with me was that I would be musical, like my

father. She claims she is tone-deaf herself, and has enormous admir-
ation for those who are musical. Music is a gift that no one can
take away from you. Music can mean life.

Hela: There were other times when Poldek and Herman had
to play. Once, a prisoner escaped and was caught soon afterwards. He was paraded around the camp wearing a board
with the words, *Komme Zurück* (Come Back), the title of a
well-known song. The melody was the same as for the
French song *'J'attendrai'*. Poldek and Herman had to play this
tune repeatedly while following the prisoner around. We all
had to see this pitiful example of the consequences that
awaited anyone crazy enough to attempt escape. The prisoner was later executed.

Small groups of several hundred continued to arrive, but
transports of 500 or 1000 or 1500 people left daily without
us knowing what happened to them. We would hear
rumours about crematoria, and burning bodies, but somehow we just didn't want to believe them. Each one of us had
a theory, and tried to deny the awful reality of the mass
murders that were occurring.

After each *Aktion*, there were fewer and fewer people. We
still didn't know where all the hundreds and hundreds of
people who were being rounded up were taken. Tearful fare-
wells took place, amid unspoken questions whether this was
the last time we'd see each other; we knew in our hearts the
answer was yes, but we couldn't afford the luxury of grieving or thinking about the future. Daily survival was the only
thing on our minds.

Janka: While we were in Płaszów we heard about a factory
called Emalia which manufactured enamel-ware. It was run
by Oskar Schindler, a German industrialist who, although he
was a member of the Nazi Party, seemed to have some
humanitarian feelings. He employed Jews as cheap labour,
but the people who worked for him were much better off
than we were. Nobody shot them; they had better food and
relative comfort.

When there was talk of Płaszów being closed down, Schindler asked Goeth for permission to move his factory from Płaszów to Brünnlitz in Czechoslovakia, near his home town. In autumn of 1944 he had begun to draw up a list of names of people he claimed he needed for his munitions factory, asserting that they were essential to the German war effort. He was eventually given permission, but only about a thousand Jews could go with him. On this list were the names of the two musician brothers, Poldek and Herman. Schindler knew them from hearing them play at Goeth's parties, and he loved their music. He agreed to put all of their surviving family on the list as well. So Poldek's wife Hela, my brother Kuba and I were on the list, as well as all of Poldek's relatives. There was Herman's wife Manci and their little son Olek (who had escaped an *Aktion* by hiding in the sewers), Poldek's sister Regina with her husband Dolek Horowitz and their children Ryszard and Niusia, and Dolek's brother Mundek, his wife Roma and their daughter Halinka. This list promised life.

Hela: I didn't know what was going on and felt the panic in the air. There were rumours that the Russians were approaching and that the camp would be closed down. Things were chaotic, we had no idea what would happen to us. There were also rumours about a list being drawn up by a German industrialist, Schindler, containing names of people who would work for him, but I knew no details. All I knew was that for several days the women guards were running around, screaming, counting, taking people away. I knew that our time would come soon. On 15 October 1944, groups of men, including Poldek and Herman, were marched out the gates, as well as many of the women. I didn't know where they were being taken. I lay in my bunk at night and couldn't sleep. Was this the end?

It was a week later. From early morning I knew that today the trains had come for us. Our guards ran around frantically. They put us into groups and counted us again and again, waving their truncheons wildly. One of the women in our group whispered that she wasn't going anywhere, she would rather be shot on the spot. No one knew what was happening. There were rumours about extermination camps. It seemed preposterous. Massacres and mass murders were committed right there in our presence. The Germans were not ashamed of genocide. Why would they go to all the trouble of sending multiple trains of Jews to some supposed extermination camp? It must be a bad joke of the vicious Poles. As we stood being counted, some women were taken from our group, others brought in. It was said they were the workers from Emalia, the enamel-ware factory. Janka was not with me; I didn't know where she was. The counting took hours.

Janka: At the last moment people were frantically giving away gold or diamonds which they had managed somehow to conceal, to get their name on the list. I found out that my name, which had originally been on the list, had been removed. I felt a terrible despair, because even though we didn't know for sure what would happen to the people on the list, I wanted to get out of Płaszów and be with my sister.

There were others I knew of whose names, like mine, had been on the list. One was Suchestowa, a glamorous singer who was married to a Polish prince. Someone else had offered a bribe and had their own name put on the list in place of hers. There were those who later boasted of how they had been able to offer money to get their names added to the list.

I went to an OD who had been involved with drawing up the list, Marcel Goldberg, and asked to be reinstated, insisting I knew that my name had been on it. He began to hit me around the face and head until I fell to the ground, and still he continued to beat me. Many people claimed afterwards that because of his greed some members of their family lost their lives. Others stated that he was their saviour and didn't take a penny for it.

But there was nothing I could do. So that's how it was that my sister and the others went with Schindler's transport to

141

Brünnlitz, and I was left behind in Płaszów. A few days later the order came that Płaszów was to be liquidated, and we knew we would all have to leave.

Hela: As I stood there with the other women, clutching a scrap of bread in my palm, I wondered whether it was better to put it in my mouth or save it for later. But I knew I couldn't swallow it now; I was so thirsty. It was 21 October 1944. We began to march, gathering what energy we had left, hungry, dirty, with the guards' screams all around us. We marched in our wooden clogs, clutching whatever was left of our belongings—a few rags and a spoon. That spoon was very important to me. I could tear bread with my hands, but to eat watery soup like an animal was the final degradation; the spoon was my last precious link to humanity. But even this was soon to be taken from me.

I had no idea where we were going. Soldiers were lined up, aiming their rifles at us. I suddenly thought of the absurdity of these strong, powerful men, afraid of a group of weak starving women. We marched to the accompaniment of screams and the thudding of truncheons.

We were now outside the camp. I wanted to see normal, free people, but there was no one about. Maybe it was better, maybe I would have burst out crying. We were marching towards the cattle wagons of the train that stood nearby. There were screams again as they pushed us together towards the wagons, not wanting us to get mixed up with other lines of women. How could I climb up on that high wagon without being beaten? But one helped another. Hands reached down to drag up those below. About a hundred of us were pressed into one wagon. I had lost one of my clogs. I tried to stay near the side to avoid being crushed. The doors were closed, then nailed shut, and the train began to move. At first there were several strong shudders that threw us all backwards on top of one another, then we were all thrown forward. Eventually the train moved off with a rhythmic motion.

The crush was terrible. I needed to urinate. I should have

done it earlier, while standing. Some of the women decided that it would be better if half of us stood while the other half sat down on the ground. For some of us there was no alternative; we had to sit in the puddles and mess. One of the women started to sing in a high voice, a camp song about life outside the wires. The train stopped often, and the stale air and the stench became unbearable. At one of these stops we heard some words of Polish. We began to thump on the door. 'Where are we? Where are we going?' our voices called out.

Eventually a voice replied, 'To Oświęcim.'

'Give us some water!'

'Not possible. The doors are nailed shut, and the windows are too small and too high. I'd give it to you if I could.'

The train began to move again. The words of the Pole kept echoing with the rattle of the wheels. Questions were flying. Are we going to be gassed? Are we going to be rescued by Schindler? Is he really a friend to the Jews?

We found out only later, the three hundred of us, that we were on the list drawn up by Oskar Schindler. At the time I knew very little about who Schindler was, and how he had been helping the Jews who worked for him at Emalia.

Again the train stopped. We could hear dogs barking, quite close. '*Raus!*' we heard being yelled over and over again, coming closer to our carriage. We held on to each other tightly, and it seemed less crowded in there. All I could think about was my thirst. I dreamed of a large glass of cold water.

∞

My mother's hands fascinate me. She has nimble fingers that can knead and shape pastry into an even circle on the floured table, while the bit of pastry I am working with gets sticky and ragged. On ironing days, with the smell of hot cotton hanging in the air, she wields an iron with such speed that I am sure she will burn her fingers, changing it swiftly from her right to her left hand as she tugs and smooths the fabric. I am not allowed to go anywhere near the iron, for fear that I will burn myself. When she strips the beds, clouds of white billow around me and eventually the pile of laundry in the centre of the room grows, while she smooths clean sheets over the discoloured mattress and tucks the corners in neatly. I try to help, but can never reach far enough or hold the edges firmly enough to make the sheets smooth. I wander off and decide to jump onto the high pile of stripped bed linen before she comes to tie the four corners tightly together, ready for the laundry man (we don't have a washing machine, and the sheets come back from the laundry gleaming white and starched stiff, needing to be pulled apart with strong hands before they can be spread on the beds). I leap onto the laundry pile imagining it to be a huge soft cushion, but I sink through it and land against the hard ground beneath. I conceal my disappointment and, realising my mother hasn't seen me, I don't tell her I hurt myself.

My mother's hands are reddened, particularly on the fleshy part of her palms and down the sides; she tells me that all the Haubenstocks have these distinguishing marks. My aunt has the same colouring, but I am disappointed to find that my own small palms are identical in colour with the rest of my hands. Sometimes (and these are the times I associate most vividly with my mother) her hands are red from kneading meatballs, and the smell of onion and garlic is on them. It is the first thing I notice when I walk in the door after school and she gives me a hug. Her eyes, she tells me, are watery from peeling the onions. Her hands are cool and dry after she has washed them, but the smell lingers. It is a smell associated with home and comfort, the warmth of a small crowded kitchen, and a sense of security that my hunger will soon be appeased.

11

Hela: Our journey from Płaszów was over. We had arrived at dawn. The doors were prised open with a loud crash, and my first view was of a red sky, grey smoke, black shadows, and flames.

'*Raus!*' screamed the men in striped clothes. 'Everybody get out! Quickly!'

We jumped down from the train as quickly as we could, trying to avoid the blows of truncheons. As I stood in a line with the others, my eyes adjusting to the light, I could make out the shapes of chimneys in the distance belching smoke— and still I was looking for rational explanations. My nose filled with the smell of acrid smoke, yet my mind refused to think of the source. It's a smell I can never forget: the smell of burning flesh. We were marched from the train amid the noise of dogs barking, rifle butts hitting flesh, the whistling of truncheons, and people screaming.

We had arrived in Auschwitz–Birkenau.

Auschwitz was a place of mud. The moist clay stuck to our wooden clogs. We were led through a gate with the large words *Arbeit Macht Frei* (Work Makes You Free) in metal letters across the top. There were beautiful tall trees, and behind them buildings, row after row. We continued straight ahead, bypassing the tall chimneys billowing smoke. The stench was constantly in our nostrils.

In front of the buildings stood people who looked like corpses, with no expressions on their faces. None of them even raised a head to look at our group. We were halted in front of a grey building. The female guards hit us at random. 'You Płaszów sluts! We will have order here. You are in

Auschwitz–Birkenau. This is not a brothel!' I trembled. In the ghetto I had thought things couldn't be worse, and then again in Płaszów. But this . . .

First they counted us. One of us was punished for something she had done by having to squat, up and down many times, and then she was brutally beaten with truncheons. I wondered whether she would come out alive. Other SS men came and counted us again. We had to stand in the mud for hours, our feet numb and frozen. I was past caring. All I wanted was something to drink: for two days we hadn't had a drop. A group of women went by. No one looked at us. Could they see? Did they know whether they were alive or dead?

The guards then attacked us and shouted at us to move. They pushed us through the metal doors of the grey building, down a corridor that led into a larger room with several doors leading off it. We didn't know where we were. We saw some more men in striped clothes, milling around. Some women said we were in the bath-house. Someone had heard rumours about gas, and tremors of panic ran through us.

We were told to undress as quickly as possible. The stares of the SS did not matter. We had to leave our clothes and belongings in a corner and were told we could collect them later. But that was not true. The Slovak women who had been in Auschwitz for some time had told us we wouldn't survive another day. Hadn't we seen the chimneys, the flames?

We were taken to a room to be shaved. The hair under our arms and our pubic hair was ripped and pulled with blunt blades. I couldn't stop my eyes filling with tears. Some of the younger girls, including Niusia and Halinka, had their heads shaved too. This was followed by a stinking wet rag rubbed over the shaved areas, smelling of some kind of disinfectant and stinging our eyes.

We were then taken to the showers. We huddled cold and naked in the large concrete room, eyeing the metal pipes overhead with fear and clutching each other. Someone said they could smell gas. There were ripples of hysteria. The time dragged on interminably and my thoughts were a jumbled panic. Was this where it ended? My vision became blurry. I saw the faces of my sister, my husband. Had all my suffering been for this?

At last a thin trickle of icy water began to fall on us from the metal pipes above. We gasped in shock and relief. I began to laugh hysterically, letting the stream of cold water pour over my head. We emerged from the showers, a sea of naked shivering bodies. There were no towels. I could see that some of the women's bodies were badly bruised and scratched. Everyone was skinny, with bones protruding. Breasts were just folds of hanging skin. We were all trembling with cold.

My mother knits little woollen hats for me with two points that look like rabbit's ears. She worries about my feeling hungry or cold. She dresses me in hand-knitted woollen dresses and thick woollen stockings in winter. I am often warned not to sit on the ground, especially on concrete, as I might catch a chill. Walking barefoot is also forbidden, even in summer.

My mother's concern for my warmth is particularly evident at bathtime. The little bathroom is filled with steam and the two-bar radiator glows orange in the corner. She bends over me as I splash around in the old-fashioned, claw-footed bathtub. She soaps and rinses me gently, then stands up, her hands on the small of her back as she stretches. Next to the electric heater she spreads out the towel, turning it this way and that to warm it. As I get up out of the water, pink and glowing, the soft roughness of the towel envelops me, as does my mother's love. I feel safe and warm.

Hela: We learnt that other women arriving in Auschwitz who weren't in Schindler's group had numbers tattooed onto their forearms, which meant they would be sent to work. If you were destined for the gas chambers, however, they didn't bother with a number. We weren't tattooed.

They took us to a storeroom set up with tables piled high with clothing. They gave us old clothes to wear, chosen at random and thrown at us: men's shirts, socks, underwear or tablecloths. I was given a light-blue night-dress that was too big for me. Others had ridiculous garments that were much too small. We also had rough wooden clogs thrown to us. They didn't care whether we got two left feet. These clogs gave me terrible blisters.

Then some Slovak women guards screamed at us and pushed us around. These women were Jewish, but they came from little villages where they were brought up as rough peasants, with much more strength and cunning than we had. They were quite different from us and they had contempt for the 'intelligentsia'. They seemed to enjoy tormenting us with their brutality.

We were counted and allocated bunks in barracks without windows in the women's camp. The floor was of damp clay, seeping water. There were three tiers of bunks here, but they were wide, and eight women had to fit on one bunk. The thin straw pallet was damp and stinking, and crawled with bedbugs. The little bit of grey blanket we had to cover ourselves with was filthy. Four women were sent out to the kitchens for 'coffee'. They came back with a cold watery liquid, which the female guard dished out into the dented tin cups we were given. All the while, she was hurling insults at us. We were dying to have a drink, despite its taste. I drank it in one gulp. There was no bread, nothing to eat. When it was time to sleep we all had to roll onto our right sides so that we could fit on our bunk. We could hear rats running around.

Our first house in Australia is large and many-roomed, but there are some rooms I seldom go into. There is a dark room at the back of the house, with spiderwebs hanging from the rafters, and empty boxes and newspapers on the floor. There are strange creakings when I go in there and the needles of light that filter in through cracks in the walls show up the dust floating around. I see frightening shapes, which re-emerge in my dreams.

Another place I don't go near is the woodpile next to the back shed. My mother tells Auntie she has seen a rat there. She doesn't know I am listening. I've never seen a rat, but the word in Polish—

szczur—embodies all that is ugly and evil and terrifying. I hear the shudder in my mother's voice when she utters it. There are places you don't go, things you don't talk about.

Hela: Everywhere here the wires were electrified. Several people threw themselves onto the wires to kill themselves, unable to stand any more. One of these (I found out later) was Janka's friend, Kuba Stempel. He was one of the first to be deported from the ghetto, and was sent to Montelupich, the prison in Kraków, and then to Auschwitz. They even told his parents that they could send a parcel to him, but it was all lies; the Jews all went to Auschwitz to be exterminated. There was nowhere to escape, no way of avoiding the torment. What could you do, when there were Germans with guns and truncheons, ready to beat you and kill you on the slightest pretext? But I don't think I ever considered giving up my life in this way.

The following day was the first selection. Before dawn we were woken to the shrieks and blows of the guards, ordering us to fold our blankets and assemble outside. We stood in rows, silently, and were counted again and again. A drizzling rain was falling. That's when I saw Dr Josef Mengele, the 'Angel of Death', and looked into his terrible eyes; eyes that would haunt me forever. We had heard that he not only murdered people but performed the most appalling medical experiments on them. Beside him stood four women guards with white scarves on their heads. My heart was thumping. Calmly he sorted people, pointing with a baton to the right or to the left, separating the older women or anyone who looked sick from the others, selecting for life or death. I heard later that in a quarter of an hour he could decide the fate of five hundred people. No one was selected from our group.

There were frequent medical inspections, at any hour of the day. We were made to strip and had to run, naked, back and forth in the clammy mud or in the bath-house while we were looked over and examined. We tried to appear healthy, straightening our bent shoulders, pinching our cheeks or rubbing red clay into them to colour them. In daylight we looked grotesque, pale with two red patches on our cheeks. We knew that looking unhealthy meant being selected to die. What instinct of self-preservation made us want to live? With the incessant shouting and screaming and brutality, I thought I was in hell. Where was Schindler now?

We soon lost track of time. Our group was kept separate from the others. Everything here was meant for death. Two and a half million people were killed here, and half a million died from disease, hunger and torture. Our days were spent in fear of being gassed, or shot, or dying of disease. Icy winds blew in through the gaps between the walls and the roof. There was no soap, there were no stockings or underwear, no toilet paper or sanitary aids. We spent most of the time standing outdoors in mud up to our calves, suffering hunger and, above all, thirst. Roll-calls lasted three or four hours, twice a day. At three in the morning and five in the evening, we had to line up in fives to be counted. We would stand for hours, immobile and numb, waiting for the SS to arrive and start counting.

They told us the water was contaminated with typhus and we were not allowed to drink. We were sometimes given a tiny bit of dirty warm water that passed for coffee, in a dented tin mug, or some watery soup in a bowl that five of us had to share. There was nothing floating in it, not even a bit of potato. I don't remember being given anything solid to eat.

When I saw a truck loaded with rotting vegetable-scraps drive past, I noticed that a few decayed old cabbage-leaves fell off and I ran with several other women to pick them up. I shoved a handful into my mouth. Shots suddenly rang out and some of the women fell. I didn't look at them but ran off. Many people died like this because they were overwhelmed by hunger and forgot all precautions. Other women, who had been in Birkenau longer than we had, moved around like shadows with huge eyes. They wore rags and had shaven heads. They were so hungry that they no longer had any control of their actions or emotions, and behaved like crazed animals. That's what terrified me the most; the total hopelessness and loss of human dignity.

We all developed dysentery. None of the Germans cared that we had nothing to eat or drink. The latrines weren't even like those in Płaszów—which had been primitive enough, a row of holes in a long bench. Here there was just a cesspit, with a wooden board caked with filth and excrement. They also called this, ironically, the washroom. On one wall, along the whole length of the latrines, was a metal gutter flowing with water and a sign above: 'This water is not for drinking. It is contaminated with typhus.' But even for a few drops of this infected water, desperate women were beaten. Our standard of hygiene deteriorated dramatically. We all developed rashes and ulcers. The skin around our mouths cracked, and we appeared more and more grotesque.

We stood for hours on end on the *Appellplatz*, not daring to move. If someone weakened and started to fall, another would hold her up and hide her. No one had yet died from our group. My thirst tormented me; maybe I was already suffering from typhus or dysentery, because I felt hot and feverish and wanted water so desperately that I drank from the gutter. We also suffered from lice. They crawled in our clothes till we were ready to rip off the rags together with our skins.

Days ran into each other. It was getting colder and the hunger was relentless. Sleep became the only respite. I dreamt dreams of the past, and they seemed more real to me than what I was going through. I talked to my mother, and saw Tadeusz, my blond Polish boyfriend, smiling at me, reassuring me that things would be all right. Janka was calling to me. It was hard to know whether I was asleep or awake. I also dreamt constantly of food, of thick slices of fresh rye bread, of steaming bowls of thick hot soup and potatoes, of cheese blintzes with sour cream. We'd often be woken up out of our dreams by fists or truncheons belonging to the Slovak women guards, who were no longer the newcomers and maybe were taking their revenge.

My mother knows how to knit with four needles at a time, those with points at both ends, and I am amazed that her stitches don't drop off the ends. My attempts at knitting are uneven and loose, but my mother with her magic fingers can always pick up a dropped stitch and finish off the row with lightning speed. She has an amazing ability to cast on stitches by winding the wool around the fingers of one hand and using only one knitting-needle. She holds the needles differently from my teacher at school and winds the wool around the wrong hand, or so I am told. Also, my mother knits without a pattern; the intricacies of the printed shorthand English language defeat her, but she is very skilful in producing hats, jumpers, and even matching blue dresses for me and my sister with a fluffy edging of white angora. I continue to work doggedly at scarves and hot-water-bottle covers.

Sewing is another feat at which my mother excels. With an old metal thimble firmly set on her middle finger, she weaves in and out of the fabric, darning socks, letting down hems, fixing tears. My only efforts are for my doll; I try to make dresses for her but they are poorly cut out, and as I don't really understand the need for knots to start with, the stitches unravel soon after I have finished. Most of all, my mother is annoyed that I won't use a thimble; how can you sew without a thimble? But I tell her that if I can push the needle through successfully without one, why should I try to work with such a hard, unyielding metal tool on the end of my finger? It only gets in my way and falls off every few minutes.

But it's not only practical things my mother is good at. She loves to play cards, and can shuffle and deal with an offhand grace that comes only after years of practice. My favourite game is when she tells a story of three robbers and three kings, arranging the cards in stacks and inserting the main ones at random into them. Miraculously, each time she comes to the end of her story the required cards have migrated mysteriously to the top of the stack, and she triumphantly reveals the kings: one, two, three! I watch her again and again but can never discover the magic.

Sometimes she takes a long loop of wool or string. At first we play cat's-cradle, as countless mothers and daughters have over the centuries. But there is another trick she teaches me that none of my friends know. With the string wound around the little finger of her left hand, she weaves the two strands in and out between and around her fingers, around the thumb and back again. This seemingly tangled maze is released by easing the loop off the thumb and pulling the string: it flows out freely through all the fingers! Again and again I try, each time getting caught with the string wrapped stubbornly around one or other of my fingers. But with persistence, watching her repeatedly, I master the trick at last. This is one that none of my friends have seen and I dazzle them for a while, but soon they give up, bored, and look for other entertainment. Nevertheless, I think my mother is the cleverest and most beautiful woman in the world.

12

Janka: Hela had left Płaszów before me. We were one of the last groups to leave. We had to start pulling down the barracks and carrying the timber to the top of the hill, where they used it as fuel to burn the bodies. The day came when they put us all into a cattle train, cramming so many of us into each carriage that a lot of people suffocated before we reached our destination. We were given no food or water for more than two days. I lost all sense of time and was aware of nothing but the lurching of the train and the suffering we all felt in the darkness.

At last we realised that the train had stopped. I was still with my friend Marysia Sperling and her mother, and Mila Braw, but I had no idea what had happened to Hela. We couldn't see anything, as the only gap in the carriage wall was very high up. Someone lifted up young Mila to try and see where we were. She peered through the slats for a moment, then was lowered down. 'Girls,' she said in a subdued voice. 'We are in Oświęcim.' She had seen the sign on the railway platform, and noticed the railway clock showing eight minutes past eight. No one spoke. We had all heard the rumours and could imagine our fate.

It was night-time. They opened the doors and let us out of the locked wagons, filthy and hungry. The dogs were barking and Germans were screaming at us to move quickly. We were taken to Birkenau, adjoining the camp at Auschwitz. We saw barbed-wire fences broken only by tall watchtowers, and rows and rows of low buildings. As we walked along the gravelly road, a world of barracks and barbed wire stretched out into the darkness and the awful stench of smoke was everywhere. There was nothing else.

We were assembled in a big hall and had to wait there for hours. We were told, 'The only way you leave Auschwitz is through the chimney.' All night we stood there, sometimes with the lights on, sometimes in the dark. A sense of resignation fell over us.

In the morning about fifty men and women came in. They marched us to the shower block, and with a lot of shouting and pushing told us to undress. Then they took everything from us, our clothes and any other possessions we had, including my little cloth bag containing a spoon and a bowl. I had my period at this time, and they took even the small shred of rag I had been using. We stood there naked, huddled together for selection in front of a group of young German soldiers with Alsatian dogs. Being stripped of our clothes, trying to cover ourselves with our hands, was bad enough. I felt exposed, abused. But as I stood with the group of women, I felt with horror the sticky blood starting to run down my legs. I was a young woman, acutely aware of my state. My sense of modesty and self-respect was totally outraged. I felt desperate, suffering such humiliation in front of these jeering men. But there was nothing I could do. They pointed and made lewd comments, while I clenched my fists and tried to keep breathing.

We had to walk past Mengele, who calmly divided us, to the left or to the right. Many of our group, those who had to go to the left, were led away and we never saw them again. I had been selected for the right group. I was still alive. Anyhow, that was the last time I had my period for a long while; whether from bromide that they put in our food, or from malnourishment and hunger, I stopped menstruating altogether.

We experienced shock after shock. Once the selection was over, we were led to the showers. Heartbroken after the loss of friends but relieved to be alive, we waited for our turn. Marysia, her mother and Mila were still with me. Survival was now foremost in our minds. One woman expressed her doubts. 'Look around,' she said. 'There are hardly any guards in here. By performing this quick selection they have lulled us into believing that we were chosen to live. We don't make a fuss, we sit here like lambs. That's how they can now fool us, make us enter the showers quietly and ...' She paused; '... turn on the gas.' Everyone gasped. Panic ran through the huddled group.

But I refused to let her words terrify us. 'Shut up,' I told her. 'Your ideas are crazy; they could have done it without selection. Besides, with that kind of attitude we may as well all give up hope right now.'

Hardly was this exchange over than we were taken to be shorn. They were probably in a great hurry because only a few of us, those infested with lice, had to succumb to this treatment. They were content to shave off our pubic and underarm hair. Luckily I didn't have lice, so they just cut the hair on my head very short. I was fortunate that in Płaszów, Mila, with whom I had been very friendly, had a special fine-toothed comb that she let me use. She was still very young when she came to Auschwitz, and kept her pretty black hair. I borrowed the comb sometimes and that was how I avoided having lice. It was very important at the time.

The man who was cutting my hair started to talk to me. I found out he was a 25-year-old Polish Jew from Kraków, my home town, and we continued to talk in whispers as he worked. I didn't have much time but I told him that I was very hungry, as we had had almost nothing to eat for several days. From then on, for the three months that I spent at Auschwitz, he managed secretly to send me two pieces of bread every day. I was able to share this with Marysia and her mother.

Once we got into the showers, the metal pipes did indeed release water and we could take a deep breath of relief. After the shower we were sprayed with some sort of disinfectant. Wet and shaking with cold (there were no towels), we now awaited the distribution of clothes. We were taken to a store-room where they handed out old clothes to us at random. Not only were most of the clothes thin summer dresses (no coats for this cruel winter) but some were too small, some too large. We tried them on, looked at each other, and exploded in laughter. They gave me some shoes that didn't match, one with a high heel and the other flat. I therefore walked with a limp. Some of us were wailing, others laughing as if possessed, swaying and rocking, pointing at each other. 'Stop that hysterical laughter!' shouted one woman, slapping a young girl who was laughing and crying at the same time.

'Leave her alone,' I said. 'Let them get rid of all their pent-up emotions after the shock of selection and the fear of the showers. Let's pretend that we are merely putting on fancy dress for *Purim*. The reality will catch up with us soon enough. We'll be crying tomorrow; right now, let's have a party.'

One of Mila's friends recognised her uncle among the workers; she was able to obtain a fine woollen jumper, a navy-blue one trimmed with a coloured border, and a skirt that fitted, as well as a good pair of leather shoes. I was always envious of her clothes whenever I passed her. This uncle was also able to get Mila and her friends some bread.

Then came the time to have a blue number tattooed onto the inside of my arm. It was a painful, slow process, but I felt quite numb by this stage. I emerged with my arm throbbing and the number A-26259 recorded permanently along it. Mila, who had been ahead of me in the queue, was number A-26077. Gradually each of us was losing her individual identity. With our short hair, our odd clothes and now a number instead of a name, we were taken over by a kind of apathy. They had reduced us to the lowest level. I stopped worrying about the future and walked around in a sort of daze. But I clung to the idea that a number meant I was going to live. If you didn't have a number, it meant you weren't even worth identifying, as you were going to be exterminated straight away in the ovens. We knew this to be true, because the crematorium chimney billowed smoke day and night.

We visit an old relative who has no children of her own. She wears a white lace blouse with a high collar. I am fascinated by the dark circles beneath her eyes, and the crinkled soft skin of her cheeks and neck. Although I am quite happy with my own company, the old lady searches for something to amuse me. Her pearls click together and the gold rings on her knobbly fingers shine as she searches in a drawer. She finds a book in Polish, with hard covers and thick brown pages the colour of paper bags, which I think very odd. I begin to turn the pages slowly, with a growing uneasiness. They give off a peculiar musty smell. Of course, I can't understand the unfamiliar combinations of letters, with dots and strokes and hooks everywhere. But I realise that's not the reason I dislike this book. The words are printed in the same blue-green ink as the tattoo on the inside of Auntie's arm.

I close the book quickly and put it back on the coffee table. The rest of the afternoon I play with the miniature porcelain table and chairs on the old lady's mantelpiece.

Janka: They then allocated us to our barracks. These were long wooden buildings. When we were taken there I asked the woman in charge, the *Blochälteste*, whether I could have a bunk on the top, where I thought it would be a little lighter and more private. She glared at me, and responded by hitting me so hard that I fell to the ground. They would hit and beat you on the slightest pretext. But she gave me that bunk, and I shared it with Marysia and her mother. We were crammed in with several others, but it was very important to me because I had a bit of light and was later able to write. Mila was in the same barrack as we were.

At last they gave us a small piece of bread. I decided to eat only half of it, wanting to save some for the morning so as not to faint during roll-call. I knew the dangers of eating it all at once. I hid the remainder under my pillow, but when I came back to get it later on, it was gone; someone had stolen it. I was so unhappy I started to cry, from hunger and despair. My friend Marysia, the one to whom I had once given my night-dress, saw my plight and said, 'Don't cry, my mother and I will share our bread with you.' I knew the two of them could have devoured their bread without witnesses. So when they offered me their last piece, I began to cry even harder. We were all swollen with hunger, and yet women like them could preserve their dignity and remain human, even under such conditions. Only by sheer willpower were they able not to abase themselves despite the circumstances. It meant taking care of the sick and the bereaved among us. It meant not begging for bread while we were naked and a male prisoner brought several loaves. It meant washing our skeletal bodies with snow or urine when water was not available, to try to preserve some cleanliness. These little victories over one's basic instincts were a passport to survival in dignity.

We were driven out of our bunks daily at 5.30 a.m., to assemble in the cold darkness on the *Appellplatz*. We had to stand there for hours, arranged in rows of five, one behind the other. Sometimes if the count wasn't right, we had to kneel with our hands in the air. It was a harsh winter and we were still dressed only in thin summer clothes. As we stood with chattering teeth, we clung instinctively to each other, one body warming the back of the one in front of her. Thus the first one had her front unprotected, while the last one, the fifth, had her back exposed to the wind. I suggested a fairer arrangement: we could take turns. We had no watches, so after counting to 200 two of the middle girls would move quickly to the 'outposts', and the half-frozen first and last became the protected ones in the middle. But it had to be done while the SS woman guard had her back to us. Once the roll-call started we didn't dare hug each other.

Sometimes the Germans would make us stand on the *Appellplatz* for hours at a time, cold and hungry, not allowed to move. When two Russian girls ran away, we had to stand in the cold all day long as punishment, with nothing to eat. The Russians were tough and had formed their own gangs. They stole bread rations from us whenever they could. Once, when they wanted an old piece of blanket on which we were sitting, they just came over and shook us off like meatballs. They were afraid of nothing.

159

Many times we were told to undress, and we never knew whether we were going to the showers or the gas chambers. We would crowd together in a cold room and hear a hissing noise. Women would begin to scream 'Gas, gas!' and cry hysterically and shout to be let out, trying to break down the door. But it wasn't gas, it was water.

One day the *Blochälteste*, a really nasty woman from Kraków, called about a hundred of us to leave the barracks. She had previously called the Slovakian girls and the Hungarian girls, and they had never returned. We walked for some time, accompanied by the shouts and snarls of German guards and dogs, in the direction of the crematoria. We could see smoke pouring out of the tall chimneys. We met up with lots of other groups and had to wait with thousands of people. I don't really know why—maybe the Germans were impatient, or hungry, or cold—but after some hours our group was turned around and led back to the barracks. The *Blochälteste* was amazed to see us return. Those who didn't were never seen again.

News reached me that my sister was somewhere in Birkenau. All the women who were headed for Brünnlitz had finished up here. I volunteered to empty the latrine cans, because I thought I might have a chance of seeing Hela if I was moving around. I did indeed see her once at roll-call, from far away, but could not speak to her. She spent only a short time here.

One day at roll-call a group of us were given two grey army blankets and told we were moving. We were marched through Birkenau past the men's camp, past the 'Union' factory, and eventually came to two brick buildings separated from the rest of the camp by wire.

These barracks were called the *Musterlager*. We saw a large room with double bunks, but we were told we didn't have to be crammed together like sardines and were allocated two to a bed. We had proper beds with pillows and feather eiderdowns, and electric lights, so everything looked quite civilised. We pinched each other, we couldn't believe this was still part of Auschwitz. It was like heaven compared to what we had come from. We were very lucky, because this camp was set up as a model camp, so that when inspectors would come from the Red Cross they were always shown these barracks to demonstrate to the world what good conditions we lived in.

There were maybe a hundred of us in these quarters. My friends Mila and Marysia and her mother were there with me. Once during roll-call, soon after our arrival, an SS man started asking for people with various skills: shorthand, office work, German typing, and so on. When he asked if there were any artists amongst us, Marysia's mother, who was an artist and had studied before the war in art academies in Paris and Vienna, stepped forward and said she was a painter. Her daughter then said she was a painter too and volunteered. I didn't even know how to hold a brush, but I didn't want to be separated from Marysia and her mother so I said I was a painter as well. I was lonely without Hela and desperate to stay with my friends. I thought that perhaps when the Germans discovered I was lying they would kill me, but what was the difference whether they shot me now or later? I could not visualise ever surviving Auschwitz.

It could have meant a death sentence for useless weaklings, but as it turned out it led to a good secure job. They were looking for people who could draw and copy famous pictures, to work in the *Druckerei*, the print factory; the copies were later sold by the SS as originals. They had selected only us three to work there. I thought about the thousands of other inmates in Auschwitz who had to work outdoors, carrying heavy loads or shovelling snow.

We, on the other hand, were taken to the print factory, where Marysia's mother started to copy all the great masters' paintings for the Germans. Marysia also worked at drawing. The *Oberscharführer*, Deutscher, came to look at my progress. He very soon found out I couldn't draw. He gazed at me for several moments, then the shadow of a smile played around his lips. There must have been something he liked about the way I looked. Marysia and I were both reasonably attractive in those days. He spoke to me in German, which I understood because I had learnt German stenography at school, but I didn't speak to him and kept my eyes lowered. He told me I was to go to the storeroom, where they kept all the paper and pencils. I had to keep records of everything and be in charge. He explained things to me very slowly, so that I would understand. My heart leapt. With my knowledge of the language, I knew I could manage that job. I also had to watch that no one stole anything, and that nobody who was not authorised was allowed in, not even the German woman guard who supervised us. I would be given the key and be responsible for everything.

So I began to work in the storeroom of the printing factory. I was warned not to steal anything, but like everyone else I survived by stealing. I was in charge of five other women. I was even given a dress to wear instead of the striped prisoner's uniform most inmates wore. It was a beautiful dress of brown wool trimmed with soft white feathers. It must have been taken from some Hungarian Jewess, because it had a Hungarian label sewn in the back of it. I felt a shudder, thinking of the Hungarian women who had been the most recent arrivals in the camp: they had been gassed and their bodies burnt straight away. Later my dress became infested with lice. They also gave me a fine brown woollen coat, which I managed to hang on to even after the war. The only thing they did was to cut a small square hole out of the back of it and sew in a patch of the striped material that all the Jews had to wear.

I was permitted to leave the camp occasionally to go to the city to buy supplies. Of course I was accompanied by a German soldier who watched over me. I would be taken in a truck past fields of corn, cows grazing, neat little houses. The other women would ask me, when I returned, 'What does the world look like out there? Do people still have curtains in their windows? . . .' It was quite bizarre going out of the camp, seeing the traffic, the people hurrying about their business and barely giving me a glance. I felt I was in the middle of a crazy nightmare. I was indeed lucky to get occasional glimpses of the outside world and to realise that, somewhere, normality still existed. My cousin Różyczka, who had played dolls as a child with Hela, was not so lucky; she had to carry out backbreaking work in the snow and suffered daily from cold, hunger and exhaustion.

I was also fortunate enough to have two pairs of underpants. What a luxury, to own underpants! I had sold a piece of bread for the second pair. I wore both pairs, so that I could hide some stolen paper or pencils between the two layers. That way I could give them to some of the men who worked in the other camp. For these goods they could buy some extra bread for us. I knew I was risking my life, but at that time life wasn't worth all that much so I continued to smuggle out small items.

Only once while I was there, the Red Cross visited our barracks. We were lined up for inspection but of course we weren't allowed to speak openly. We were given beautiful silk nightgowns to wear for the occasion, confiscated from other women who had brought them to Auschwitz. The people from the Red Cross started to ask us questions, but nothing that we could answer truthfully because all the time the Germans stood around us. We had to say that we were well treated and that we did indeed have enough to eat. We couldn't talk about the thousands of people forced to work breaking stones in freezing conditions. We couldn't talk about the constant degradation and suffering we experienced. We couldn't tell them that sometimes we had to wash ourselves with snow because there was no water. After the Red Cross inspectors left, the silk nightgowns were taken away from us.

In all this time, the man who had cut my hair continued to send me two slices of bread every day. I would write to him, when paper was available, and with every piece of bread he sent he included a letter, full of romantic ideas, very beautifully written.

Once, while I was working in the printing factory, I saw a Jewish man washing the windows and he started to talk to me. It was against the rules, and we both knew we could have been shot. He spoke French to me, but my French was very poor so I called Marysia over. She spoke French fluently and began a conversation with him. He told her his name and where he used to live in Paris. When he heard we were hungry he promised she would have some bread. It was easier for the Jewish men to obtain bread and they were very helpful to the Jewish women. Marysia really only saw him that one time, but from then on he sent her bread regularly.

I was still limping on that day because of the odd shoes I had been given. With the Frenchman was another Jewish man whose name was Rubin. I found out he was from Białystok. He asked me, 'Why are you limping? What has happened to you?' So I told him the story, and showed him my one flat and one high-heeled shoe. He told me not to worry, he would send me a loaf of bread so that I could buy some shoes from the illegal traders who somehow continued to do business, with bread as currency. The next day he did indeed send the loaf of bread and I was able to buy myself a matching pair of shoes from a Jewish *kapo*. Not only this; every day he put a bowl of hot soup in the oven in our barracks, so that I found it there on my return from work. These kind acts were performed by people whom we met once and never saw again in our lives.

The French fellow, Marysia's friend, sent her a letter containing a story. 'There were once two frogs who fell into a pail of milk,' he wrote. 'One frog said, "It's no use struggling, we are going to drown anyhow." And thereupon it gave a gasp and drowned. The other frog started to move its legs, backwards and forwards, backwards and forwards, churning the milk until it had turned into butter. Then the frog jumped out of the pail and hopped away.' We read the story and understood his message of encouragement.

Auntie's little red notebook is full of handwritten sayings which give hope and encouragement. I come across a typical one which she often quotes: 'Two men look out through the same bars. One sees mud and the other sees stars.'

Janka: We hardly ever knew what would turn out to be good for us and what should be avoided, possibly by subterfuge. Sometimes being led to a train could mean being sent to a small camp with a factory, and easy work; other times it could mean being sent to death. Sometimes you could save your life just by lingering, which was dangerous in itself. There was no way of knowing how to survive; we felt we were victims of some macabre game of chance.

There was a day when a thousand women from Theresienstadt, in Czechoslovakia, arrived. We were all herded towards the gas chambers together with them. I was as close to them as from here to the wall. But I always seemed to have an instinct for survival. I began to pull Marysia back, the same way I had once pulled my sister Hela back. Marysia was saying, 'I am so cold, I am so hungry, if I go to the oven at least I will be warm and my misery will be over.' I ignored what she was saying and dragged her with all my strength away from there, despite the blows and screams around us.

I kept telling her, 'Don't be stupid, go back a bit, let's keep moving towards the back.' In the midst of the clamour and the pushing, a kind of calm certainty came over me. At that moment I thought of a tiny photo of our mother which I had managed to hang on to until Auschwitz. I had this feeling that mother was watching me and this gave me strength. I was not a strong believer in God but I felt mother's presence guiding me at the last moment, the last second.

We were just a couple of feet away from the entrance, with women surging forward all around us, when we were halted. Mengele, the infamous doctor of Auschwitz, came towards us. He looked us over, and said, 'They still look in reasonable shape, leave them. They can work a bit more.' He gave the order for the women from Theresienstadt to be taken to the gas chambers instead. They were immediately sent to be undressed and within minutes had perished. Their bodies were burnt in the ovens, while we were spared. I said a silent prayer to mother. Was she really watching over me? Was it just luck? I felt weak with the relief of being alive for another day.

They had taken our bras away, and all I had to wear under my dress was a shirt and two pairs of underpants. When I washed them it was hard to get them dry. There was a large tiled stove in our barracks, and when we had to get our clothes dry I was allowed to stand facing the stove, holding the pants or the shirt there, to dry them for Marysia or myself. The German in charge of us allowed me to do this. Others were not treated with such consideration.

We had a roster for duties like lighting the fire for the stove. When it was my turn, I would nervously arrange the paper, then the pieces of wood with the lumps of coal on top, just as I had been taught. Then I would light a match, but inevitably the whole thing soon fizzled out, the coal finished up at the bottom, and there was no fire. The other women would say that if it was my turn to light the fire, they knew that when they returned from work it was sure to be cold. They started to do my duties for me. When it was time to wash our shirts they stood around and laughed because I had no idea how to do the washing. We had always had a woman come in to do the family wash and I was quite spoilt. But they knew that I was knowledgeable about books and films, and I filled in many desolate hours with exciting stories of the adventures and romances I had read about or seen. They also admired my fearlessness, and I felt they were fond of me, despite my clumsiness.

Auschwitz–Birkenau was a strange place. Sometimes there were concerts that the inmates organised, with an orchestra formed from those who were talented. People sang or danced and told stories, to try to recall the past and forget what we were going through. Once we were invited to watch an evening of drama staged by German Jewesses, but it wasn't much of a performance. The only good line was, 'To be or not to be—that is *here* the question.' There was a French girl who told us that her name was Fifi and that she had danced at the Folies-Bergère. She claimed she was famous and had danced for the princes of Europe. She was attractive, with short dark hair and stunning eyes. I found her very entertaining and admired her a lot. Only after the war did I find out more about her.

The German officer who had given me the job, the *Unterscharführer* of the printing factory, continued to be nice to me. Once, at work, he caught me writing a letter (I was still writing to this boy who used to send me food), so he called me in to his office, which was enclosed by glass and soundproofed. He asked me what I was writing. Without hesitation I told him I was preparing a ballet, absurd as it might sound; I was writing down my part so I could learn it for a show that was being organised. Of course I knew nothing about ballet.

Marysia, her mother and the other girls observed us from around the corner, peering in through the glass. They were terrified, certain that he was about to kill me, or lock me up somewhere, or make me stand out in the cold for three days, where you were sure to die.

Meanwhile he was being so nice to me: he was worried about me, he said, because I appeared so simple and didn't know how to do anything properly. He paced up and down and told me he was concerned about how I would manage. Suddenly he stopped in front of me and looked directly into my eyes. 'What sort of job is it,' he asked me, 'to be a ballerina?' I looked at the floor. He continued his pacing. A few moments later he resumed. 'After the war, as soon as things quieten down, I'm planning to let you stay here at the printing factory, to learn the art of printing and bookbinding in the workroom. That way you will have an occupation at least.' He sat down behind his desk and beamed with satisfaction. He continued to talk to me for a while longer and then pulled out photos of his children from his wallet. Wasn't that amazing, for a Nazi officer?

On 7 October 1944 we heard a tremendous explosion that shook our barracks. We looked at each other with raised eyebrows but knew not to ask questions. We later found out that there had been a small group of members of the underground who had been planning a general uprising in the camp. Explosives had been smuggled to a young woman called Rosa Robota, and one of the four crematoria in Auschwitz had been blown up. Within a short while they caught Rosa and three other girls. Rosa was questioned and tortured for several days, but she did not reveal the names of others involved in the plot.

Several days later everyone was ordered to go outside and watch the execution of the four young women, but my boss said that I could stay indoors and didn't have to watch. He was much more humane and understanding than many of the other Nazi officers.

There were so many strange things happening there. Marysia worked in the households of the German families, there at Auschwitz, as well as at the printing factory. When it was my birthday in November, she noticed some pelargoniums growing in a garden belonging to the family of one of the officers. It was edged with a low white picket fence. Without thinking too much of the consequences she leaned over and broke off a pink flower. She gave it to me as a birthday gift. That was the most precious present I ever received. If they had caught her stealing the flower she would have been shot on the spot. On every birthday I've ever had, someone always remembered me, even in Auschwitz. I must have been born under a lucky star.

∽

She isn't what I'd call a close friend, but we meet fairly regularly on the weekends. Julie goes to a Catholic school, while I attend the local high school. I live in a house with a garden, she lives behind a shop. We have a toilet next to the bathroom; at her house they all use chamberpots in the night, and during the day they have to go to the outdoor toilet.

But I'm fascinated by her difference and want to spend time with her. Her face is pale and oval, and she has dreams of being a film star. Her mother lets her pluck her eyebrows and wear lipstick, which makes me very jealous. Julie has discovered a pile of love

New life, new lives: Hela with Anna, Janka with Louis, Paris, 1947.

Anna riding high in Paris, 1948.

Hela, Janka and Poldek with the two children, Louis and Anna, in front of Sacré-Coeur, 1948.

Kuba at Jelenia Góra in 1946 with his first wife, who was to die tragically.

Janka in a pensive mood.

Hela and Poldek looking to the future.

Hela and Poldek spending a romantic evening in a café.

Poldek playing to entertain the passengers on board the *Cyrenia*, 1949.

Poldek, Hela and Anna, with an attentive ship's officer, during the voyage to Australia, 1949.

At home at Glenhuntly Road, Caulfield, 1950.

Double act: Poldek plays as Anna sings, 1953.

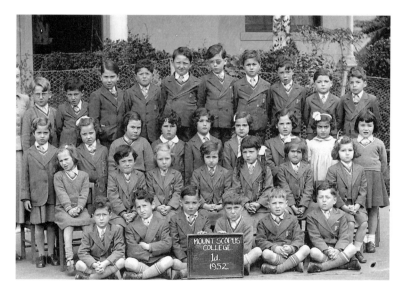

Anna playing with Shirley in the front garden of the Glenhuntly Road house, 1953.

Janka with Anna and Louis, Caulfield, 1953.

School photo, Mount Scopus Memorial College, 1952. Anna is in the second row, at far right; Louis, with eyepatch, is in the back row.

Hela and Józek tackling the garden with a passion.

'There are fields and forests and thickets of thorns stretching as far as the eye can see. At least that's how the garden seems to me.' Anna and Louis playing in their backyard, early 1950s.

Anna and her sister Frances, Surfers Paradise, 1958.

Putting the past behind them: Poldek and Hela at a ball in the 1950s.

Manci and Henry (Poldek's brother) on a trip back to Kraków in 1977.

A reunion of three generations. Paul (one of Anna's three sons), Niusia (Poldek's niece) and Hela in front of the Mariacki church, Kraków, 1988.

Józek, Janka, Hela and Poldek enjoying a *Shabbat* dinner together, Melbourne, 1988.

letters tied up with a blue ribbon, which her father sent to her mother many years ago. We take turns to read the words aloud in mocking, passionate voices. We do each other's hair in front of the mirror of her mother's dressing-table, and sometimes dress up in her mother's wedding gown. Julie finds some dusty netting that she uses as a veil, and a dried bunch of flowers. She teaches me the words the priest would recite at a Christian wedding ceremony, and makes me kneel and bow my head. I feel the thrill of experiencing the solemn and forbidden. We take turns at fantasising about our future, but it always remains misty and unspecific; a vague rosy glow settles on all our ideas.

But it's not only Julie who fascinates me; it's her whole family. Her mother is plump but still pretty, with soft skin and dark curls. She buys many women's magazines, and spends a lot of time reading them and drinking tea. She is nostalgic for the past and often reminisces about her childhood in the country, while I listen eagerly. She dresses in outrageous colours, hot pink or purple or orange. Her living-room is painted black, with large shawls covered in roses hanging on the walls. Sometimes Julie's mother plays the old piano in the corner. She gets a dreamy look in her eyes and holds the pedal down continuously as she runs lush arpeggios up and down the keyboard. While she plays she sings to herself softly, a tremulous soprano voice that tells of lost loves and weeping hearts.

Everything here evokes mystery, romance, excitement.

Julie's father, however, is a different story. Julie and her mother share a conspiracy: they believe all men are slightly uncouth, insensitive, unaware of the finer things in life. I listen to their gossip, while Julie's father sits outside the narrow back door on a rickety wooden chair, having a smoke. He looks out onto a dilapidated fence and the vine-covered outdoor toilet. As he sits there he drinks beer from a bottle and listens to the races being called on a Saturday afternoon. I try to listen too but can't understand a word. My father never listens to the races, or to the football. Sport is never a topic of discussion at our place.

Julie's father holds a dark fascination for me for another reason too, ever since Julie and I found a pile of old Playboy magazines on a low shelf behind the counter in the shop. It is the idea of them, rather than the contents, which I find so exciting and disturbing.

169

After I have been seeing Julie regularly for some months, my mother's questions become more insistent. She wants to know what we talk about, are there any crosses in their house, do they know that I am Jewish? I decide to keep secret my visit with Julie to her school for a weekend celebration. I do not tell my mother about the holy water just inside the door of the classroom, and the large paintings of Jesus pointing to a throbbing red heart. Better that she doesn't know. Nevertheless, I sense her uneasiness every time I go over there. Eventually my visits become less frequent, then stop altogether. I don't understand the reason for this at the time.

13

Hela: Days and nights rolled over me in slow succession, and I no longer knew which was which. We were continually surrounded by dampness, fever and putrid water. I ate almost nothing and I grew weaker and weaker, my belly clenching in pain. We hovered on the edge of extinction for three weeks, constantly aware of aching hunger and the threat of being gassed or shot. The chimneys continued to pour out foul smoke, day and night.

In the early hours of the morning, with the sky still black, we struggled out once again to roll-call. Still half asleep, I began to be aware of a charge of excitement running silently through our group. Suddenly I realised, as we stood swaying in our groups of five, that they were not calling out numbers, but names—our names! 'Horowitz, Niusia ... Horowitz, Regina ... Pfefferberg, Mila ... Rosner, Helena ... Rosner, Manci ...' Three hundred names were called out, the names on Schindler's list. We had been no better than a herd of cattle; suddenly I was an individual again, with a name and an identity. We were probably the only group in Auschwitz–Birkenau with names.

I was taken, ill and dazed, with the others in our group to be washed and shaved once again, and then towards the trains. I looked at the closed carriages with fear and a wave of nausea swept over me. I was terrified of having to climb up into the dark, crowded carriage and had no strength to hoist myself up, but somehow I was lifted and pushed in with the others. It was stifling and black in there, but the women with me still had hope and believed that maybe at last we were going to be rescued.

After a long wait the train began to move and we heard the steady rhythmic sound of the wheels turning. In later years, it amazed me how we can forget. Sometimes now I worry about trivial things; I get caught up in wanting something or being upset about a minor incident. At that moment in the train, all I thought about was being alive, and leaving that terrible place, Auschwitz. Dizzy and feverish, I crouched on the floor of the carriage surrounded by other bodies and let the movement lull me. Survival was my only concern. I had seen many people die, but I had not died. That was all I could focus on. I began to think about Poldek and wondered whether he was still alive. Was it possible that he had already been taken to Brünnlitz with the eight hundred men that Schindler had given refuge to?

I don't know how long we travelled. Sometimes the train moved quickly, sometimes slowly. We had nothing to eat or drink. There were hours of standing still and waiting. At other times we rolled on and on through the countryside, barely aware of whether it was day or night. I drifted in and out of a semi-conscious state. At one point I stirred and realised I had been asleep. I was shivering. I noticed it had become quiet in our carriage, we had come to a standstill. After an hour or more we heard voices. We could hear someone speaking in Czech. I tried to get up but I felt very weak. Somebody asked where we were, and a man's voice told us we were in Czechoslovakia. She asked, 'Why aren't we moving?' Because the Germans had taken the locomotive away for the army. We continued standing there. One of the women was sure that soon we would be let out of the carriage and shot. Some of them started praying aloud.

Suddenly we were thrust forward, and then there was another jolt. A different locomotive had been found and joined on. We started to move again. We couldn't quite explain to ourselves why we felt so happy to be moving without knowing our destination, but the feeling was obvious. When we moved, there was hope, and possibility.

Soon, however, the women started complaining, saying we would die in these wagons. It was freezing, and we were hungry and thirsty. Maybe the train would just continue travelling in circles till we all died. Time played tricks on us. It was hard to tell how long we had travelled. Was it one day, or two? Sometimes it was grey and sometimes black. The train stood still more often than it moved.

We stopped again. There was a voice, asking if anyone was there. All of us yelled out together. We were told that they wanted us to return to Auschwitz. No, not that! Better for them to kill us here than lead us back to that hell-hole. The train stood still again for a long time. Women tried to use the corners to relieve themselves, but the whole wagon was dirty, because it was so difficult to make your way through so many women crowded together. We moved again. Our bodies were numb from the cold. One woman kept repeating to herself, 'If Schindler doesn't save us, it means he himself has perished.' Others tried to quieten her down.

We became aware that we had been standing still for a while. We could hear the sound of footsteps running past the carriages. We all stood, pressed close to each other, waiting. I felt very sick. No one said so out loud, but we thought this must be the final destination. We could hear conversations, mostly in Czech. Someone was speaking in German, but calmly, without shouting. There were no dogs barking. Suddenly the doors were opened with a grating sound and the light made us blink.

We had arrived in the early morning. It was cold and the sky hung grey and passive above us as we jumped down from the carriages, helping one another. The soldiers stood by with guns, but no one was pushing or hitting us. Was this the calm before the end? We could see in the distance an old two-storey building, and chimneys. Oh, no! Not chimneys again! The smell had not left my nostrils.

But as we stood there, a shiny black car pulled up and two men got out. One was quite tall, in an SS uniform. The other, very large, in a different sort of outfit, appeared to be smiling. A whisper went around. Was this Oskar Schindler? We were counted, and it was established that none of us had died on the train journey. The soldiers backed away from us. One of them said, holding his nose, '*O, wie die Frauen stinken*.' But I noticed he didn't use the usual term, *die Schweine*, pigs; he had called us women!

We began to walk along a path with long grass growing on both sides. We passed little houses but there was no sign of anyone. Sometimes I thought I saw a curtain move in a window. Suddenly the road turned to the left. Before us were the gates to the camp, leading to the long grey two-storey building we had seen from a distance. My heart was thumping. We were marched through the gates and into the building through a wide doorway. Where were the men?

We were in a huge hall, divided down the middle by wire mesh. I noticed lots of huge machines, some of them as high as the first storey. And then I realised that on the other side of the wire were rows of heads. There were the men! Everyone started talking at once, till a loud voice commanded us to be quiet. He started calling names. Wives were reunited with husbands, mothers with sons. I tried to see over the heads of others. My head was swimming and I felt very ill. A cold sweat drenched me. Suddenly there was Poldek's face in front of me. As he embraced me I collapsed.

I remember very little of the next few days. I could not keep any food down, and I was taken with two or three other sick women to the little hospital that had been set up in the cellar. It was warm here. I was placed on some straw among the boilers, where I lay drifting in and out of consciousness for several days. I had a very high fever and was sure I was dying. Sometimes I could hear the voices of Regina and Niusia, Poldek's sister and her daughter, and of Manci, Herman's wife, talking above me; the sounds seemed to be fading in and out, coming to me from a great distance. I heard one of them say, 'There's nothing more we can do, only God can help her now.'

Gradually I began to be more aware of my surroundings. They told me I'd been talking feverishly for three days. I couldn't take in any solid food. One woman who was a nurse, Wala Begleiter, fed me watery semolina and soup, and slowly helped me to recover. Later I ate white bread with marmalade and hot tea; not real tea, but made from some kind of herbs. Also, I remember that Poldek somehow managed to get a few tiny apples that had fallen from a tree, or maybe they were given to him by some Czechs that he played for. Anyway, these apples were cooked for me over the stove and their sweet moist flesh nourished me. Slowly, as I was able to take in more soup and bread and fresh water, my strength returned.

Poldek had been overjoyed at finding me alive: they had been told that the women had all been gassed. He knew that Schindler had tried every method to get us out of Auschwitz, but the Germans didn't want to let us go. The eight hundred men on Schindler's list had left Płaszów a week before us. With Poldek were his youngest brother Wilek and my brother Kuba, as well as Herman with his son Olek, and Dolek Horowitz with Ryszard. They were loaded onto a freight train, thinking they were going to Brünnlitz, but after three long days locked in trains with thirteen hundred other prisoners, they finished up in Gross-Rosen, a terrible concentration camp in Germany. In the freezing evening air they had to undress and stand naked all night on the *Appellplatz*. For several days they suffered the torments of beatings, hunger and overcrowding. Poldek remembered a moment during one of Goeth's parties when Oskar Schindler had come up to him and put his arm around him, saying, 'Rosner, don't worry. Everything will be all right.' The words echoed hollowly in his mind as he stood there in silence in the bitter cold of the *Appellplatz*.

On the third day they were called together, the eight hundred of them who had left Płaszów with such hopes, and were once again loaded onto cattle trains. This time, however, they headed towards Czechoslovakia and eventually reached Brünnlitz. Poldek told me his story gradually, during the days when I was slowly recovering. Manci and Regina came to visit me. I asked about Herman and Dolek, but found out the awful truth.

They had been arrested together with their sons on a day

when Schindler had not been in Brünnlitz. An inspector had arrived with orders to find children for Dr Mengele's medical experiments. Olek and Ryszard had been running around the camp, unaware of danger. They were caught and sent to Auschwitz, together with their fathers and a few other children. Regina and Manci had in fact got a brief glimpse of them, ironically on the day the women were taken out of Auschwitz. Manci now held my hand and nodded silently, her eyes full of unwept tears. There was nothing I could say.

Conditions here, though not luxurious, were infinitely better than before. The sleeping quarters were on the first floor. This was a large hall above the factory, with no bunks or mattresses, just straw spread on the ground and some folded blankets on one side. We were separated from the men by a wooden partition. There were several gaps in the slats through which we could have a whispered conversation, but that was the only contact. I couldn't sleep with Poldek, but we were still so hungry, and so happy not to be living with the daily threat of being beaten or shot, that there were no thoughts of making love. I was content just to see him from time to time. In the women's sleeping quarters, when we lay down all together we were jammed in like sardines, with nowhere at all to walk through. It didn't matter; no one was screaming at us or hitting us.

The main thing that tormented me now was that I was infested with lice. They crawled all over my body and through my hair, alive, big with my blood, biting mercilessly. Someone had a special two-sided comb with fine teeth. This was like a treasure—the women would beg to borrow it, to try to remove some of the lice, especially in the pubic hair. That was the worst torment, making us scratch uncontrollably.

Once in the night a woman had a stomach ache and needed to get up, but she didn't manage to get out of the hall in time. Some people yelled at her, calling her a pig. There was no shortage of mean-mouthed ones. The next night the same thing happened to somebody else. It turned out to be typhus. Typhus was carried by the louse bite, and took several weeks to incubate. Schindler, fearing an out-break of huge proportions, organised a delousing unit with showers and a disinfection plant. He managed to get hold of some medicine and to isolate the sick women, so that an epidemic was avoided.

At last the bunks and mattresses arrived. They were narrow and we had to sleep two to a bed, head to feet. I slept with Manci. She seemed to have a lot more energy than I did, and was a good organiser. I felt helpless and did what-ever she told me. I was very down and depressed, and she always helped me and looked after me.

I was never very courageous or strong. Everyone was somehow stronger than I was; there was fear in me all the time. Even in the ghetto, at the beginning of the war, I was sure that we would soon all die. Again and again, I was sure death was at hand. I lived day to day, never saving or plan-ning for the future, unlike Janka, who saved things for special occasions. I wasn't like that; I always wore whatever was new because I was sure I would die soon. That feeling stayed with me for a long time. It was Manci who helped me morally, who tried to cheer me up and make me laugh. She helped me to make a frock out of the night-dress I still wore from Auschwitz. It was important to try to be normal. Maybe because she was older, or just because of her person-ality, she was the one I leaned on.

The building we lived in had once been a woollen mill but was set up now as a munitions factory. Still, we had to work, and the rest was Schindler's business. (Later we heard that his anti-tank shells always failed quality-control, through deliberate miscalibration of machines or the rigging of furnace gauges. Schindler was delighted that his products would not kill anyone, and continued to fool visiting inspec-tors.) I began making casings for ammunition. I had to work with very fine sheets of metal, which I had to feed in and out of a huge noisy machine. My hands were all cut and scratched from the sharp metal. But I was eating regularly and starting to feel human again. Although I was still very weak, and hungry a lot of the time, there were hot-water pipes running through our sleeping quarters, so we were warm, and we could dry our clothes on the pipes or even warm a piece of bread on them. I also thought a lot about Janka, and tried to push away the ideas that kept surfacing about what might have happened to her.

I saw Schindler often on the factory floor and he spoke to us kindly. When he walked in, it was as if the sun had come out from behind a cloud. All the girls looked up to him, and smiled shyly when he glanced their way. He was a very big man, broad-shouldered and muscly. We looked at his handsome face and knew we could trust him. He never carried a gun or wore a uniform; he was always in civilian clothes. He had a strong voice that carried and he often laughed loudly, but he was usually gentle. He would light up a cigarette, take one puff, then throw it onto the floor and keep walking. One of the men was always ready to pounce on the forbidden treasure. He spoke with an accented Polish, telling us he understood that we had been through hell and was sorry for the discomfort here, but that we were brave women. He called on our good sense and self-discipline to get ourselves organised. His soothing words calmed us.

Food was increasingly scarce, purchased somehow by Schindler on the black market. We were given a small piece of bread that had to last all day. Some of us ate it all at once; others rationed it to try to stave off the hunger. Kuba could not resist gulping it all down; he didn't have much self-control. He used to talk about his dream of eating a huge slice of bread sprinkled with sugar. That was all he wanted.

My mother is always anxious at mealtimes. She coaxes me to eat more and checks how much I am putting in my mouth. My father is impatient at how slowly I eat and doesn't let me leave the table until I have finished. I sullenly push my food around on my plate. My father starts to tell me to hurry up but my mother cuts him off. 'We shouldn't have arguments during meals; it interferes with the digestion.' She changes her tone and coaxes me into finishing.

Childhood patterns are strongly ingrained. Even as an adult, I find that whatever I am eating, I always leave a little on the plate;

178

I get to the last mouthful and just can't fit it in. I push my plate away, remembering that when I used to finish everything on my plate, my mother thought I was still hungry and gave me more.

Hela: Our peace was somewhat disturbed when Liepold, the Commandant who was Schindler's superior, sent a *kapo* to supervise us and, shortly after, some tall Dutch female guards. Schindler assured us they wouldn't harm us, but he could do nothing about their presence. The *kapo*'s name was Müller, and apparently he had a metal plate in his head from being injured on the Russian front. From the first day, he ran around very energetically, waving his truncheon and calling out, 'Avanti!' This quickly became his name, and we always knew when he was approaching because of the noise he made. It made us uneasy when he or the women guards came close; we tried to work more quickly when they were around.

Once, Avanti was in a bad mood and beat one of the men. Schindler came into the factory, quickly surmised what was going on and, with a flourish, offered Avanti some vodka. We could see him trying to refuse, pointing to his head and indicating that it would harm him. But Schindler wouldn't take no for an answer and made him drink a whole glassful. When Avanti had finished he went to his corner and slept for several hours. As the weather became colder, he stayed more and more often in his corner with the women guards, huddled around the stove.

Whenever Liepold and his men visited Brünnlitz, we could hear late into the night drunken voices and music, played once more by Poldek (Schindler had somehow rescued his accordion from Płaszów). Schindler's voice was louder than anyone else's, but he never appeared drunk on the factory floor. After these parties Poldek would sometimes return with some extra bread or a piece of sausage. Regina, who had lived with her brother till the war began, had difficulty understanding that his young wife was now his first priority. Manci tried to explain why it was me he brought the food to, but I had to share the piece of sausage with Regina and her daughter, Niusia, and sometimes with Dolek's family: his brother Mundek Horowitz, his wife Roma and daughter Halinka, as well as Roma's parents—the whole family had to be appeased. Halinka was one year older than Niusia and had her head shaved. I was a bit afraid of Roma's mother: she had a glass eye that was often crooked and Regina was the one who had to straighten it. (Dolek and Mundek had been wealthy before the war, and had soon become members of the *Judenrat*, with some influence and protection—this was how all the family had been put on Schindler's list.)

Poldek told us that at one of these parties, when the guests were completely drunk, he had overheard one of them telling Schindler, 'You know, Osi, it's time you organised to liquidate this camp.'

To this Schindler had replied: 'No, let the Jewish swine keep working for the Third Reich till their last breath.'

Another of the guests had then proposed a toast to this wonderful patriot, who was such a good example for the others. He said he deserved a special decoration for his commitment to the war effort. Poldek recounted that, after more congratulations and back-slapping, he saw tears in Schindler's eyes. They all thought he was overcome with emotion, but he was trying, poor thing, to stop himself from bursting out laughing.

Our men had found an untouched storeroom full of greasy wool, and, as winter was approaching, the women began to knit the wool into jumpers. Some of the men made splintery knitting-needles out of pieces of wood. In our spare time we knitted with this strange, thick, hard wool that hurt our fingers. The jumpers we made would scratch the skin, but still they were some protection from the cold on the factory floor. Manci also taught me how to use four needles to make socks with a shaped heel. She and Regina were very sad, grieving for their missing husbands and sons.

Regina walked around crying all day. She was small and fragile, wrung out by all that crying. She went to Schindler, begging him to rescue Dolek and Ryszard, but there was nothing he could do. He tried to reassure her that the war would be over soon and that they would survive. Even her daughter Niusia couldn't convince her. The Germans showed no sign of slowing up their process of liquidating human beings.

I discovered that Schindler had a wife, Emilie, but I rarely saw her. She was small and blonde, with a calm and gentle manner. She managed to bring medicines in to the factory. Often she invited the women guards to her place for a cup of tea, but we had no doubt that she did it not for pleasure but to give us a bit of peace.

I heard towards the end of the war that she rescued people from frozen wagons that arrived in Zwittau, the station near Brünnlitz. Some of our men were given warm jackets to wear, and were loaded with blowtorches, axes and blankets. They made their way to the train and released the prisoners from the locked carriages. We were told that Liepold had been sent by Schindler to friends for a drinking party, and to be entertained by some woman. Anyway, he was nowhere to be seen that night. Many of the occupants of the train were dead or dying, but about sixty people were brought in to camp, in a state that could not be described. They were mere skeletons draped with skin and could barely walk. You couldn't tell whether they were men or women. Emilie some-how had kept some cereal for emergencies, and cooked this for the survivors. Slowly she nursed them back to health, although many of them died.

We knew she was behind the scenes all the time, super-vising the kitchens, trying to find food on the black market to feed the *Schindlerjuden*, as we were now called. Portions of food became smaller. Amazingly, at the time of one of the Jewish holidays, Emilie procured *challah* for all of us, half a loaf per person, which meant she had to find more than five hundred loaves of *challah*! I have no idea where she could have got it from.

My mother never throws away a piece of bread. She tells us she likes the end, the 'heel' of the loaf. She particularly likes challah with honey or rye bread with caraway seeds. She cuts a chunky

slice and spreads a thick layer of butter on it. In the playground I
sometimes see children throw their lunches into the rubbish bin. I
don't always want to finish my sandwiches, but I have been told
to bring them home. It's a sin to throw bread away. I believe that
I am being watched, and if I ever dared to put my lunch in the
bin my mother would know. I dutifully carry my squashed half-
sandwich home, and wait for the sorrow to cloud my mother's eyes
when she unpacks my bag.

Hela: Schindler was struggling to keep feeding his prisoners. He was often away from the camp, trying to scour the
countryside for food. Every few days he would take several
men with him and set off in one of the trucks. He knew the
surroundings well, knew where the farms and restaurants
were. He knew what the Germans had missed. He took what
he could, but it was not enough. Once he got hold of some
cheese, a very smelly cheese that was considered a delicacy.
It came in little rounds and was very salty. We were so
hungry that we thought it was wonderful. At other times he
brought herrings, or barrels of mustard, or the head of a calf.
Our diet was quite bizarre. Some enterprising men collected
cigarette butts from Schindler's living quarters, and extracted
the shreds of tobacco, exchanging this tiny treasure for bread
from those who craved cigarettes and worked in the kitchens. Schindler still seemed to have great stores of alcohol,
with which he entertained visiting Germans in return for
sacks of potatoes. We could see how important his sociability
was.

While he was away Liepold would sometimes appear,
handing out harsh punishments to the workers. The women
guards would let us go to the toilets only at set times, something that never happened while Schindler was around. He
kept sending out messages that those on his list were absolutely essential for the war effort, to save the Third Reich.
Despite this, however, we were very hungry. Some of the
workers were able to leave the factory and steal a little grain
which they brought back secretly. They ground it between
two stones, mixed it with something like sawdust, and

added a little water. This they shaped into patties, which they baked in the fire. The patties were strange: they tasted like woodshavings, took a long time to chew and were difficult to swallow. A new disease appeared: scurvy. People's teeth began falling out, as if they had never been attached to the jaw. I lost several teeth.

One day I was sitting on a bench, very hungry and miserable. I had finished eating my tiny portion of bread. The last crumb had been swallowed hours ago and I wished I had more. When I had arrived in Brünnlitz, suffering from typhus, I was close to death. Now I was here, still alive, but I wondered how I could go on.

Suddenly I noticed, on the bench beside me, a piece of bread. It was small and dry. My whole mind was focused only on that piece of bread, and on the hollowness within me. I reached out with my trembling hand and, without another thought, I very quickly ate it.

Then my conscience began to prick me. This bread must have belonged to somebody. How could I have stolen it from one of my friends, someone who must be just as hungry as I? I knew that now she would be hungrier than ever.

Suddenly Vera appeared. She was a tall, thin girl who must have been pretty once. Now her cheeks were hollow and her skin was yellowish. She looked around. She started to search frantically, on the bench, under the bench, but she could not find the piece of bread she had left a few moments ago. I will never forget the pain on her face. I saw her big sad eyes as she searched around, tears rolling down her face. I dropped my gaze and said nothing.

∽

I am fifteen. I fall in love with a good-looking, black-haired boy with fiery dark eyes. He pays a lot of attention to me and I can't stop thinking about him. We go to dances and parties, and walk home holding hands in the warm night air. My mother, brimming with anticipation, is waiting up for me, sitting at the kitchen table.

She wants to know what we talked about and whether he kissed me. Her eyes shine as she dreams of her girlhood. But I sense as well her anxiety and fear, and am reluctant to talk about details. 'It was fine,' I say off-handedly. 'But I'm really tired, I need to sleep.' And I go to bed, clutching my feelings to myself.

A few days later my mother tells me she's feeling sick. She doesn't have a temperature but she stays in bed all day. Her eyes look red.

I am soon to go to a youth camp in the country. My boyfriend will be there. My mother is still unwell. She is afraid for me and doesn't want me to go away. The doctor has given her various medications but doesn't have a real diagnosis. She's beginning to see double and she has a bitter taste in her mouth all the time. Sometimes her eye twitches. I write about her in my diary almost every day. She is moping around, making an occasional effort to get up, then going back to bed. Often she stares into space and her lips move silently, but when I ask her what's wrong she tells me she doesn't know. She just feels afraid, all the time, and the only safe place is bed. She thinks a lot about death.

She reads the family medical encyclopaedia, searching for symptoms, and says she might have to go to hospital. I wish she were better. I feel selfish and guilty as I pack to leave.

It is visitors' day at the youth camp. I wake with an ominous feeling in my stomach. My parents arrive. My mother cannot walk straight and is supported by my father. Half of her face is numb and rigid. She tries to smile but tears fill her eyes. I feel agonies of conflicting emotion. When my boyfriend tries to take my hand, I hiss at him, 'Not now.' He walks away, bewildered.

Camp is over. My boyfriend has broken up with me. He prefers a dark-haired girl with a cute nose. I feel devastated and abandoned. My mother is very sick. She is depressed and cries all day. A doctor visits daily but all he can suggest is vitamin injections.

One morning I wake to find her on the sunroom floor, unconscious. I scream for my father and we carry her inside. She begins to regain consciousness, but is very shaky. The doctor comes and checks her blood pressure, heart, temperature. He declares that there is nothing wrong with her, so my father goes to work. Later that day she begins to vomit. I hold her forehead. She starts saying

184

she's going to die and wants my father. He comes back from work four times that afternoon.

My mother is afraid to go to sleep because she'll faint and die. Her face is still numb. I sit by her bed all day, and sleep beside her till my father comes home late that night. She settles down and sleeps.

The next day she feels better. My father says it must have been the schnitzel and cabbage she ate the night before. Slowly over the next few days she recovers. She can walk to the bathroom now unaided. I brush her hair and massage her feet. For several weeks she is very weak and tires easily. The crisis is over. I turn sixteen.

14

Janka: I heard that the group of three hundred women on Schindler's list had left Auschwitz and were on their way to being saved by Schindler. That was Schindler's miracle, that he took three hundred women out of Auschwitz—it was the first time in the history of the war that people came out of that death camp alive. I'd had only a brief glimpse of Hela from a distance while she was there. I had also seen my husband once, but again briefly and behind barbed wire.

We began to hear rumours that the Russians were coming. They were already in Kraków and were heading towards Auschwitz. So the Germans began to liquidate Auschwitz. We saw planes flying low above us, and heard bombs and Katyusha rockets falling on the barracks and exploding. I felt more curious than afraid. Was this the way we were going to die? The Germans started to panic. My boss was so afraid that he hid under the bed whenever he heard the sound of planes screaming overhead. Perhaps that's why he liked me: because I seemed so unafraid.

One night there was an order given for a total blackout of the camp. The towers and barbed-wire fences stood out eerily in the faint moonlight—we were used to having searchlights swooping over us all night. One of my friends who had gone to the latrine didn't hear the order, and came stumbling back to the barracks wondering why it was so dark. She cursed and fumbled for the light-switch. The moment the hut was flooded with light, a shot rang out. Our eyes squinting from the sudden light and noise, we could see her body slumping to the floor near the open doorway. With their revolvers ready, the frightened Germans were prepared to shoot down any of us who caused the slightest trouble.

Hela: The New Year of 1945 was approaching. How could we mark this time with the possibility of hope? Some of the women collected metal strips and offcuts from the machines and created a bouquet of flowers for Schindler. It seemed that even the most religious Jews were now praying not to God but to Schindler. When he was presented with the bouquet he was visibly moved, and said to us, 'As long as I remain alive, you will survive. The war is ending; let's try to hang on. I know things are difficult, for you as for me. Trust me till the end. We never know what battles we will still have to fight to survive.' People were crying, thanking him. His voice broke as he took the bouquet and then gave us the rest of the day off.

We went upstairs to the sleeping quarters and sat in silence. It was hard to know what to do with a day of freedom. It was hard to imagine freedom, just as once it had been hard to imagine war. Was it possible? That the gates would just open and we would walk through them, without anyone screaming at us or beating us? That we would walk freely, not in rows of fives? ... No, it was impossible to imagine.

One day someone said that Amon Goeth had been seen entering Schindler's home. We panicked. What could he be doing here? Had he come to take us back? Were they planning to liquidate us? All night we talked in whispers. I felt my stomach clench with fear as the threat of death once again stole closer.

In the morning Mietek Penner reassured us that we didn't have to worry. He had found out that, soon after we left Płaszów, Goeth had been denounced for hiding stolen goods and had been charged. He had indeed made a secret visit to Schindler but had disappeared before morning.

Janka: It was 18 January 1945. All the men and women who were left in Auschwitz were told to assemble outside. It was late afternoon and snowing heavily. Orders were given that we would march out of the gates in rows, by blocks. There was some bread that had been brought out, but with the pushing and shoving you had to be strong and quick to get any. The Russians, like the Gypsies, had formed their own gangs. They terrorised some two hundred of us, including the supervising SS woman, and stole all the bread. So Marysia and I missed out and we started to march on empty stomachs.

The snow kept coming down and there was a strange stillness in the air, despite the shouts of the SS. I looked at the unfamiliar landscape, aware of the hunger gnawing at me. But as we began our march we saw a woman we knew, Mrs Stenser, who was carrying three loaves of bread, which she had been shrewd and quick enough to grab. She was having some difficulty carrying them, so I told Marysia that I would ask Mrs Stenser whether we could help her carry her bread in return for half a loaf for the two of us to share. She agreed, so we carried one loaf of bread for her, and promised to return half of it later.

After a couple of hours marching, when we stopped for a rest, we couldn't find Mrs Stenser. We sat down on the snow, and we were so hungry that we tore off a whole piece each. Then Marysia and I looked at each other. Without a word needing to be said, we both ate the remainder of the loaf. Afterwards we always had a guilty conscience that we had betrayed her trust and eaten the bread we were supposed to return. I suppose it's some comfort to know that she survived.

As we continued our march, past fields and villages, someone brushed against me and placed a spoon in my hand. I had my head down to keep the snow out of my eyes and didn't have time to see who it was, but I knew that a spoon in those days was like gold; it meant you could eat. Bread could be eaten with the hands, but not soup. I still have that spoon today.

We marched in a snowstorm for three days and three nights with only brief stops, and with shelter for only one night, in a shed in Pless. The SS kept trying to make us walk faster, with threats and blows. Soon we were so numb that our bodies just kept going, no longer aware of the pain, fatigue and hunger. If anyone stopped or fell, they were shot. Whether in darkness or in the grey light of dawn, we just kept going like robots.

At last we reached a railway station and were herded into open cattle wagons. We didn't know where we were being taken, but sank to the floor, a pile of bodies barely alive. The snow kept falling and an icy wind was blowing all around us. Those who could huddled together for warmth; others just died where they lay. We didn't know where we were, but after a short journey we arrived at Ravensbrück.

Ravensbrück was a concentration camp that was hell on earth. Aching and shivering, barely able to move, we were herded off the train and into the camp. We were placed in the Polish barracks, with some non-Jewish Polish women who had been captured quite recently in Warsaw. They were still permitted to receive parcels from home and were in excellent shape. The Polish commander of the barrack relegated us to a small back section, and while the Polish 'ladies' were accommodated one per pallet of straw, we were squeezed three to a pallet. These sadistic Poles treated us like vermin.

At last they gave us something to eat. They distributed a watery soup from the top of the pot, saving the thicker part for themselves. Another time we were fed a very thin soup, with no salt, and we discovered that the people in the kitchen were stealing the salt. Often they didn't even give us time to eat, chasing us back to our corners like dogs.

The ground was oozing with mud and we huddled together for comfort. We were filthy and constantly hungry. Unable to sleep, we began to talk in the dark, fantasising about how to cook our favourite dishes. Each one of us added details and descriptions, momentarily caught up in our frenzied recollections. We talked about food endlessly. Marysia and I also began to recall all the books we had read, and all the films we had ever seen. We would tell each other the stories of the plots, in order to hang on to a shred of normality and take our minds off our terrible suffering.

Although Auntie uses expensive perfumes and cosmetics, it is the smell of garlic that I associate with her. I am in her kitchen next door, watching her prepare a delicacy from the early war years. No one else is around. Auntie takes slices of rye bread and places them under the griller till they are lightly brown on one side. She then takes them out, rubs a cut clove of garlic all over the soft moist side, then places them back under the griller. When the slices are ready and the warm pungent smell fills the kitchen, we both devour the crisp, fragrant bread greedily. Another of her 'delicacies' from those years is a dish made with thick slices of Polish sausage covered with thinly sliced onion rings and moistened with vinegar. It makes my mouth water. We giggle together as we eat this peasant food. Even though Auntie can afford all kinds of luxurious things, she tells me this dish is one of her favourites.

Janka: In this camp we were very badly beaten by both the German guards and the SS women. There was no particular reason for their brutality. It was frequent and relentless. Once a woman guard bashed me so severely that my head was gashed open and my cheekbone broken. As I lay on the ground moaning, covered in blood, all the girls stood around me to hide me, because if the Germans saw someone covered in blood they would shoot them. The girls cleaned me and took care of me as best they could, and in that way I survived the ordeal. The head wound healed eventually, but even to this day my left cheek has remained swollen.

We were constantly covered in lice and filth. They even barred us from access to the wash-house. There was no water, no toilets, nowhere to wash. I suffered as much from the filth as from hunger. We couldn't even sleep because of the bitter cold and the stabbing hunger. The straw on the bunks was infested with bedbugs, which tormented us all night long. We would scratch in our sleep, and the bedbugs would fall onto our faces from the bunk above. My whole body was covered in sores.

Although I was usually quiet and fairly stoical, I was now past caring about the future. One day, seized with incredible anger at the way we were being treated, I spoke to the barrack leader. 'What have we done to you that you treat us like scum? If you had been kept a prisoner in a concentration camp for the last two years, you would look just like us.'

The Polish woman turned slowly to me, gave me a look of disgust, and said, 'You are here simply because you are cowardly Jews, while we are here as heroines of the uprising, so don't you dare compare yourselves to us.'

I stood my ground, feeling a white-hot fury rising in my chest. I began to give her a whole speech about the Jewish uprising which had taken place in Warsaw less than two years earlier. About fifteen hundred fighters, poorly armed, had taken on several thousand Nazi soldiers, fully supported by their whole range of weapons. The uprising had held out for twenty-eight days, despite the inevitability of eventual defeat.

While I talked about the courage of this small band of fighters who succeeded where whole nations had been unable to resist, the others stood around me and listened in amazement. I even attacked the Poles without fear.

'And you call yourselves socialists?' I continued. 'You are fascists under your skin; you only wear the noble mantle of the socialists.'

This speech didn't change our situation, but it certainly changed the tone in the barrack. Perhaps their cruelty was a little less intense.

Hela: Work in the Brünnlitz factory continued as normal. There were frequent inspections by officials in uniform, checking the output of the factory. Schindler always seemed to give them satisfactory responses. Apparently there were trucks arriving at night in secret, and unloading ammunition bought elsewhere, to make it look as if it was produced in the factory. Some people, fearing that Liepold would try to kill us at the first opportunity, wanted the ammunition to be stored on the factory floor, among the packages, so that it would be at hand if needed. Others feared that if it was discovered by Avanti or Liepold, we would all lose our lives on the spot. We had to wait, hoping that Schindler would think of something.

Food became more and more scarce. Sometimes there were some beetroots that were made into soup, or a bit of grain that was turned into a sort of porridge. We ate only one meal a day. At times we could hear thuds that told us there was fighting going on somewhere not too far away. The men thought the Russians were closer to us than the Americans. Day after day we could see columns of German trucks and tanks driving past the factory gates, filled with soldiers. We could smell spring in the air, and a feeling of anticipation lightened our otherwise miserable existence.

Janka: From Ravensbrück we were transferred to Jugendlager, a sub-camp, and then taken to Malchow, another concentration camp. In Malchow I saw two Russian girls attacking a huge wolf-dog. They took a juicy bone from its snout and went away to gnaw it. The Russians also taught us, during our 'death march', how to gather and cook nettles.

We continued to suffer from hunger. Our bodies were emaciated and our bellies swollen. Sidonia, a young woman who had been a journalist in Lwów, would recite poetry to us. She was terribly frail and her soft voice quavered from weakness, but there was a glimmer in her eyes and two spots of colour would appear on her cheeks as she spoke. Another way she made us forget the present was by retelling the stories from her favourite books. We decided to reward her with crumbs of bread. These fell copiously when our mouldy brick of bread, mixed with sawdust, was sliced into eight portions.

While in Malchow, we were once led through the forest on our way to a delousing station. As we stumbled along I wondered: can hungry, exhausted people yearn for nature? We hadn't seen trees for three years. Sturdy, dark-trunked pines bordered our path on both sides, and the fragrance of pine needles filled the cold air. Marysia's mother, marching in the outside row, broke off a small branch. She got a thrashing, but she brought the branch piously back to camp. So much for romanticism.

From Malchow we started on a journey, once again in open cattle wagons, to Leipzig. We pulled into Magdeburg, an important railway station. The station was being bombed by the Allies and there was terrible shelling going on all around us. The train stopped. It was freezing. A small group of us tried to cling together for some warmth and we found an old blanket that we could share. We were stopped there for quite some time; we were left like sitting ducks in the open carriages while all the Germans, terrified, hid under the train. We didn't care if we perished there with the abominable Germans. Despite our suffering, we were in an elated mood, seeing the Germans so fearful. What did it matter whether we died now or later? We were even cracking jokes and singing songs while the bombs rained down. They could crush our bodies, but not our spirits. When the shelling eased I stood up, as I wanted to get a glimpse of the city. It looked terrible, with all the houses bombed and devastation everywhere.

I was so thirsty by now that, in desperation, I scooped some water in my hands from the engine of the locomotive. It was so bitter and metallic that I can remember the taste to this day. I used to dream all the time about sweet orange juice, because of the terrible thirst. We had no food either, but it was the thirst that drove me mad.

Auntie squeezes several oranges, strains the juice (because I hate 'bits' in it) and stirs in one teaspoonful of sugar. It is only served to the children. Oranges are still seen as luxuries, exotic fruits that were only dreamed about in Poland. My cousin Louis and I are dressed up to go visiting so we have to be careful not to spill a drop. The sugar never really dissolves, despite all the stirring I do with the spoon. The best part is at the end, scooping up the crunchy remains. You are drinking liquid sunshine, she tells us. If only you knew . . .

Janka: Three days later the train was approaching Leipzig. The Swiss Red Cross arrived to collect the sick and wounded. We were lined up for inspection. Despite everything I had been through I still looked reasonably healthy, so they didn't take me.

They took both Polish and Jewish women who were sick. Even one week before the end of the war you could feel the anti-Semitism, because the Polish girls were put into a separate group from the Jewish ones. If a Jewish girl stood next to a Pole, she was beaten and sent back to her own group. They took only twenty or thirty of us. The numbers in the group dwindled.

Brutality was a constant threat. Even in the last days, when we had to walk through the forest and through small German towns, we had to walk in fives. Unluckily I was once the sixth in the row, so I was hit so much with the butt of the German soldier's rifle that I couldn't move my left arm for two or three weeks. Even today I cannot straighten that arm because of the damage done. They hit us, also, because they were afraid. I could see it in their eyes, in April 1945.

We arrived in Leipzig, where we were sent either to a munitions factory or to work in the latrines. I was put to work in the factory, but it lasted only a short time because the Russian front was drawing closer. The second death march began from Leipzig on 9 April. They drove us from one place to another, not knowing what to do with us. The convoy of thousands had been split several times. I had lost track of Marysia and her mother by this stage, because I thought that if I stayed with them I would go crazy. There was so little to eat, and neither of them wanted to deprive the other, so they were constantly arguing over who would eat the last scrap. (They went eventually to Paris, pretending that they were French.)

Here we were, a thousand women, hungry, dressed in rags, in late April with the weather still very cold. We trudged through the forests and slept in fields, with the civilian Germans looking at us as if we were witches. They were afraid to come near us.

There were two Ukrainian women in our group who were so hungry that they dug up a dead dog that had been buried and were preparing to eat it. The Germans caught them at it and killed them on the spot.

We decided, two girls and I, to run away from the group and hide in the forest. We could see that if we stayed with the group we would surely starve to death. We were so hungry that when we found some potatoes left in the ground after harvest, we crammed them into our mouths, dirt and all. I was amazed to discover that raw potatoes could taste like almonds.

The seder *plate, filled with all the traditional offerings, glows like a jewel against the white tablecloth. The usual items are there, the shank bone, the roasted egg promising life, bitter horse-radish and sprigs of celery leaf and parsley for hope. But tonight there is one more item. This potato peel, it has been suggested, should be placed on the* seder *plate to represent our memory of the six million Jews murdered in the Holocaust. In those years of horror a piece of potato peel could mean the difference between life and starvation. It was worth more than gold. To steal a potato peel could mean instant death.*

Janka: In the villages the German population was afraid and avoided us. Sometimes we went begging from door to door. Often a plump, round-cheeked German woman would slam the door in our faces, fear and disgust written all over her. But occasionally one of them gave us a boiled egg or a piece of bread. Maybe she liked my face, or felt sorry for us and wanted to help.

We had heard that the Russians were advancing through Germany, not far behind us, and we were afraid because of the rumours of their wildness and drunkenness. We'd been told they raped and pillaged wherever they went. They travelled at night, hungry and sex-starved.

We were scared to sleep outdoors. One night we knocked at the door of a little house just as it was getting dark. We were tired and cold, and hunger continually tore at our insides. A German woman opened the door cautiously and eyed us up and down. We got her to understand that we only wanted a place to sleep for the night, so she agreed to give the three of us shelter in her house. She opened the wooden door a little wider and we entered a low-ceilinged room, warm and smoky from a bright fire burning in the grate. The woman's fair-haired daughter, who was sitting near the fire in a rocking-chair breastfeeding a baby, nodded to us as we passed through the living-room, and we were shown into a little room at the back of the house. It smelt musty and there were rat droppings in the corner. There was only one single bed, and a couple of pieces of old furniture, but we were grateful for the shelter.

That night, as we hid in the German woman's little room, we woke to hear loud footsteps approaching. We could hear harsh Russian voices echoing in the dark, discussing their sexual exploits in vulgar language. We crept towards the door and barricaded it as best we could, with a rickety table and an old wardrobe. The voices were coming closer. The front door banged and there was a commotion in the next room. We didn't know how many of them there were, but they were making a lot of noise, obviously drunk. We held our breaths as we realised they were right next to our door. They called out to us to let them in and pounded heavily on the door. We were terrified. After all these years of suffering and torment, to be raped by our 'liberators'! At first we remained silent, but as they became more insistent and the door threatened to give way, I called out to them that we were sick, that we all had typhus. The shouting stopped; we heard some muttering and heavy breathing, then eventually it became quiet. They left us alone.

Towards dawn, when we came out of our hiding-place, we found the old German woman crouched in a corner of the room, her apron over her head. The fire was out. She was sobbing quietly and didn't stir. We learnt that the Russians had broken into the house, grabbed the baby as it slept beside the mother and hurled it against a wall. Then they had raped the daughter. We couldn't stop trembling.

The two girls and I continued on, not really knowing where we were going. Daily survival was uppermost in our thoughts: where to sleep, how to avoid the marauding Russians, how to find food to eat. I moved like an automaton, knowing that we had to keep going but believing less and less that this deprivation and suffering would ever come to an end. It was late April now and we were walking through forests. We were starved, and dressed in the same clothes we had worn for months. As I continued to put one foot in front of the other, my attention was caught by something on the ground. I stopped and looked more closely. There before me was a clump of white growing at the base of a tree. It was lit with a strange light from a stray sunbeam that filtered through the branches overhead, and seemed to glow against the dank, shadowed background of the forest trees. A sweet, delicate scent drifted up to me as I recognised the flowers: lily-of-the-valley. I was overcome by nostalgia. These had been my favourites in childhood. I picked the fragile whitish-green flowers and inhaled their perfume.Then I found a rusty nail and pinned them onto my filthy coat. The fragrance kept wafting up to me, making me forget my hunger for a while.

As we kept on walking, we suddenly became aware of the sound of crackling twigs. Seeing some German soldiers coming towards us, we froze. One of them, a major, noticed me with my flowers. He came up to me and asked me what I was doing there in the forest. Wasn't I afraid of the Russians? The German soldiers were themselves very frightened. When he asked me if I was *Volksdeutsch*, I said yes. He smiled at me, gently touched the flowers on my lapel, and gave me half of his portion of food, which I could then share with my friends.

We saw other German soldiers discarding their uniforms and hiding them, so we knew that the end must be near. We came upon a French camp for prisoners-of-war, and when we approached cautiously, they welcomed us with kisses despite our appearance. They killed some chickens for us, cooked them and fed us, so at last we had something decent to eat. That's when we found out the war was over.

I seldom read books with a historical theme, and I never read any war books. I sense that I won't like them, that I'll find them boring. When Louis and I go to the local public library, he heads for the non-fiction section; I go to the fiction shelves. I much prefer to escape into the fantasy world of Enid Blyton, or study the 'how to' books that will inspire me to make useless shell ornaments or pictures from seeds. War is something that I know has happened, and it was a terrible thing, but I don't know any details. Members of my family speak of war to each other but never directly to me. Since they don't tell me anything, I assume I am not supposed to know. They often divide events that have happened into two categories: before the war and after the war. Even the words in Polish for war breaking out are terrifying; the sound is explosive, like bombs going off—jak wojna wybuchła. The words literally mean 'when war exploded'.

Hela: I stayed in Brünnlitz until the end of the war. A letter was organised, signed by all the *Schindlerjuden*, testifying that Oskar Schindler was not a murderer, and that he had done all in his power to save Jews. It was hoped that this letter would save him after the war. It was written in three languages, Yiddish, English and Russian. Late one evening in the last days of the war, some of our men loaded a truck with the Schindlers' luggage. Oskar smoked a cigarette nervously as he paced up and down the factory floor. When it was time for them to leave, he made a short, emotional speech to us about not taking revenge. Then, dressed in striped prisoner's clothes, Emilie and Oskar got into the back seat of his Mercedes and were driven off towards the American front. Seven of our men followed them in the truck for protection.

Before leaving, he had arranged for each of us to be given a brown-paper package. When we opened it we found some navy woollen material from the storeroom for suits or dresses, pyjamas, and a few essentials. Manci later sewed a dress for me from some of the material we were given. (Poldek still has the navy-blue suit made from this material.)

As I watched the car receding I didn't know what to think. The guards had disappeared. We were still afraid of German trucks passing by on the road outside the gates, thinking they could kill us like flies if they came into the camp. We heard next day that Schindler and his wife had reached safety. We stayed indoors all that day, afraid to move. The Czechs from the nearby villages were probably afraid to approach us too, as they had been told we were murderers, criminals and prostitutes. I didn't sleep that night.

The next morning the sun rose in a clear blue sky. It was 9 May 1945. Through the gates we saw a cloud of dust and a Russian officer approached on a white horse. He galloped through the gates with a great clatter, followed by other men on horseback and in trucks. We were told that the Germans had surrendered. The war was over. All those years I had tried with great difficulty to imagine what freedom was like. I had waited and yearned for so long. Now that it had arrived all I could feel was numbness.

The Russians set up a long table and built a fire under a big pot, from which came a delicious smell. We lined up with our bowls, and soon a very young soldier was dishing out hot soup for us. Our portions were not big; we were told that we would be fed a little, but more often, as it was dangerous in our condition to eat a lot at once. We were also told to eat slowly. I was surprised that I didn't feel all that hungry. I had imagined that when food was available I would eat and eat until I was bursting. It turned out to be different. I had imagined that when freedom came I would be happy and rejoicing. That too was different.

Regina and Manci were with me, safe, but we didn't know what had happened to their husbands, Dolek Horowitz and Herman Rosner, or their children, Ryszard and Olek. I also trembled when I thought of Janka. Where could she be now? Was she still alive?

We decided to try to make our way back to Poland, back to our home town of Kraków. I couldn't think where else to go, but I was frightened of what we would find. Could we ever live a normal life again? We walked out through the gates clutching our packages, no longer yelled at by guards, no longer in rows of five. We headed for the railway station, where we'd been told there would be a train leaving, but no one could say when. I felt a pang of anxiety when I saw the lines of cattle wagons waiting there. Somehow I had imagined that we would leave in a normal train. But we boarded quickly, and eventually began to move. When the train stopped we had to get out and walk.

After some hours of walking Manci stole a horse and cart and we travelled for a while, together with Poldek, Regina and Niusia, along quiet country roads. Then we reached a railway line and saw some carriages standing there. We got on, and eventually the train moved. Later, when it stopped, we got off again. This happened several times. Many bridges and tunnels had been blown up by the Germans and there was no way through except to walk around, so we had to walk to another train line. Trains often stood for hours without moving. Sometimes at train stations there were Red Cross people, giving out hot tea and bread.

At one point, as we were travelling through the country-side, we heard rumours that the train had been boarded by Russians who had begun to steal from the people in the carriages behind us. Poldek had his accordion with him and we clung to our possessions, meagre as they were. We were very afraid. The Russians got closer—we could hear their shouts in the next carriage. Then with a sudden screeching of brakes the train came to a halt. Uniformed officials made their way through the carriages, and we saw the band of Russians leap down from the train and run away.

Janka: We stayed in the French camp only one night as we wanted to keep moving. I hoped somehow to make my way back to Poland. After trudging through the forests, we found ourselves back in Leipzig. I was still dressed in my clothes from Auschwitz, which were filthy and full of lice. Now that we were free, we felt that the worst horror was behind us, although it was hard to feel elated. I was slowly emerging from my nightmare, but I felt lonely and numb. From the time I had been taken to Auschwitz until a few weeks after the war ended, I hadn't had my period. After I started to eat normally my normal body functions resumed, but I was still very skinny.

In Leipzig I met a Russian officer, a Jew, who recognised that I was Jewish. Despite my fears, he had a reassuring face. He spoke to me for a couple of moments, then came close and secretly put something in my hand. It was three hundred German marks. He whispered, '*Bleib gesund*' (stay healthy). Although he was an officer, he was afraid to be seen giving me money. I later used it to buy myself a dress.

We had mixed feelings, because while we were in Leipzig both the Russians and the Americans were arriving. On a street corner the Russians were giving out a bit of soup and bread that we accepted gratefully. But near us stood a group of hungry German children. For me, despite all that I had been through, they were still children, so I couldn't help giving them some of my bread. My friend said to me, 'What are you doing? Are you crazy? *Rache*! Revenge! They are German!' But all I could see was a hungry child.

We kept travelling towards Poland, staying in abandoned German houses along the way, left empty because the Germans were fearful of the advancing Russians. Sometimes we stayed in cellars that were crammed full of silver dishes and cutlery, cameras, crystal vases and candelabras—but the only thing I ever took from the stored loot was a small bag of beans, because I was so hungry. I kept the beans with me till Kraków; no other material things were important to me.

∽

Soon after getting married I travel with my husband to Europe, pushed by an invisible wind of which I am barely aware. In our tiny Fiat 500, young and inexperienced, we travel through many countries, cramming our minds with impressions, thirsty for new sights and sensations, carefree in the way only the very young are.

Part of our itinerary is to visit Kraków, where my father's sister Regina still lives. It is cold and grey. She welcomes us warmly, but is frightened by 'foreigners' and is afraid of the power of the communist authorities.

'Why do you want to go there?' she asks puzzled. 'You should be happy, you are young. Go to the Wawel Castle, which is so old and beautiful; go to Mariacki church, to the Wieliczka salt mines.' Her lined forehead (just like my father's) wrinkles and her hands restlessly clutch each other. We will go to all those places too, but our minds are made up.

That afternoon we drive the short distance to Oświęcim and park the car. I feel as if the world is flowing around me and I am standing still. My body feels tightly clenched and the wind is whistling loudly in my ears. Although we're walking side by side, my husband seems to be a long way away, as if through the wrong end of a telescope. What is in front of my eyes moves, slides away, won't stay still. There is the railway track, and the famous archway which says 'Arbeit Macht Frei'. I feel I am on a movie set. The place is vaguely familiar. Low brick buildings, oppressive in their sameness, flow past. I look down and try to focus on where my feet are stepping. On this very grass . . . here, here . . . but the ground keeps shifting.

The sky is a dirty white and the air is cold. I feel shivery. I breathe in deeply and we walk on. We go through the cells, the 'hospital', the crematoria. There are echoes of screams floating just out of reach, on and on, or is it the mournful cry of the crows flying overhead? I feel helpless, yet a part of me stays clear-headed, determined to make sense of all this. I need to see, to imagine. The place is almost empty today, with only a few stray visitors wandering around. Once there were thousands of people here. I read all the signs and explanations carefully.

Somewhere in the back of my mind I have stored the knowledge that Auntie has a number tattooed on her forearm, but my mother hasn't. I don't know why. For a brief moment I try to visualise the sisters, my mother and my aunt, as young people here in this place. But all I feel is numbness. I can't grasp realities. This is a place of terror, a place of deadness, like watching a horror film but knowing that it doesn't really touch you, that you're safe. My close family are alive, on the other side of the world. My mind refuses to make the links. I am only twenty years old.

We move into another building. Once inside, I feel a wave of panic, but it subsides as I thrust my hands deeper into my pockets and concentrate on walking, placing one foot in front of the other. We are in a long corridor-like room that seems to go on for ever and ever. On the wall are rows of photographs, small black-and-white faces staring out solemnly, each numbered methodically. My eyes roam ahead of me and behind, overwhelmed by the sheer number of them. Rows and rows, mutely they wait, not accusing, not condemning, but patiently waiting for my eyes to focus on them, to acknowledge them, to know that once they existed, and breathed, and even laughed. Women, men, children, how can I grasp them all? I am searching, frantically moving from one to the other. It's too fast; I can't take them all in. What am I searching for? I keep scanning the photos as we walk steadily on, with only the sound of our steps breaking the oppressive silence. But as we walk, I strain to hear other sounds; it seems as if there are whispering, urgent voices, suppressed but compelling. Again I feel as if a wind is blowing around my ears, a loud hissing closes in on me. I shut my eyes for a moment, holding myself still and willing my breath to go in and out slowly. The noise subsides and we continue walking. My husband looks at me concerned but doesn't speak.

I continue looking at the faces, but no longer search to recognise familiar features. On and on, dark hair and light, young and old, intense gazes meet mine. But they are strangers, and they are gone.

15

Janka: I wanted to return to Kraków, desperate to find out whether Hela and Kuba, and my husband Salek, were alive. But it was not so easy to get out of Germany. The transport system was in chaos, and the two girls and I often walked for many miles, only occasionally getting lifts in the backs of horse-drawn wagons. When we came to Wrocław we met some Polish officers who were stationed there. They didn't realise that I was Jewish because I spoke Polish fluently. They were very friendly to me, and one of them got into a deep conversation about Polish literature and culture. He offered to lend me some books. He asked us why we wanted to go to Kraków, and then told me that the Jews were already returning there and starting to 'raise their heads'. He said this with a sneer, and I understood that not much had changed in Poland. Despite the anti-Semitic sentiments, this was very good news for me, because it meant there were other Jews who had survived and it was safe for me to return.

After days of walking and riding we came to a railway line. There were many people struggling to get onto the train that was standing there. A Polish railway worker approached us, and looked us up and down. He scratched his head under his cap and asked us what we wanted. I was young and still quite pretty, despite my thinness, so he agreed to find a place on the train for me and my girlfriends. But he told me that he would come afterwards to find me, and smirked at me in an unpleasant way, then ambled off. My friends had stood by during this conversation and now they looked at me without needing to say anything. They understood that I was worried, so when we found a corner in one of the carriages, the girls covered me with an old sack and sat on me to conceal me. Eventually the railway man came back, calling out, searching angrily from one carriage to another, but he couldn't find me. In this way we came at last to Łódź, north of Kraków.

In Łódź we slept on the floor in the Red Cross building. It was very dirty and we were still very hungry. I didn't have it in me to take something away from someone else. All I had with me was a tiny bit of sugar and those beans—that's all I had thought of bringing, because of my hunger. I had not taken anything out of Germany, although I knew some people took things like cameras and other valuables.

Hela: Eventually we arrived at Podgórze, the suburb of Kraków where the ghetto had once been. Regina's maid had lived here before the war, so we decided to see if she was still there. She was shocked to see the state we were in, but she welcomed us. We were given a little corner in her kitchen, and I lay down, overcome by a terrible tiredness. We stayed there for several days. Regina ran around the city, trying to find out whether Dolek or Ryszard had survived.

I started to get intense flashbacks of my mother, her soft skin and gentle eyes. I had been missing her for so long, yet I was acutely aware of my sense of loss and loneliness. My father too was in my thoughts. I had loved him so much, and I think he loved me the best, because I was the youngest. I could feel the warm rough fabric of his jacket as he piggy-backed me around the room. I could smell his skin and hair ... but I knew I mustn't go on torturing myself. I never really found out what happened to my father; I knew only that he was torn away from me suddenly, as were so many of my family.

Despite my determination to stop thinking of the past, the images of familiar faces swam before me. I could see the face of Aunt Itka, Różycka's mother, who was always so close to me; and Aunt Lajka, in her little crowded room with her daughters; and Big Kuba, with his broad smile that showed all his teeth ... As the tears trickled down I wiped them away resolutely. I was here, alive, with Poldek beside me. There were no other relatives in the whole of Kraków that I could find. The time just before the war seemed like centuries ago: walking in sunshine along the Planty, looking sideways at boys and giggling at their winks; living in a comfortable home; visiting all our relatives ... Now there was no one but Regina's maid to remind me that the past did indeed exist. I took a deep breath and felt the hollow numbness in my chest that was to stay with me for a long, long time.

I was too afraid to go outside. But after a few days Poldek convinced me to go with him to number 12B Wrocławska street, where we used to live. Not much had changed. Luckily Kraków had not been bombed, and I had the strangest feeling walking up the familiar staircase, as if a whole lifetime had passed since I was last here. But I didn't allow myself to dwell any further on the past; we had to think about the future. We found Mrs Święchowa, our old caretaker, who remembered that she had lived with our family for half a year at the start of the war, and that we had fed her and looked after her. She was very happy to see 'the young miss' alive, and arranged for us to have an apartment in the same building. However, again we had to share it— with another couple—because of a shortage of accommodation.

We started to meet people that we had known before the war, and to recognise shops that were now in new hands. I looked for the Polish tailor who had promised to take care of Janka's brown English suit, her leather boots and some dresses. When I found him and asked him for her things, he looked at me mournfully and said the Germans had taken everything. This did not surprise me.

Many people greeted us with incredulity. 'Are you still alive?' they asked. 'We thought all the Jews were dead!' We found out later that about four and a half million Polish Jews were among the six million Jewish men, women and children who had been murdered by the Nazis. The figure was staggering.

Poldek now began to make contact with musician friends and immediately got work, even though he didn't yet own a suit. He found a job in Floriańska street, in a nightclub called 'Bajka' (fairy tale). He started to earn money straight away. Till now I had been wearing the clothes I had in Auschwitz, but now we could begin to buy essentials like food and clothes, so we were more fortunate than many of the other people who were by this time flooding back to Kraków. Manci, together with a friend she had found, moved into a room above the nightclub. They began to sew to earn a living. All this time Manci still didn't know what had happened to Herman or her son Olek. There was no mail, no telephones, no public transport, and services were only slowly beginning to return to normal.

Regina, who had also had no news of her son or her husband, went to stay with Dolek's parents; they had been in Brünnlitz with her and were living in Kraków, on Starowiślna street. One day, feeling depressed, she decided to go and see a film on her own. She sat in a darkened cinema, watching a newsreel, when suddenly on the screen in front of her she saw children's faces—the faces of her son Ryszard and his cousin Olek! They were among a group of children who had been rescued by the Americans from Auschwitz at the end of the war. The children were all rolling up their sleeves, showing the numbers tattooed on their forearms and looking seriously at the camera.

Frantic, Regina ran out of the cinema and started to question everyone she could think of. Through one of the agencies she found out that a family called Liebling was looking after Ryszard and her husband Dolek, right there in Kraków. The Lieblings had known the Horowitz family before the war, and had identified Ryszard in an orphanage and taken him in, not knowing what had happened to his parents. Dolek had later found them and was now living with them too.

Regina was joyfully reunited with her family. They moved

into an apartment which they shared with the Rabers (Mr Raber was the accountant who had employed Janka before the war). She heard the full story of how Dolek and Ryszard, as well as Herman and Olek, had been taken from Brünnlitz, from Schindler's haven, to Auschwitz, where they would have perished if the Americans hadn't liberated them. Manci still had no news of her family, and I knew nothing of the fate of my sister and brother.

Every evening I went to the nightclub where Poldek was playing, as I didn't want to stay home on my own. I would sit at a little table near the bandstand, listening to the musicians, or go upstairs to be with Manci. One evening I was sitting in the nightclub, enjoying Poldek's music. The cabaret was noisy and smoky, full of Russian soldiers in uniform. A tall, well-built Russian with a big moustache came over to me, put out his hand and said, *'Tańcować'* (Let's dance). I didn't want to dance with him and pretended not to hear. He took my arm and repeated, in a louder voice, *'Tańcować! Ja cie oswobodził!'* (I freed you!). He was determined that I would dance with him and could not understand a refusal. Poldek, hearing the Russian's raised voice and seeing what was going on, put down his accordion and ran over to us. He threatened to punch the man if he didn't leave me alone. The Russian looked from me to him, then back at me, and, thinking it wasn't worth the trouble, slowly walked away. Poldek gave me a kiss and returned to his playing. I remained very frightened of the Russians who had just returned from the front; there were some terrible types.

Janka: At last we got to Kraków by train. It was 15 June 1945. I started to ask people, 'Have you seen Poldek Rosner?' because my brother-in-law was well-known as a famous musician. At last someone told me that they had seen him, and that he had been playing in a nearby cabaret, 'Bajka', in Floriańska street.

I went there that evening and walked into the noisy, smoky interior. I looked around, my eyes slowly getting accustomed to the hazy scene. People were laughing and dancing all around me. I could hear familiar music, and there on the bandstand I saw my brother-in-law, dressed in a white shirt, a bow tie and a black dinner-suit, playing his accordion and smiling to the crowd. My heart leapt. Suddenly he caught sight of me and stopped playing in the middle of a song. He put down his instrument and ran towards me. The patrons of the nightclub looked on in amazement. The other musicians also raggedly stopped and stared. A hush grew over the crowd. Without saying a word, Poldek grabbed me by the hand and led me, breathless, up two flights of stairs.

Hela: I was in Manci's apartment above the nightclub one evening, drinking tea with her. Distant music floated up from below. Manci was feeling rather sad and I didn't know how to cheer her up. Suddenly Poldek burst through the door, much earlier than usual, and I was afraid that something was wrong. I jumped up and ran towards him. He moved aside and suddenly I saw, standing behind him, my sister Janka.

Janka: When Hela came to the door, she took one look at me and fainted in the doorway. It took several anxious minutes of patting her cheek and calling her name before she recovered. She hadn't dared to believe that I was still alive after all this time. As you can imagine, it was a wonderful, emotional reunion.

I moved in with my sister, but I was afraid to stay in Kraków, not only because of the Poles and the Germans but because of the Russians too. I was afraid whenever I came across a group of Russians, remembering their brutality. My fear was so great that I wanted to leave Poland as soon as possible to get out of their reach.

I began to be aware of Polish anti-Semitism, something which I hadn't personally felt before the war; it was plainly evident now. We heard of pogroms that were still occurring, now, after the war, where Jews were being rounded up and beaten or killed. In the town of Kielce forty-two Jews had been attacked and beaten to death.

I heard a woman shopper at the market saying, 'Why are you selling that goose to a Jewess and not to me?' We could feel that we were not welcome. Feelings of anti-Semitism vibrated everywhere. To make things worse, food was still scarce. I once again tried to eat a raw potato, but quickly spat it out, wondering how I could ever have imagined that it tasted like almonds.

Everyone was going regularly to the *Gmina Żydowska*, the Jewish Agency on Długa street that had been set up with records of who had died and who had survived, to try to locate missing relatives. I went there almost daily, looking for news of my husband Salek Immergluck, but I didn't find out his fate till later. At the agency I met a man called Jozef Gross (known as Józek), who was also looking for news of his family. I had met him briefly in Płaszów but didn't really remember him. I knew his friend, Pilcer, who had been a jeweller before the war, with a wife and child. He was the one who had made me the copper ring in Płaszów.

I asked Józek whether he knew what had become of Pilcer. He didn't know what had happened to him, but he knew that his daughter had survived by being hidden in a Polish house. She was now five years old. We went together to see her and found the little girl, her hands stained brown from peeling walnuts for the Poles with whom she lived. She had little recollection of her father. We returned to the town centre and continued chatting. I asked Józek what the time was, but neither of us had a watch so we went for a walk to the clock-tower. We continued to talk. I told him that maybe I would remarry one day if I didn't find my husband, but I would never have children.

Józek and I often met up at the Jewish Agency, but we could find no information about either my husband or his family. Józek had been married before the war, with a five-year-old son. His wife and child had been taken away by the Germans and never heard of again. He had also had a large family of six brothers and two sisters, all with their own wives, husbands and children, as well as aunts, uncles and cousins. He searched the records at the agency meticulously but not a single name could he find. We were both very lonely.

After a time Józek fell in love with me and told me, 'Stop looking for Salek, because I won't give you back to him.' Later a friend of his told us what had happened. They had been together in the last days, crammed in cattle wagons with hundreds of others, travelling for endless days and nights. Almost at the end of the war, in April 1945, they were taken to Sachsenhausen, deep in Germany. They had arrived there after being transported to different camps several times since Płaszów. Salek was twenty-eight years old. This friend had seen him getting down from the wagon and falling over, exhausted and starving. He was unable to get up again and didn't survive.

I'd never had a child with Salek, and I felt overcome by pain and loss. I had nothing to remember him by, just absence and emptiness. But then I recalled my father's advice at the beginning of the war: he had told me not to get married or have children, as terrible things were going to happen. And indeed, I witnessed so many of my women friends suffering or perishing because of their children that I was determined not to have one of my own. Some didn't want to leave their children behind, so they threw themselves into the graves with them. What was the use of loving, of caring for someone? All it brought was pain. Only much later was I able to allow my maternal instincts to overcome my fears.

We play some strange games at school. Every playtime I go with a few girls to the dark sunless side of the building, where there is only asphalt and no trees. We play fantasy games of soldiers and prisoners. 'I'm the soldier,' one tall girl says to me. 'You be the mother, and she,' pointing to another small girl, 'will be the baby. You must smack your baby, otherwise I'll shoot you.'

'No, no!' I protest. I feel tormented by the dilemma. But I am drawn back to the game day after day.

Janka: Józek and I started to see a lot of each other, but we didn't discuss marriage yet, of course. At this time he was already working and had a steady income, as he had a very good profession as a jeweller and a good reputation from before the war. Soon after my arrival in Kraków I had met some friends of my uncle's who helped me initially by giving me some money, for I had no means of support. But once I met Józek and we became close friends, he began to look after me. Even though he was a redhead like my brother, he was strong and didn't let it worry him.

Hela: Janka talked a lot about Józek, describing him as a kind and gentle person, a tall man but with thinning red hair, which she wasn't too pleased about. I said to her, 'What's the difference? If he's good to you, you should stay with him.' So they began a relationship, although they weren't married yet. He moved in with us too.

We all lived together in Kraków for a short while, but I was not happy living in Poland. Poldek and I wanted to leave: there were too many bad memories here. Manci was still anxiously waiting for news of Herman and Olek. There was some man who was interested in her, as she was still young and attractive. He tried to make her forget her family but she couldn't. And at last, after several months without news, she found out from a cousin that Herman and Olek had been liberated from Dachau, had survived, and were living in Munich in Germany. She left immediately to join them.

Meanwhile Poldek got a job in Katowice, an industrial city not too far from Kraków, so we went there while Janka stayed in Kraków. Poldek played in a club called 'Wojko', and we lived in an apartment together with a pianist, Arzewski, and his family. (He later played with Herman in America for many years.) I didn't take to his wife Bronia. We had separate bedrooms but shared a kitchen. Arzewski worked with Poldek in the nightclub and for a little while we were content, but the urge to move on overcame us. Poldek, who had lost his parents and several brothers and sisters, knew that Herman was working in Munich as a musician, and he wanted to be reunited with his brother.

We decided to leave Poland, but we had no passports or official documents of our own to allow us to travel. We couldn't go legally across the border, so we had to pretend not to be Jewish, and pay someone from our tiny savings for false papers.

A few weeks later, we packed a few things for the journey and left early one morning. We went by train, on false papers classifying us as Greeks. We had been given instructions by a man from UNRRA (United Nations Relief and Rehabilitation Administration) who was organising our journey, not to speak to anyone, not to say a word, in case we gave ourselves away.

We travelled for hours, sitting in silence, trying to attract as little attention as possible. We slept that night on the floor of a train station, waiting for another connection. We had to proceed in an indirect way, and spent many hours waiting, travelling a bit, then waiting again, speaking only in whispers when necessary. Sometimes we rattled along in trains; other times we sat jolting about in the backs of trucks. Once, we had to cross a river in a small boat. At times I despaired of ever reaching our destination; I was tired of living in a state of fear, insecurity, uncertainty. We couldn't trust anyone. At night I crawled close to Poldek for a bit of warmth and reassurance, but neither of us knew where this strange journey would lead us.

I never trust strangers. When I am small I like to stand inside our low white-painted front gate, watching the cars and trams go by. One day an old lady comes along, moving slowly with a walking-stick. She has a long nose and a hunched back. She wears an old black coat and is carrying a large heavy-looking paper bag. As she comes closer she pauses and examines me. I step back from the gate, but she offers me the bag with an encouraging smile. 'There you are, little girl. Give it to your mummy,' she says in a croaky voice, and I reach out for it gingerly. She keeps smiling and nodding her head, then turns and continues on her way.

I clutch the bag uncertainly, feeling its weight. As soon as the witch is out of sight, I place the bag on the ground and crouch down to look inside it. It is full of greenish pears, meant to poison us. I hide the bag under a hedge in a corner of the garden, then run inside all breathless to tell my mother.

Hela: We were stopped by officials in Kudowa, a holiday resort near the border of Czechoslovakia. They took away our papers and we couldn't get across the border, so we stayed in Kudowa for several weeks. People looked at us strangely at first, thinking we were criminals of some sort on the run. But there were so many unusual things going on after the war that no one took too much notice of strangers. Eventually some people found out who we were and Poldek began to work there, playing on his accordion. While he was entertaining a group of holidaymakers, we met two men, Andrzej Ślimak and his uncle. Andrzej began to flirt with me. I was a young woman, Poldek was working and there was nothing to do in the evenings, so we would sit together and enjoy each other's company.

Eventually the relief organisation, UNRRA, heard of our plight and that of many other Jews who were without papers. They arranged transport and papers for a whole group of us to allow us to get across the border. We travelled through Czechoslovakia, and then through Austria. We slept at night in large halls on bare floorboards and kept traversing unfamiliar landscapes during the day. When we arrived in Vienna, we were permitted to go to the public baths, as we hadn't washed in quite a while. Poldek and I were delighted to discover that you could rent a cubicle with a double bath in it, for married couples. We had a hard time convincing the management that we were married, as we had no wedding papers, but eventually they took pity on us. We became shy with each other in the confined privacy of the cubicle; but soon we discarded the rags and grime that clothed us, and could luxuriate for a short while in cleansing our bodies and renewing our intimacy while soothing warm water flowed around us.

We made it to Munich and found Poldek's brother and his family. We were relieved to meet up with family members again, people who were close, who understood us, who had shared our past. Poldek and Herman were very alike, despite the difference in their age, and they couldn't stop telling each other stories. Manci and Herman looked contented and we kept breaking into laughter, happy to be with them. Their apartment in Munich, at Aussere Prinzregentenstrasse 67, was large and old, with many high-ceilinged rooms, large wardrobes and enormous beds. An added surprise, one which overwhelmed me at first, was that Oskar Schindler, our saviour, had made his way to Munich too. When we moved in with Herman, Manci and Olek, we discovered that Oskar was in fact living with them as well, together with his latest girlfriend, Giza Schein, a Jewish girl he had met through Manci. She was plump and not very pretty, but they seemed to get on well together.

Things weren't easy; we had arrived with almost nothing. We had no possessions of any value, and no money, only the clothes we wore. Food was still scarce. Poldek started to work with Herman on stage in a Munich theatre, and was able to provide food for all of us in the apartment. Manci, a dressmaker by trade, measured me and helped to make some clothes for me using the navy woollen cloth from Brünnlitz. She made me a lovely dress, adding a little white collar. But the first thing Poldek bought for me with the money he earned was some underpants. What a luxury! Later, as his income became regular, he brought home other necessities.

Schindler didn't leave the apartment much; he would lock himself in the bedroom with Giza for hours at a time. When I saw him he was always smoking, and often drinking. He was a very large man physically, and his presence commanded attention. But he was always polite and friendly to us. He had lost all his wealth saving 'his' Jews from death and providing food for them for so many months. We learnt that after the war he had gone to Argentina with Emilie for a short time, to try to set up a business. He had then returned to Europe, leaving her there. Now he seemed to have a very nonchalant attitude to life, not in a hurry to achieve anything any more. He didn't know what to do with his life at this stage, and just seemed to live from day to day. He seemed to be afraid to go out.

The war years had left me very nervous. I remained extremely sensitive to noise and any unexpected sound frightened me. Every knock or shout made me jump. The sound of footsteps mounting the stairs, or of boots walking on the pavement outside, made me catch my breath, particularly if the wearer also wore a uniform. Whether it was a Russian soldier or a local policeman, the sight of the uniform made me tremble. Another sound I could not get used to was the resonance of the German language. Again and again, I felt its grating harshness as a direct assault on my being, and no amount of reasoning could make it otherwise.

I was still very frightened of being alone and clung to Poldek constantly. We were together almost all the time. I also missed Janka. Living with so many people wasn't easy. Everyone else seemed happy and confident, but I felt very out of place. I was withdrawn and shy and couldn't speak out. Manci and Herman were the owners of the place; I was the intruder, who felt guilty for taking up space and food. I began to crave fresh fruit. There were some apples in a bowl on the sideboard and I really wanted one, but being so shy I was too embarrassed to ask for one, and too frightened to take it without asking. My cravings kept tormenting me. Another problem was the lack of privacy; the walls were thin and everyone knew what everyone else was doing.

Janka: We found out that Kuba had survived and was living in Jelenia Góra, a town near Wrocław. He had not stayed long in Kraków after the war: he felt afraid of people who knew of his role during the war, and made his way to Wrocław. I was told that Mundek, my lover from Płaszów, lived there and had a very good position. He helped Kuba by organising an apartment, and he also set up a dental clinic for him, as Kuba had trained to be a dentist before the war. Mundek was a great help to my brother.

I heard that Mundek wanted to see me again and was looking for me, but Józek didn't want me to renew contact with him. I didn't want to start married life with any secrets, so I told him all about the relationship, and how young and lonely I had been. Times had been abnormal, and after my short-lived marriage my senses had been aroused and I needed a man's company. Mundek had been good to me and bought me nice things. When people in Kraków tried to gossip about all this in front of Józek, telling him I had had a lover in Płaszów, he was not perturbed because I had already confided in him. It was time to make a new start.

We were married on 14 February 1946, St Valentine's day, though we didn't know the significance of the date at the time. I wore the same brown woollen coat I had been given in Auschwitz. Józek had a friend who was a tailor, and he shortened the coat for me and removed the patch of striped prison material, using fabric from the hem to mend it so that it looked almost like new. We had a civil ceremony; we couldn't have a religious wedding because there was no written proof of the death of my first husband.

We continued to live in Kraków, although we didn't want to stay there. I knew that two of my father's brothers were living in America and were looking for news of us. They sent us letters through the Jewish Agency, and we made contact via Munich. Hela and Poldek had gone there six months before us, crossing the border illegally, but we had legal passports that my husband had paid for.

Hela: At last, Janka and Józek came to Germany and joined us. I was comforted by my sister's presence and began to be less afraid. They moved in with us, into one of the rooms of the large apartment, and the nine of us continued to live there: Poldek and I, Janka and Józek, Herman, Manci and Olek, as well as Oskar Schindler and Giza.

My food cravings became stronger. I found that I was pregnant. Soon after the war had ended, while we were living in Kraków, my period had started again. We took no precautions, and I was happy to discover physical joys which till then had been denied me. We would steal moments of intimacy whenever we could, enjoying the present and not thinking beyond each day. I felt well with my pregnancy and had no signs of morning sickness. The only symptom was the persistent craving for fruit. I was very happy, but also frightened, as I didn't know what the future would hold. Janka, when I told her the news, surprised me by announcing that she too was pregnant and was due to have her baby a few weeks before me. We embraced each other and wept.

There were many late nights full of laughter and loud noise. Everyone smoked a lot and drank large quantities of brandy. There were also great hunks of chocolate eaten; everyone was mad about chocolate after the war. Days and nights passed in a smoky haze, and I tried to focus on the present. We discovered that our cousin Różyczka had survived and was in Germany. She came to visit us in Munich and invited us to her wedding to Moniek, in Feldafing, a small town south-west of Munich. Another wedding we celebrated was that of Wilek, Poldek's youngest brother, who married Erna. Gradually the rhythms of life began to assert themselves and a desperate urge for rejoicing bubbled to the surface. I was acutely aware of the satisfaction of being warm and having a full stomach. My fears, however, didn't leave me. I began to have nightmares.

I didn't think too much about God any more. I could see that people around me, like Józek, had become atheists and no longer believed in anything. They said that God couldn't possibly exist or He would never have let such terrible suffering happen to us. If He existed, where was He when we were in Auschwitz?

God is not a strong force in my life. I never hear His voice. Only in my later teenage years do I begin to explore the idea of God, and to search for some kind of an understanding. I find very quickly that the rituals and laws a Jew is supposed to observe are quite foreign to me, and I develop a strong feeling that God is something else, beyond individual religions, beyond human understanding, but nevertheless a force or energy that is central to life's meaning. God cannot, however, be loving and omnipotent, if He has allowed the horrors of the past to occur. The words of praise feel dry in my mouth. I continue to grapple with the mystery.

Hela: And yet, I came back again and again to an awareness, despite the logical arguments, of a belief in some power greater than myself. I prayed often, and continued to do so in later life. I didn't, however, worry any more about trying to keep kosher or observing all the laws; that just seemed pointless.

Herman and Manci had applied for a visa to go to America so we decided to do the same, but there was a long wait. Maybe because Manci had been born in Austria, their visas came through first and they left for America, leaving us in Munich. Full of emotion, we farewelled them, promising to follow soon. Poldek continued to work in the theatre, and Schindler stayed with us for a while longer.

I was happy to be close to my sister but I could see that Józek was very uncomfortable in Germany. He wanted to take his wife as far as possible from Europe, where he had endured so much, so he too applied for a visa to America.

Janka: We lived for a while in Munich with Hela and Poldek, and with Schindler and his girlfriend, but Józek was desperate to get out of Germany. He couldn't stand being surrounded by Germans, hearing the harsh guttural sounds of the German language and being constantly reminded of his losses and suffering. We tried to organise affidavits to be able to emigrate to the United States. There was a cousin by marriage, Sidney Maisel, who lived in Buffalo, New York. He filled out and signed an application for an immigration visa for us, attesting that he was concerned about our welfare and had a 'strong sense of moral responsibility' for us. He gave assurance that he would properly receive and care for us upon our arrival in the United States, and would not permit us 'to become a public charge upon any community or municipality'. This document was dated 12 March 1946. We waited and waited for the American Consul to approve the visa, but without results.

Eventually we obtained a visa to go to Paris and decided to leave. At the train station I parted tearfully with my sister and we commenced yet another journey. We travelled from Munich to Paris in comfort, by the Blue Express. This was very different from some of the other train journeys I had suffered, but I felt anxiety at moving again. Would we ever find a secure home?

∽

At Passover, although we don't follow the whole service before impatience and hunger pangs make us abandon the reading, there is one song we all sing, with many verses and a bouncy chorus. It is basically a list of all the wonderful things God has done for His people, and expresses appreciation for each of them. If He had taken us out of Egypt, but not led us to the Promised Land, it would be enough. If He had led us to the Promised Land, but not given us the Ten Commandments, it would be enough. And so on.

But as I grow older, and learn the term 'grateful for small mercies', I begin to wonder about all this gratitude. If we are the 'Chosen People', what are we chosen for? My ignorance in this area doesn't stop me from drawing my own conclusions. It seems that to be Jewish means to be different, to be an outsider, and to be constantly vigilant. There are those out there who want to annihilate us for no good reason, and we have to be ultra-aware and sensitive to any sign of discrimination or intolerance. News of anti-Semitic daubings on walls or racist comments are taken personally by the whole community; desecration of graves or attacks on Israel assume monumental proportions and remind us of the ongoing threat to our existence.

I begin to wonder about what it means to be Jewish, in the absence of most forms of religious observance and rituals. If I am not religious, how is it that I am still acutely aware that I am a Jew? On the other hand, those who argue that we are a race cannot really define what that means, given the enormous geographical and cultural differences between one sort of Jew and another. The black Ethiopians are nothing like the East European refugees; the Yemenite Jew is totally different from the Jew whose family has lived in Australia for five generations. Yet these differences counted for nothing during the Holocaust; having Jewish blood was enough reason to be exterminated. How can I not be influenced by my parents' views and experiences? How can I not see my world through the lens of Holocaust persecution, and not identify myself as a product of their suffering?

And so at Passover, as we sing the traditional songs, other words begin buzzing in my head. 'If they had thrown us out of our homes and taken our belongings, but not herded us into ghettos, it would have been terrible enough. If they had herded us into ghettos, but not killed all those over fifty-five, it would have been terrible enough. If they had killed all those over fifty-five, but not starved and beaten us, it would have been . . .' And so on. The enormity of the injustice and of the horror defies expression. Even one day of hunger, even one night of sleeplessness, waiting to hear the sound of heavy boots marching up the stairs, would have been torment. How could this have been repeated, again and again, for six long years? How could you live on, day after day, not knowing whether today would be the day that your sister, or your father, or you yourself, would die? How much discomfort, pain, cold, anguish and suffering can a human being endure, and not crumble?

I look at my parents smiling contentedly as the grandchildren take up the chorus again with renewed gusto; I see Auntie and Uncle trying to join in with the singing, the candlelight reflected in their eyes, and I have no answers. The power of the human spirit to survive, despite everything, is limitless. I feel humble in seeing their joy tonight, and the buzzing words of despair fade away.

16

Janka: We arrived in Paris armed with only two suitcases, my schoolgirl French and a piece of paper with the name of a jeweller who was originally from Kraków. We found his address and Józek went in to the apartment building to look for him. I stood on the footpath beside our cases as people bustled around me, taking no notice. My belly had started to grow and my legs ached. After what seemed like ages, Józek came down smiling.

This jeweller, Fendler, had never met Józek in his life, but he knew his name from before the war, and told him he could stay with him and start working for him straight away. But Józek replied that he couldn't, as he wasn't alone; he had a pregnant wife waiting below. The jeweller thought for a moment, then had an idea. He had an apprentice whose parents were Polish Jews and he would help us find a room.

This apprentice found us a room on the Rue Richer near the Folies-Bergère, in an apartment block where the ground and first floors were rented out to prostitutes, but the second and third were for refugees like us. After all the travelling we had done we were grateful to have a place to stay, and wearily climbed the narrow, dirty stairs to the second floor. We shifted into a room with a bare lightbulb, a stained mattress on the bed and a rickety wooden wardrobe. Compared to what we had been through, this was luxury. We looked into each other's eyes, then hugged for a long time.

Fendler and his wife were very kind and good to us. After a week, they were leaving Paris to go on holidays and they left their seven-room apartment and the jewellery workshop open for us. They gave us the key and had total trust in us.

We could go to their home to cook and wash whenever we wanted. Our life began to take on a sense of ordinary routine. My husband was to work for three years for this man.

Fendler's wife had been in the camps with me and we now became friendly. Once, when I broke the heel of my shoe, she told me that there was a shoemaker downstairs. She asked me if I remembered a girl we knew from Auschwitz, a French girl called Fifi. She was the one who had told us she used to dance for the Folies-Bergère and gave concerts to entertain us. I had admired her enormously at the time. Mrs Fendler told me that Fifi was no dancer; she was the wife of the shoemaker.

I went downstairs and there she was, Fifi the dancer. She looked very unkempt and poor, and I didn't want to confront her with the past. She seemed embarrassed, but we didn't say a word to each other. Sometimes, in extreme situations, one can have fantasies of a more exciting life than one has really lived; maybe that helped her to survive the long nights and fearful days. I had to let the deception stand and allow her to save face; there was no point in pinning her down to the truth.

Hela: Poldek still wanted to join his brother in America and we waited daily for notification of approval of our visas. At last we received papers from the Central Committee of Liberated Jews in the American Occupied Zone in Germany, dated 17 September 1946. These were transit visas allowing us to pass through France to go to Venezuela. I looked hard at the document, read it over carefully again and again. Venezuela. America! That was so far from Janka! I began to visualise how permanent this move would be. I had been missing her very much and began trying to convince Poldek to reconsider. We had several sleepless nights discussing our options, but eventually, seeing how distressed I was, Poldek agreed to apply for a visa to France, so that we could join Janka and Józek. We followed them to Paris soon after. It was autumn 1946.

We arrived with almost nothing and couldn't speak the

language, but the very day we arrived Poldek went with his accordion to a local café and came back loaded with bread and sausage. We met up with a cousin of Poldek's, Herman Schneider, who was living in Paris. He and his wife offered us a beautiful apartment—in those days you needed 'key money' to move into an apartment, but they let us move in for nothing. We stayed there for a short time, but I wanted desperately to be with my sister. Schneider didn't know my sister or her husband, and wasn't prepared to provide accommodation for them as well.

Janka: We visited Hela and Poldek in a lovely apartment on one of the boulevards. It had three rooms and a bathroom, but I could see Hela was not content. She wanted to be close to me, so they shifted in with us into our little room.

Very soon we realised how cramped we all were in the room in Rue Richer. We began to look round for somewhere bigger for the four of us. With all the changes and movements of people after the war, it was very hard to find an apartment at this time; you needed about 100,000 francs. Józek had a diamond that he had buried in Kraków before the war and had managed to retrieve while we were there. With this diamond he went to Poldek's cousin, Schneider, to ask him for a loan for an apartment, leaving the diamond as security. Schneider considered Józek's offer but then told him to keep the diamond; he didn't want it and would lend him the money without security. With the borrowed money we found a small apartment in Barbès-Rochechouart in the 18th *arrondissement*, a poor district full of Algerians and prostitutes, but it was near Montmartre and the Sacré-Coeur, a beautiful basilica set on a hill, and we were happy to have a place of our own.

Hela: We had to climb the stairs to the second floor of an old building in a poor part of Paris, at 20 Rue de la Charbonnière. There was basically only one room and a kitchen but Janka and Józek were happy to live with us, and I was content to be with my sister. I felt an overwhelming need to be close to her now that I had found her again. I was totally dependent on her and looked to her for advice in everything. Being older, and knowing a bit of French, she was the one I turned to for direction in my life.

Both Janka and I were well into our pregnancies by this stage. I prayed for two things: for my baby to be healthy and that it should be musical, like Poldek. One of his greatest disappointments in me was that I couldn't sing in tune. I liked to sing, but after the first time I opened my mouth and saw the look of horror on Poldek's face, I never tried to sing again in his presence.

To my mother's great relief I can sing in tune. I learn to sing as soon as I can talk. My father's pride in my abilities displays itself from my earliest years in a familiar routine. At any party, or when visitors come, he lifts me up onto the table so my head is on a level with his. He plays his accordion as I sing. At first the song is always the same, with Polish words which I carefully pronounce, not really aware of what they mean. Whenever I reach a certain line everyone always laughs, and they clap when I finish, so I feel gratified, but never understand why they laugh and wink at each other.

In private it is a different matter. I love to sing for my mother. Whenever I sing, her eyes light up and her face softens. I want so much to make her happy. One special time, she and I have a bath together. I am ten or eleven. My younger sister is asleep and it's just the two of us. She fills the bathtub with fragrant oils and bubble-bath, and we delight in the steamy warmth. While she lies back opposite me I close my eyes and begin to sing songs for her, one after another. They are love songs, or songs of farewell, sad songs, often in a minor key. (These always seem to be my favourites.) I sing about things of which I have only an imperfect understanding, but I am reassured and grateful that my mother enjoys them so much, and her love washes over me.

Hela: Being with Janka and Józek helped me to overcome the initial adjustment period that any couple has to face when living together. I didn't spend all that much time with

Poldek; he worked at night and slept during the day. His lifestyle seemed very glamorous to me and I often went to the cabaret where he was working, to breathe in the joyful atmosphere of people determined on having a good time. At four in the morning I shared in raucous parties and ate hot garlic snails which Poldek brought to my table. There was a lot of drinking and singing, and I felt intensely happy.

Nevertheless, thoughts of death were always with me. I was afraid a lot of the time. Whenever I felt pain or experienced anxiety I began to think of dying. I watched my body changing with my pregnancy and didn't know whether I could withstand it. I felt confused, as I wavered between fear of childbirth and euphoria. I was afraid I might damage the child growing within me. When I woke one morning with a pain in the region of my bellybutton I raced to the doctor, who had to reassure me that nothing was wrong. I was never sure of my health and lived each day anticipating that something might go wrong.

Life was difficult because I didn't speak the language and our conditions were fairly primitive. There was no bathroom, so we would go to the public baths on a Sunday morning. We were told that we should get there early to avoid the crowds of prostitutes who came later from the surrounding district. The toilet in our building was on the landing halfway between the first and second floors, and served everyone living on both levels. It was only a hole in the floor that you had to crouch over, and the stench was awful. But after what we had been through, nothing mattered.

Janka and Józek shared the tiny bedroom, which contained only a bed and a wardrobe. The kitchen was the main living area, with a double bed where Poldek and I slept next to the window, as well as wooden table, a cold-water tap, and a little wood stove over which we cooked our meals.

There were still food shortages. We had to go downstairs with a ration card and a tin to buy milk, and we had to boil it because it wasn't pasteurised. There were long queues to buy the milk but pregnant women and mothers with babies had a different-coloured card from the others, which gave us priority. Everything was rationed then. When I silently handed over my ration card in return for the milk, the woman serving me turned to Janka and said, shaking her head, 'Poor young woman . . .' She assumed I was deaf and dumb, as I didn't know how to say one word in French.

Schneider's wife helped me a lot, bringing me things I needed for the household, because we were starting out with nothing. Even a dishcloth was an unexpected gift. She took me to the market to show me where to buy vegetables and how to choose the best buys. She had to show me how to use the Métro so I could get around. I knew nothing; everything was unfamiliar.

But for the first time in ages I felt a contentment settle over me that was only occasionally penetrated by fears. I deliberately pushed memories of the past to the back of my mind and began to live my new life with a passion, making up for all the years I had missed. Simple things gave me joy: a bunch of flowers brought to me by my husband, the feel of my baby kicking inside me, the scent of lily-of-the-valley in the streets of Paris in April.

Poldek was now working in a Russian restaurant called 'Dinerezade', and later in a cabaret. Before our child was born I would go with him to listen to him play, and I spent my evenings sitting at a little table near the bandstand watching the crowds enjoying themselves.

Janka: On 3 January 1947 I gave birth to a boy, Louis, in a private hospital in Paris. (He was named after Ludwik, the son that Józek had lost during the war.) It was a very difficult birth; after struggling through two long days of labour I was exhausted and weak by the time the baby was born. The doctor had taken hours to arrive and I was left suffering for a long time. But I was overcome by relief and gratitude for a new life, mingled with loneliness for Józek, who could only visit briefly. I spent seven days in hospital and filled in the long hours by writing letters to my husband. He was my fairy-tale prince and I really believed it was fate that had brought us together. Whenever I suckled Louis I imagined

Józek was standing by my bed watching us. I think the little one sucked all the longing from my breast because he cried so much! But we had our own little son, who would light up our life.

Hela: When I came to visit Janka I was carrying a large teddy bear we had bought in the Galeries Lafayette department store. I had travelled on the Métro, balancing the teddy bear on my belly until I reached the hospital. Because I was in the seventh month of my pregnancy, the nurses mistook my reason for being there and immediately wanted to whisk me away to the labour ward. Not speaking French, I had a hard time convincing them that it was not I but my sister who was having the baby!

We met up again with Marysia Sperling, with whom Janka had lived through so much of the war. Marysia and her mother had survived and were living in Paris. They didn't have any family left in Poland. They had told the Americans they were French, so they had been taken to Paris. There it was discovered that they weren't French at all but Polish, and they were put in jail. Feeling the anguish of being a prisoner again, Marysia had had a brainwave. She remembered the name and address of the Frenchman she had seen for just a few moments in Auschwitz, and she told the authorities. Shortly afterwards he arrived at the jail and arranged their release. He looked after them and fed them, and they remained good friends.

Marysia had married a very kind, gentle doctor, Dr Dolek Nick. We became close and saw a lot of them. Five weeks after Janka gave birth, we were having dinner at Marysia's place when I began to have labour pains. Dr Nick arranged for me to be taken to the Rothschild Hospital, a huge hospital in the middle of Paris. It was the evening of 8 February 1947. He attended the birth and everything went normally, although I was very afraid. When the nurses told me to push, saying '*Poussez, poussez!*', I didn't know what they were talking about. All I was aware of was the surge of insistent pain. I thought I would die, and just wanted it to end.

In the large maternity ward were long rows of beds lining two walls, with tiny cots for the babies all down the middle. I was placed in one of the beds, exhausted. When they brought the tiny bundle to me, I could barely believe that I had given birth to this little scrap of new life: a baby girl. Enormous relief and tiredness swept over me. Someone was asking me what I wanted to name my daughter. I thought of mother, and knew I wanted to name my child in memory of her. I heard the voice questioning me as if from far away, and managed to mutter 'Anna', before falling into a deep sleep.

When I awoke I lay back in my bed, wondering whether it had all been a dream. I was waiting impatiently for visiting hours so I could share my joy with Poldek. Visitors started to arrive and one by one the beds were surrounded by admiring friends and relatives; all except mine. The minutes ticked by and my despair grew. Why wasn't he here? What had happened?

Meanwhile Poldek, clutching a huge bunch of flowers he had bought hours earlier, was running all over the endless corridors of the large hospital, but couldn't find me. Visiting hours came and went and I sobbed into my pillow, unable to explain to the nurses, with my lack of the language, what the problem was. I didn't even know how to ask for a drink of water and felt overwhelmed by isolation. My sense of abandonment dissolved when the next visiting hours came around; there he was, full of apologies, kisses and wilting flowers.

But once he'd gone I was again left alone. I didn't know how to feed the baby properly, and the nurses must have got impatient with me as I was unable to follow their simplest instructions, except with sign language. It must have been difficult for them too, faced with waves of these 'foreigners' arriving after the war. They ran around busily, checking on the babies and putting hot-water bottles in the cots to keep them warm. I was so afraid they would burn my baby that I got out of my bed during the night, on legs still shaky from the birth, to check whether she was all right.

The nurses looked quite unconcerned and carried out their duties with brisk efficiency. When it was feeding time they would carry four infants at once, two under each arm, and stride purposefully along the long ward. I was always worried they would drop one of them, or bring me the wrong child.

I came home from the hospital and the routine began: washing and boiling, feeding and cleaning. Nappies and babies took up a lot of room in a one-bedroom apartment. Janka couldn't stand the sight of dirty nappies, it made her begin to retch; so Poldek took on the job of scraping the nappies, washing them by hand and boiling them in a big pot on the stove, then hanging them from cords strung across the room and afterwards ironing them. Cleaning the nappies and changing the two babies was a never-ending process. As for feeding, we both breastfed, but Louis was a very hungry baby—Janka didn't know at first that she didn't have enough milk. He cried a lot and never seemed satisfied, whereas Anna took a few sucks and fell asleep. I began to feed both of them, but Louis was such an energetic feeder that when he'd finished, my breasts were sagging and hollow.

We went regularly to a health centre to have our babies weighed, and every gram they gained was documented and worried over. We were given strict instructions there to feed our babies at precise times, even if it meant waking them when they were asleep. On the other hand, no matter how much they cried from hunger, we were to wait till the appointed time. Not having any experience of babies, I was terrified I'd do the wrong thing and tried to follow the instructions even when I found myself crying together with my child.

Despite all this, she gained weight normally and the doctor declared her perfect. In fact she was never really ill. But it was so hard to feel reassured; I had so little French that I couldn't explain my concerns, and even when I did I couldn't understand the quick, slippery syllables of the replies.

I was always fearful for my daughter. I stared at her while

she slept, never tiring of her smooth rose-petal cheeks and her gentle breath, and at the same time wondering how such a fragile being could survive unhurt. I would lay her gently on a large pillow and wrap her in swaddling-clothes, as was the custom for newborn babies. This way she could not wriggle around and hurt herself, her arms were wrapped firmly by her side so she couldn't scratch herself with her tiny fingernails, and her head and neck were well supported when I carried her around. I wasn't sleeping very well, as I was keyed up to hear the tiniest peep from my baby. When I did fall asleep, exhausted, I had disturbing nightmares and woke in a sweat. During the day I was so busy shopping, preparing food, surviving everyday life, that there was little time to think of anything else.

Nor was there much time to develop a relationship with my husband, with circumstances the way they were. When he returned from work in the early hours of the morning, we slept in the bed in the kitchen without any real privacy, as someone always needed a glass of water or had to warm some milk for one of the babies. We felt like thieves, sneaking a few moments together. Janka and Józek could close the door of their room, and even though the two little cots for the babies were in there, they had more privacy. Anna woke more often than Louis and would whimper the moment she was wet, whereas Louis could be drenched yet slept right through. Janka would often be the one to get up and change Anna's nappy when she started to cry. After a feed I liked to take my little Ania back into bed with me, to feel her sweet warmth.

Janka: Our apartment had become very crowded. Poldek worked all night in a cabaret, while Józek worked during the day in a jeweller's workshop, so sleeping arrangements were always a bit difficult. Poldek learnt to sleep with earplugs during the daytime and the children learnt to play quietly.

There were food shortages, with rationing and a flourishing black-market trade, where all sorts of goods could be obtained but were very expensive. Packets arrived occasionally from America, from UNRRA, containing things like sardines, which were Anna's favourite. Hela also searched the markets to buy calves' brains or a piece of liver, which she believed would make Anna strong. But both our husbands were working so we had some money. We were young, we took turns to go out to cabarets, we enjoyed life. We had survived.

Hela: I tried to live every day as it came. I bought new shoes, tried out a new hairdo. I had to push the past back and to forget.

We both bought prams and proudly wheeled our babies around the district. The prostitutes who lived on the floors below helped us to carry the prams down from the second floor. They were very friendly and helpful, but I was always afraid that my daughter would get an infection from them. I was terrified when they peered into the pram and played with her. But Janka laughed at me.

I was forever anxious that Anna wasn't eating enough. I thought she was so fragile and delicate that the slightest thing would upset her. When I noticed a bit of milk that she had brought up on her pillow after a feed, I thought she had been vomiting. No one had told me that you had to bring up a baby's wind after a feed; I mistakenly thought that the less I moved her, the less chance there was of her bringing up milk. I even attempted to breastfeed her while she lay in her cot—painfully bending over her, my breast in her mouth—so that she could fall asleep undisturbed!

We spent three years in Paris, in a cloud of domesticity: shopping, cooking, looking after our babies. We loved to visit Sacré-Coeur and the gardens surrounding it. Other days we took the children to a park nearby, the Parc Monceau, where there was a sandpit, and when they were old enough we sat on the bench watching them play with other toddlers from the neighbourhood. When we returned from our walks, soot and grime covered the little white pillows in their prams. Everything was dirty to touch, with traffic and factory chimneys smoking around us. But in spring the air was fragrant with lily-of-the-valley and there was hope in people's faces.

Once, on our return from a walk, I had a surprising visitor. In the doorway, standing with a huge bunch of red roses clasped in his arms, was Oskar Schindler. He had been back to Argentina but couldn't settle there and, once again leaving his wife behind, had made his way to France. He had heard we were in Paris and dropped in on us, unannounced, as was his custom. He looked somehow smaller and more tired than when I had seen him in Munich. Of course we were prepared to do anything for our saviour. He was full of smiles and very courteous, but after a quick cup of coffee he left again. That was the last time I saw him.

One warm afternoon we went out for our usual walk. Anna was fussing and wriggling around in her pram. I turned away for a moment to talk to Janka, and from the corner of my eye I saw my child climbing out of the pram. I reached out towards her—and saw her falling, as if in slow motion. I couldn't grab her before she hit the ground. There she lay, silent, unmoving.

My Ania, my child, my life! She wasn't breathing. I took her in my arms and started to run. I had to find a doctor. Passers-by, seeing a frantic madwoman, directed me: straight ahead, two blocks, turn left . . . I was carrying the tiny inert body, which was getting heavier and heavier with each step. I pushed past people in the street, not seeing their stares. I had to keep going, had to reach a doctor. God, don't let her die! Step after step, the words kept echoing in my mind. I don't know for how long I kept running.

At last I reached a clinic and gasped out my story to the nurse. She took Anna from me and placed her on a table. The doctor came in and began to prod her and move her limbs. Suddenly her eyes flickered. She gasped. She was alive! She had merely suffered concussion. After that, I felt more protective of her than ever.

One winter Poldek was engaged to play for two or three

months in a hotel called 'Le Majestic', in Chamonix in the French Alps. It was a beautiful hotel, several storeys high. Opposite our window, snow-covered Mont Blanc gleamed brightly. Rich tourists from all over the world gathered here to ski, swim in the pool and enjoy the surroundings. Uniformed nannies wheeled babies around in landau prams, while the mothers waved cheerfully from a distance. Actors, artists, bankers, all sorts of rich and famous people stayed here.

But I scarcely saw them. I was occupied in getting my daughter to eat. I stood over the stove for hours cooking the cereal till it was soft, and then tried to get her to swallow the tiny spoonfuls. I threw most of it away, as she was such a small eater, and then I cooked some more, begging her to eat. When she started eating solids I tried to tempt her with delicacies. She had developed a liking for sardines, so I would place a bit of sardine on the tip of the spoonful of cereal: that way she was more likely to swallow it. I went only once or twice down to the cabaret where Poldek was playing. The rest of the time I spent in my room trying to feed my child, believing she must be hungry.

In the next holiday season Poldek got an engagement to play in Les Sables d'Olonne, another beautiful holiday resort on the Atlantic coast south-west of Paris. By this time Herman and Manci were already in New York. (There he changed his name to Henry.)

I fell pregnant again, but with a heavy heart I decided I couldn't cope with another child at this stage. Anna was about one and a half years old. I tried to drink quinine and soaked in very hot water, but to no avail. Janka made inquiries, and arranged for a woman to come secretly to the apartment. The woman risked jail because abortions were illegal. She was terrified of being found out and had to be well paid. Without any anaesthetic, she performed the abortion on the kitchen table. It was night-time and Poldek was at work. The children were locked into Janka's bedroom. I was frightened and in great pain. But we had so little, and the future was so uncertain, that it was the only decision possible for me at the time. I lost a lot of blood and it took me some time to recover.

I tiptoe around in my socks and never slam the door. I am a serious, well-behaved child. I know I have to be quiet during the daytime, because my father works at night playing music and he needs his sleep. Although he uses earplugs, I know he will be angry if he is woken. I feel I am in the way and don't have space of my own. I can't ever be boisterous or noisy.

I also know I have to be quiet and good when my mother is unwell. She frequently suffers from 'nerves' and other mysterious ailments which are never talked about. 'Be good, or your mother will get sick.' Are these words ever spoken out loud?

Janka: We heard occasionally from Kuba, who stayed in Jelenia Góra for several years and met his first wife there. He married soon after the war, but not long afterwards his pregnant wife died in Wrocław. In a freak accident, a car mounted the footpath where she was walking and ploughed into a shopfront. Kuba was devastated, but he soon married again, a woman called Hanka. He was settled where he was and didn't want to move.

I was happy in Paris but my husband wasn't. He was afraid of staying in Europe, and remained acutely aware of having lost all his family during the war. Now that we had a child of our own, he wanted to leave. We decided to apply for a visa to go to Australia, which Józek thought was as far away from Europe as possible. We knew very little about Australia, but there was a cousin of our mother's living there who had migrated before the war. So we obtained the required documents and, in February 1949, left Paris.

∾

Not until now, when I am searching for my own path, and their wounds have begun to heal just a little, can the two women in my life begin to find the words to explain, in small, halting ways, what their lives were like before I was born. Now I hear about the richness of an era that no longer exists, a country that has changed unrecognisably yet in many ways remains the same. I hear about my roots and my ancestors, and gradually the names of people who perished half a century ago become familiar to me.

My aunt Janka, whom I have always just called Auntie, is full of stories. When we begin she is in her late seventies, still a good-looking woman, careful of her appearance, taking delight in simple joys. She loves people and her social calendar is always full.

Her thirst for knowledge has never abated. She makes her way to lectures and classes, taking notes, filling her little red notebook with wise sayings and poignant verses. Newspaper cuttings litter her bedside table, because she always wants to save the interesting snippets she finds. She goes with her husband to the theatre, to concerts and to the opera, to take in all the pleasures of cultured life. She loves to travel, and each year they explore a different part of the globe. It's as if time is running out and she must fill in the minutes and the hours with enough good, pleasurable experiences to make up for the lost years.

As she starts to tell me her story, her words tumble over each other, with each memory giving birth to countless others. She pulls down a large cardboard box of black-and-white photographs and brings it into the kitchen, grabbing handfuls of photos to search for the few precious old ones. There is no order as the photos jostle with each other.

'Here, this is the one I wanted to show you,' she says excitedly. It is a photo of her mother, the only one she has, taken some time in the 'thirties. Her mother is seated sedately beside her husband, gazing wistfully, unsmilingly, at the world. Her smooth cheek rests on her hand, the forefinger touching her face. Her hair is thick and wavy, but is parted in the middle and caught back in a loose bun. Her husband is handsome, with dark hair and a thick dark moustache. His starched white collar belies the gentleness in his eyes. I stare at the picture and try to understand that these are my grandparents.

A second photograph of my grandfather shows him in military uniform with long leather boots. He is proud and upright, eyes bright with a quiet confidence. He remained confident till the end.

Only a few other photographs from those years have survived, hidden by distant members of the family who escaped to Russia at the start of the war, and retrieved later as precious relics. That is all that remains: there are no other photos, no letters handwritten on thin paper, no leather-bound books, no items of clothing, no lace collars or furs, no antique jewellery, no silver candlesticks.

I feel an ache of sorrow as Auntie tries to recreate her lost world with so few props to show me. The stories jump backwards and forwards in time, and tiny details are interspersed with hugely tragic events. There is little self-pity in her accounts, but I sense a driving urgency to communicate, after so many years of silence, all the stories and anecdotes she remembers.

17

Janka: We had to make our way to Genoa, in Italy, where we were to board a Greek ship, the *Cyrenia*. When we arrived at the ship, I found I had to sleep in the women's quarters with my child, while my husband was put with the men. The thought of sleeping in crowded bunks again, surrounded by others and separated from my husband, filled me with dread. I spoke French quite well by this time, and I went to the captain to ask him if it was possible to get a cabin for myself and my husband. I told him I had been in concentration camps and just wouldn't be able to sleep with so many people around me. He felt sorry for me and gave me a cabin in first class, as this was the only one available. Not only did we have two beds to ourselves, but one for our little boy as well.

The journey was long and difficult, as I was often sick and couldn't eat the greasy food. Nor could I stand being in the ship's kitchen with the other women, preparing food for our children, so I was happy to let my husband look after Louis. Mostly he was fed mashed potatoes and pineapple, but he was one of the few children not to be sick. Meanwhile I lay on my bunk feeling weak and exhausted most of the time, though when there was a party on I seemed to recover my energy and enjoyed having a good time with many of the friends I had made on board ship.

We were happy to arrive in Australia. The ship sailed down the west coast of the continent to Fremantle, and then across the Great Australian Bight towards Melbourne. We were met by our relatives, and they arranged a room for us in a double-storey red-brick boarding house in North

Melbourne near the Queen Victoria Market. We had a single room on the upper floor. There was no stove so I had to cook on a small burner. We had to go downstairs for water and the toilet. I washed my son in an enamel bowl after carrying the water up the stairs and heating it over the burner. Józek found it very difficult to get work. I missed my sister and began to feel very depressed, wondering if we'd made the right decision. With a new country and a new language, it was a hard time for us.

Hela: Janka wrote to us regularly from Australia. At first her letters told us to stay where we were in Paris, as life was so difficult in Australia. But eventually we received a postcard showing a place called St Kilda, where sunlight sparkled on a calm sea fringed by golden sand and waving palm trees. This scene seemed wonderfully exotic to my eyes. I had hardly ever seen the sea, having lived all my childhood in southern Poland, and then in Paris. My first picture of Australia, then, was of a strange but exciting place. I looked often at that postcard and longed to travel there. I desperately wanted to see my sister again.

Janka: We lived for about half a year in this small rented room in North Melbourne, then decided to try to find a place of our own. Józek still had the diamond, our only valuable possession, so he sold it for four hundred pounds. This was now all the money we had in the world. We started looking for a home, and found a rambling old five-roomed red-brick house on a large block of land in Glenhuntly Road, Caulfield. Hela and Poldek were still in Paris. I wrote telling them about the house and encouraging them to join us, as there was room for all of us.

They were keen to come to Australia, to be with us. They gave up their apartment in Paris, managing to repay the money to the cousin, Schneider, who had lent it to us. We took two mortgages over the Caulfield property, knowing that when my brother-in-law arrived he would help to pay it off. Our estate agent told us he wouldn't like to be in our shoes, because we were so heavily committed, but my husband now had a job in a jewellery workshop with a man called Grainger and he was confident of the future.

Hela: My first view of the sea was at Genoa. We left in October 1949 and boarded the Greek ship *Cyrenia*, the same ship my sister had gone on. The sea journey took about six weeks. Many people around me were sick but I was a good traveller. Most of those on board were Jewish refugees like us. No one talked about the past. I only thought about each day as it came, never tiring of watching the sunrise, the dark-green waves, and the huge expanse all around us as we travelled slowly away from Europe. With each day I felt a growing sense of peace and anticipation. I concentrated on how to feed my baby, and on spending some time with Poldek.

The women had separate quarters on the lower deck. I shared a cabin with a Mrs Jacobs, who was pregnant, and several other women. There were six to a cabin and most of us had small children who slept in our bunks. Renia Trajstman had her son Albert, little Bronia Rosencwajg was cuddled by her mother, while Basia Szenkel looked after her boy Piotruś. Meanwhile Poldek was in the men's quarters. There were other survivors making this long strange journey with us: my mother's cousin Hela Neiger with her husband and son (who had spent the war years in Russia), and the whole Gescheit family.

I enjoyed going to the dining-room, trying out the Greek food. One of the officers on board liked me very much and helped to take care of the baby. He flirted with me, and organised special food for my daughter. He was very kind to us. When we stopped at Aden we were surrounded by little boats selling all kinds of goods. We didn't have a lot a money but we bought a few things, like a leather foot-cushion and a pink embroidered Chinese dressing-gown which seemed to me the height of luxury.

Poldek had his accordion and often played to entertain the passengers. One of the women, Renia, felt fine when she was dancing; the rest of the time she spent in her cabin being sick. Her husband would come to Poldek and ask him to play for a while so that she would feel better. Maybe it had something to do with balance; when she was moving she felt well. Only the last section of the journey, from Fremantle to Melbourne, was rough. Yet even at that time I wasn't sick.

We arrived at Port Melbourne in December 1949 and were met by Janka and Józek. I was overjoyed to be with my sister again. We hugged and laughed and cried, unable to believe this day had come. We admired each other's child, and kissed again. Our husbands also embraced briefly, then set about organising the journey home. Janka and Józek took us and our luggage in a taxi, and proudly showed us our new house. It seemed huge! Poldek's first words were, 'Look at all this space! You could ride a bicycle in here!'

We arrived with nothing: no furniture, no household items, no money. The only thing I had brought from Paris was a little *moulinette*, a mincing machine to prepare food for my daughter. We moved in and Poldek began to work, playing in nightclubs, so that he could pay towards the house. This was a large Queen Anne–style building with an ornate terracotta roof, a veranda paved with coloured tiles, and white window-frames. There was a white picket fence and a large garden front and back. Apple trees, quince trees, flowering almonds and roses flourished in great profusion. There was a little orange tree whose perfume drifted through the whole house in the warm evenings when it was in blossom. Everything was overgrown, but as we started to clear it I discovered a love for working in the garden, planting things and making them grow. I dug my hands into the rich soil and felt enormous gratitude. We started a vegetable plot where we grew tomatoes, something that was very exotic for us. I watched the tomatoes turn from little green marbles to hot, heavy globes that took on a rich strong red colour as they grew larger. The sun and the light and the space seemed incredible.

There are fields and forests and thickets of thorns stretching as far as the eye can see. At least that's how the garden seems to me. Louis and I gallop through the fields on our white horses, wearing feathers in our hair which my mother plucked from chickens the day before. Or we crawl along on our bellies through the long, unmown grass beyond the back shed to escape from dragons. The blackberry patch behind the fruit trees is a forbidden area, wild and untameable. It is impossible to penetrate, and at its centre lies Sleeping Beauty, waiting for her prince. We also know we must stay away from the vegetable patch.

We gallop around wildly, laughing and shouting. As the peals of laughter get louder, one of our parents comes outside and warns: 'It will finish up in tears.'

I soon learn to have self-control, and not to be too frivolous or joyful.

Hela: For a long time we couldn't afford furniture, so we sat on wooden packing-cases covered with towels. We couldn't even afford a bed: we bought a mattress which we placed on the floor.

But there was plenty of space for the children to play, and for the first time in many years I started to relax and enjoy life. I discovered I had abundant energy and could tackle, with equal enthusiasm, cooking, scrubbing, baking, washing, and travelling to the city for English lessons. Physically I felt very strong.

Very soon after our arrival I went to work. Janka was happy to stay at home and mind the children. At first I worked for Mrs Benz, the sister-in-law of Mr Grainger (Józek's boss). She had a house in the suburb of Windsor, with a workshop where we sewed lingerie. It was my first experience with an electric sewing-machine. I had no idea of the words for the simplest things, like needle or thread.

After a few months I heard about a clothing factory run by a man called Felix Ash. Having established himself in Australia after the war, he understood what it was like to struggle in a new country. He employed many of the refugees from Europe and was always willing to help newcomers.

Later I sewed leather belts at home, to earn some extra money. Life was not easy, although it was a time of great opportunity and some people made fortunes very quickly. Poldek was not willing to risk investing our hard-won earnings, and we missed out on chances to perhaps become wealthier. But it was very hard to think about the future; living each day was what was important.

My lack of English was a problem. One day I went to the milk bar over the road to buy some milk and bread, and to ask whether I could put a notice in their window to advertise a pram for sale. More by sign language than words, I tried to get the blond woman behind the counter to understand what I wanted. She wiped her hands on her apron and shook her head, saying words I didn't understand. But I realised she would not be able to help me. I said it didn't matter, picked up my shopping and turned to leave. The lady kept calling out and explaining, and I kept repeating the phrase I had learnt: 'Doesn't matter, doesn't matter!' Only when I got home did I remember that I hadn't paid for the bread and milk. That was what she had been trying to tell me!

I am surrounded by many other children, who shout and chase each other or stand around. It is my first day of school. We are herded into a large yard while someone with a loudspeaker shouts directions. I can't understand the words. Everything sounds so foreign.

As names are called, small groups are taken away by adults. I find myself with several other children being led by a female teacher into a classroom. We settle into our allocated seats and she starts to speak. She has a pleasant voice and smiles occasionally, but I don't understand what she is saying. I have learnt a few words of English at kindergarten but my parents only speak to me in Polish.

Several times I see children put up their hand and ask if they can go to the lemon tree. The lemon tree? I wonder what is so special about it. I imagine a tree in the centre of the courtyard, loaded with fruit and perhaps lollies or presents. I too would like to see the lemon tree, and ask for my turn. An older child takes me by the hand out of the classroom, down a long corridor, and into a place smelling of disinfectant.

Janka: Our house had wooden floors, which I had to scrub on my knees, and the stove had to be frequently filled with coal; but we managed. Together we bought an ice-chest which we had to keep stocked with ice to keep the food cold in Melbourne's hot summer weather. What I hated most was the sticky flypapers we had to hang to deal with the ever-present flies that always found their way into the kitchen.

We didn't have much, but a few things were important to me. In our home in Kraków before the war we had always had silver cutlery, which we were able to bring with us to the ghetto. After the war, having silver cutlery became meaningful again. Somehow it was a symbol of human dignity. Anytime you came into my kitchen, you would find in the drawers no stainless-steel spoons or any other metal; only silver.

Hela: Being preoccupied with personal existence, with trying to earn money, with cooking, eating and caring for our children, left little time for philosophising or trying to make sense of the past. We had to protect them from the horrors of those years. They were lucky to live in a beautiful country, with fresh air, good food and freedom from persecution. There was no time for grieving. I had to come to terms with a new foreign language, English, and a new way of life. I had to learn where to shop, how to ask for the right cuts of meat, how to budget on our meagre income. My life was filled with the details of daily living, and I fell easily into a deep sleep at the end of each day.

∽

My mother is more reluctant to speak. 'I don't remember much,' she tells me. 'It was so long ago, it's as if it happened to someone else.' And I know that this is the way she has protected herself for all these years. In her early seventies, she is still lively and active, although in recent times she appears to have shrunk a little, and has trouble walking.

She has worked hard to keep the family together, and to keep the peace when emotions are on the verge of exploding. She has shown enormous strength and persistence despite all the difficulties. The effort is visible in the wrinkles on her soft cheeks and around her mouth, but her brown eyes are bright.

She says she doesn't remember, and yet, when the memories begin to flow, she astounds me with her recollection of smells and sounds, and the splashes of colour that make her stories come alive. I have felt her unspoken pain all my life, and I know the time has come when I must show her I'm strong enough to hear her stories without falling apart; I have to convince her that her pain will not destroy me and it is safe to share it. Again and again, when some memory pierces her defences and tears fill her eyes, she starts to apologise for upsetting me. Again and again, I reassure her that it's all right, that I am strong enough to cope, that she does not have to feel ashamed of her natural responses. I feel awed at times in her presence, listening to her recreate some fragment of experience that has lain dormant all these years, an experience that emerges now, fresh and immediate, full of emotion, as if there had never before been time to deal with it adequately, to grieve, to remember. My mother's accounts are often disjointed, abbreviated, shreds that veer away from the painful reality. But at other times they are laid out before me, complete and pulsating with life, precious jewels that I must handle very carefully.

I listen to both of the women at different times, and spend months making links between their stories. Gradually a whole lost world begins to emerge, vital, full of real people, occupying the spaces that once seemed so empty. The relatives they speak of are all gone now, but I begin to have an unfolding sense of who I am and where I come from. I start to understand the sources of my own confusion and anxiety. I hear from the two sisters of the

245

anguish and pain in their lives, of the suffering they endured. But I also hear of the love and the laughter and the urge to live which gave them the will to survive and the faith to create new life. I am filled with overwhelming gratitude.

18

Hela: A regular rhythm was established in our lives. In the weekends we went on picnics together with groups of friends who had arrived, like us, as refugees after the war. I was amazed to see black swans for the first time; in Poland the swans were always white. I missed the soft greenness of the Polish countryside and found the flies annoying, but I was happy to be among friends. We had each suffered loss and deprivation and had confronted the horror of the Holocaust, so we were joined by a silent bond. But now we were desperate to put all that behind us, we were hungry for joy.

Groups of families would meet at a particular picnic spot in Sherbrooke Forest where the bark crackled underfoot and brightly coloured rosellas swooped in the high treetops. We heard the happy shouts of children in the crisp eucalyptus-laden air and smelled the smoke of other families' barbecues. There we were, spread out on rugs to play cards, or to have a nap. Sometimes we listened to Janeczka, a pretty blond-haired friend, singing old songs in Polish full of sentiment and passion . . .

Or else, on hot January mornings we would pile into the car with umbrellas and rubber tyres for a day at Seaford beach, where the water was deep and cold but the sand held the heat of the brilliant sun above. We found our friends gathered in the hot still air beneath the tea-trees. Loads of food were spread out and shared, and then we sent the children off to play while we told jokes and laughed uproariously. We spoke the same language and knew the same songs. These were our golden days.

After the picnics or trips into the hills, we usually finished up at Hanka's place. Our friend Hanka Wachs, who had arrived in Australia before the war, was very welcoming and always had an open house. We ate our fill and continued to enjoy ourselves long after darkness had fallen. No one wanted to go home.

Early in the morning, before anyone else is awake, I creep out of bed in my pyjamas, not bothering to put on slippers, and go to wake Louis. Together we go into the lounge-room to survey the evidence of the merriment of the night before.

Our parents must have fallen into bed as soon as the last guests left in the early hours of the morning. Overflowing ashtrays and overturned glasses cover every flat surface. The smell of cigarette butts makes me wrinkle my nose, but it doesn't deter me. We start to examine the leftovers, and to sample whatever looks appealing. First I take a round dark chocolate, like a penny, and taste its sweetness. I pick up a red pickled onion that's been left on a tooth-pick and bite on it while my eyes rove around the littered table. Louis is busy examining the little glasses strewn around, some empty but some containing mysterious coloured liquids. We take turns in tasting thick yellow egg-cognac, which you have to push your tongue into the bottom of the glass to taste. When that's empty we try some ruby-red cherry brandy. The tingle and the sweetness, the forbidden flavours, are better than anything I've ever tasted. Around the table I go, grabbing a salty biscuit, another chocolate, a cube of cheese, a piece of apple cake. We speak only in whispers, but most of the time no words are needed. We point, touch and giggle quietly.

Eventually, feeling satisfied and slightly peculiar, I crawl back into bed. If my mother ever notices that I don't eat much breakfast, or that the liqueur glasses are mysteriously clean, she doesn't mention it.

Hela: Some of the people we met who had come to Australia before the war were astonished that, after all we had been through, we could be so desperate to find happiness. We enjoyed entertaining, eating, singing and dancing. Poldek was always ready to unpack his accordion and play all the well-known tunes. Food was not a problem; we were happy when people visited and everyone helped to cook whatever was available. Often a loaf of bread was put on the table and torn apart before there was time to slice it. We'd sing and joke as if all our lives we had been waiting for these moments. We didn't talk about the past; we were too busy living our daily lives.

Janka: Our two families seldom quarrelled. Józek set up a jewellery workshop in the city and Poldek continued to work as a musician at nightclubs and parties. My husband and my brother-in-law were totally different in nature and personality: Józek was quiet and steady, while Poldek was much more outgoing and excitable. Yet we lived together for many years in harmony. We shared one purse, brought up the children together, and rarely had arguments.

Hela: We no longer lit candles on Friday nights, and we didn't go to synagogue even on the High Holydays. We didn't keep kosher and didn't fast on Yom Kippur. I had fasted enough during those long years of suffering. All of that seemed to belong to an era now buried in the past. But we could never forget that we were Jewish. When the children were young we sent them to a Jewish day-school, and like most of our friends we continued to be part of the Jewish community. At Passover we had a big *seder* and observed some of the traditions, mainly for the sake of the children while they were growing up.

We were still living together at this time in the large old house in Glenhuntly Road. I told my daughter fairy stories and read Polish poetry to her. In our large backyard I would spread a rug on the springy green grass and lie in the warm sun while Anna sat beside me. All the verses I had memorised as a child came back to me, and with my eyes closed, holding her hand, I recited to her stories of hope and disappointment, of love and laughter.

One hot day I was in our garden tending the tomato vines we had planted in rows beside the shed in the backyard.

Anna was playing beside me. I was three months pregnant and felt full of energy. As I tied the growing stems to wooden stakes and pinched the tips of the plants to make them grow bushier, I was aware of the smell of the leaves wafting up to me. The smell became stronger and stronger, and I began to feel a haze of heat enveloping me as the sun grew black. I started to sweat and to feel a cramping in my abdomen, so I went inside to lie down. The smell of the tomato plants was on my hands and filled the darkened room. The cramps became stronger and I realised I had started bleeding. Janka and Józek were out for the day and Poldek was asleep, so I called frantically to Anna to wake him. He took one look at me and immediately rang for a taxi. He grabbed Anna by the hand and sat her on his knee while I lay in the back seat, groaning all the way to the hospital. I was rushed off on a trolley to the emergency room, but they couldn't prevent my miscarriage.

Several years later I fell pregnant again, and this time there were no complications. I grew big and contented, and happily shopped for a cradle, a pram and lots of nappies! Frances Marie (named after Poldek's mother, Freydele) was born on 1 December 1952. This time I had a baby in comfort and style; I wore silk pyjamas, and Poldek brought me flowers straight away. Margaret Coles maternity hospital seemed like real luxury compared to what I had experienced in Paris. I lay back on my pillow, nursing my little daughter and admiring all the flowers that surrounded me. I felt a deep contentment.

After her arrival we still happily shared the one house for a while, until we decided each couple should look for a house of their own. What we chose was a semi-detached pair divided by a common wall, in Brighton, a seaside suburb. This meant each family now had its own home, but Janka and I could continue to live side by side, sharing our daily lives almost as before. We had still not got used to the lazy-sounding language with its impossible *th* sound; the smiling friendly people, mad about sport and blissfully unaware of the horrors far away; the food, too sweet, too sour, too salty.

Even the light was strange: harsh and burning in the hot summers, coming and going unpredictably throughout the seasons. The only constant was our family, each member a focus for concern, anxiety and overflowing love.

I always feel as if I have two mothers and two fathers. When I am small, while my mother goes to work each morning it is Auntie who dresses me for school, plaits my hair and makes my lunch. Her hands are gentle and familiar.

Even when we no longer live in the same house as Auntie, our lives continue to be intertwined. A small gate in the fence between the two houses means that I can slip in and out whenever I like. Auntie helps me with my homework and sews hats for my dolls. She teaches me to arrange flowers and recognise the names of plants. On Sunday mornings I am usually next door for a cuddle in Auntie's wide bed, followed by a breakfast of challah and honey, then morning 'exercises'. She is a great believer in learning correct posture and deep breathing. She also believes you have to have 'sunny thoughts' and be positive. These messages are repeated often as an antidote to depression or sadness. Her struggle to live with the memories of the past is unknown to me. I feel only her enveloping love and warmth.

Janka: We corresponded regularly with our brother Kuba, who continued to live in Poland. After we had been in Australia for some time we got a letter from his wife, Hanka, asking if we could arrange for them to emigrate. Remembering the past, and aware of my bitter feelings towards him, I really didn't want them to come, but Hela was much closer to Kuba. It was she who organised the papers for them, saying that he was family after all and this was more important than anything.

When they arrived by ship with two small children, we met them at the dock and were introduced to a pretty round-faced woman, who began to complain from the moment they left the ship. We had arranged accommodation for them, and some furniture. We tried to help them, but Kuba's wife was very difficult and he allowed himself to be influenced by her.

251

Maybe, in the early days, if our parents had confronted Kuba with his bad behaviour instead of always covering up . . . Maybe if Kuba had seen somebody and got some help, he might have turned out differently. But sixty or seventy years ago this wasn't fashionable.

Despite everything he was very clever, and probably that's what helped him to survive. During the war he was able to help a lot of people because of his position. But even in Melbourne there were survivors who remembered that he had been an OD, and recalled some of the bad things he had done. His past never left him.

In the mid-1960s Kuba suffered a stroke which left him paralysed and unable to speak, except to say 'La la la . . .' His frustration and pain stayed with him until he died, a few years later.

Hela: For many years I tried to block out the past. Naively I believed that if the past was never spoken about, it would disappear. Only in my nightmares did its horror surface. In daylight hours I made a conscious decision to turn away any memories or thoughts that were painful. I refused to speak about the past, or even to think about it.

When Thomas Keneally came to interview my husband for the book he was writing about Schindler, I went outside into the garden. I preferred not to speak to him, even though he was very kind and understanding; I just didn't want to talk.

I was always a nervous person, but I didn't want to accept that the anxiety and 'nerves' I suffered from were a result of my past. I had to get on with daily living. From the time I arrived in Australia, I was continually prescribed Valium and Librium, and I had to take the pills in order to face each new day. When I suffered from side-effects, different medication was prescribed. No one suggested that I needed therapy or counselling, and anyway, in those days only crazy people went to psychiatrists! I was determined to suppress any bad feelings that intruded into my daily life and to live normally. I tried to shut out that period of terror. I never spoke of it to my children. After all, what could I say?

How could I tell them?

We are on holidays, the two families as usual, at Lakes Entrance, some hours' drive from Melbourne. This should be a relaxing and happy time, but the adults are tense and often speak in whispers. They listen constantly to the news. I hear that there are Soviet missiles in Cuba, which are causing problems. I have no idea where Cuba is. The United States and the Soviet Union are threatening each other. Messages are exchanged between Kennedy and Khrushchev, filled with intense antagonism. No one speaks directly to me, but I sense the continuing anxiety and overhear my parents talking with Auntie and Uncle about their fears. The word 'war' is mentioned. I don't ask questions, but I pray at night that there won't be a war. I'm overcome by a feeling of panic and there is a tightness in my chest for days.

After a tense week the threat of war recedes. My parents begin to relax and my world falls back into place.

Hela: My children had happy and protected childhoods, with none of the traumas of my own early days. I read recently that old age is not winter time, it is harvest time. I now have my children and grandchildren living close by; Hitler is dead and we are alive, and that is the ultimate victory. I know it's important to live now, to appreciate the good things. I read books and do yoga, and know all the right paths to follow. I can advise other people, but when it comes to myself I still find it difficult. I continue to be nervous and get upset easily. I'm often sad and scared—those feelings stay with me.

I still think about dying every day. When my daughter Anna was pregnant with her first child, I prayed to live long enough to see my first grandchild. Now when I check the death columns in the weekly Jewish newspaper, I look to see if the deceased had grandchildren. Then I am comforted: at least they lived long enough to see a grandchild born. There are so many visits to the cemetery now. I am becoming more used to it, more accepting. But even in those early days in Paris, the thought of death was a constant companion.

And when I hear the world news I start to feel bitter. I thought that after all we and millions of others went through, the tragedy of war would be a lesson for the whole world. I thought the worst was over and people would no longer kill each other. Humans never learn.

Janka: Little daily rituals always remind me that I have survived, and that life is good. Every morning when I drink my orange juice I remember the bitter metallic taste of the water from the train engine at Magdeburg, and I thank God for allowing me to enjoy orange juice whenever I feel like it. When I have a shower, even these days, I take five or ten minutes more than necessary, because I am so grateful that I have hot water to wash in. When we were in Auschwitz we never knew whether water would come from the showers, or gas. Sometimes there were so many girls trying to shower at once that you had to fight to claim a tiny bit of water to wash in, and a scrap of dripping rag to use as a towel. I dry myself now on a thick warm towel, and I remember.

Hela: I never imagined that I would want to visit my homeland again, but about forty years after the war I started to think about what was so much a part of me, despite the painful memories and the distance of miles and time. I decided I wanted to see Poland again.

When Poldek and I arrived there, I was excited and frightened at the same time. Kraków itself had not changed all that much. The beautiful old buildings had survived and peasant women with shawls over their heads still walked the streets. I kept expecting to meet old friends, to see familiar places. I'd turn a corner and know exactly what would be there. And yet, there was a strangeness about everything, a heaviness, as if the burden of the past had spread a grey blanket over the whole city.

We met up with a relative, Stasiu Kaczorowski, who had kept in touch by letter over the years. He was the son of a female cousin of ours who had disgraced the family by marrying a Polish count and converting to Catholicism. Everyone disowned her, except our mother. Her son still had the title of a nobleman. He was very nice to us and took us to Tonie, the country town we had moved to at the start of the war. The peasant huts and the unmade roads had disappeared and Tonie was now only a suburb of Kraków. I began to wonder if my friend from long ago, Tadeusz Pokusa, could possibly still live in these parts. He was the blond, blue-eyed boy who had been my first love and had risked his life to bring food to us in the ghetto. Kaczorowski went from one house to another, asking if anyone knew him. He found out where a cousin of Tadeusz still lived. So we went there, and were given the address in Kraków where Tadeusz could be found.

I felt both elated and apprehensive. Off we went, into a dirty, crowded district of Kraków, with rubbish cans overflowing and children shouting. We found the address and went up a dark and dingy staircase. After knocking at the wooden door several times, we saw it slowly open, and there stood Tadeusz, with his big blue eyes moving from one face to the other. Of course he was old, and had put on weight, but I could still recognise that look. He enquired politely if he could help us. We announced who we were, and for several moments shadows flitted across his eyes. He looked again at Poldek, and said at last, 'So this is the musician who took you from me!' The memories came flooding back to me, his sparkling blue eyes, the cornflowers and poppies he brought me, the romantic times we had spent together in the countryside.

We were ushered into a small room smelling of cabbage. I saw the poverty he and his wife lived in, and was overcome by emotion. He offered us a cup of tea, but we didn't stay long. What, after all, could we say to each other? He told me that Romek, the dark-eyed boy who had been in love with me, had perished. Originally Romek had been in the ghetto with us, but his whole family had been taken away and were never heard of again. He was still courting me in the ghetto after I had already met Poldek. That was a final reminder of the brief, lost days of my girlhood romances.

When we left their home Poldek and I went shopping in the marketplace, to buy the finest food we could find: sweet oranges, a large leg of ham, chocolates and cakes. We packed them into a basket and sent them to Tadeusz, in gratitude for his kindness all those years ago.

∾

I dream that my shoulders are full of stones. Actually, the right shoulder is filled with smooth grey pebbles that grate as they move against each other. I try to break them but they are too hard, so instead I scoop them out and place them in front of me. Some are pale grey, some darker, others almost black. I handle them carefully, and notice a strange writing scratched on their surfaces, but I can't understand what it says. I pile the pebbles together and listen. 'Wait,' they tell me.

My left shoulder feels cold, solid. Inside, there is a rock, polished and hard. I reach in carefully and remove it. If only I could find the correct angle, I would be able to smash this rock. As I watch it, touch it and turn it over in my hands, it changes from a uniform grey to something more shimmery. It is almost translucent. One blow and it would shatter into a thousand shards. I take a deep breath and strike it. It crumbles. The pieces are like glass, but fading, fading and disintegrating, blowing away. I catch on to one long pointed shard and hold it in front of me. It reflects the light. I hold it up to my eye, and look through its translucency at the pile of pebbles with the strange inscriptions. 'These are not yours,' I read. 'You have carried the burden for a long time. Soon the moment will come to return them to their rightful owners. Wait. The time is coming.'

The next day, at the cemetery, I place three smooth pebbles from my pocket on Auntie's grave: white, grey and black.

Epilogue

As I traced the history of my family I felt it receding slowly, steadily, with the ticking of the clock, moving further and further away from me. At the same time I realised that I and everything around me was also slipping slowly backwards, so that my world will be history to my children, my grandchildren, my great-grandchildren whom I can't even begin to imagine. At best, I will be to them like the pages of an old book: smelling dusty, perhaps containing a few things of interest, if one bothers to search. But unless someone makes the effort it will be no more than black squiggles on a page, page after page, closed tight, locked away from light, from recognition, from understanding. At worst, this strong palpable 'now' will be irretrievable. So I continued my search with a sense of urgency tinged with despair.

There was a time when the world had not heard of the word 'Holocaust'; when our parents, growing up in Europe, believed the 'Great War' was the last war the world would ever see; when they still believed in the general goodness of man and that evil was an aberration which, however horrible, had limits. We, growing up after World War II, can have no such illusions.

In recent years groups have been formed around the world and on the Internet for the children and grandchildren of Holocaust survivors. I belong to one such group. I have found, at these gatherings, that a certain uneasiness is triggered whenever the discussion turns to whose pain it is. At one meeting, a woman, a newcomer to the group, stood up and said we have a choice, we don't need to take on our parents' pain and distress. We are indulging ourselves, wallowing in self-pity when really the pain is theirs.

I thought about what she had said. I found her words disturbing, accusing. The responses from others in the room echoed my feelings that we are inextricably linked to our parents' experiences. It is not a matter of choice.

I grew up with unacknowledged feelings of anxiety and bewilderment. I used to question my right to exist. I found it hard to permit myself to feel a whole range of emotions, to be heard, to validate my own feelings and my own reality. That was always the struggle; it was constantly fresh and real, like mourning a recent death. I have tried, as honestly as I can, to work through a dark, hidden part of myself which, though I've only come to understand it fairly recently, has been a familiar presence sitting behind my left shoulder, just out of sight, for all of my life. There were no words for my family's loss and the torment they had endured. Not when I was too young to understand; not later when they arrived in Australia and all the painful emotions had to be suppressed so that they could get on with their lives; not even after that, when they believed my young mind was fragile, impressionable, needing to be protected.

Indeed the world was a dangerous and cruel place from which my family had to protect me. Thus the old patterns emerged: 'Don't be upset . . . don't cry . . . there's nothing to worry about . . . you'll get over it . . . it's not important . . . be happy.' They're the kinds of messages I had all my life, and they led me to believe I didn't have a right to have feelings of sadness, loss, regret—I was only 'acceptable' when I was happy, successful, achieving. Any negative feelings were too close to my family's pain, triggering too much personal anguish ever to be acknowledged.

Now as my mother gets older I realise that, as much as she has been protecting me, I too have been protecting her. I have watched her become more frail physically and have shared her emotional pain. I'm always conscious of how much her anguish and suffering still affect me. The urge to atone, to console, to make her feel better is always with me.

I know I can never make up for the suffering she has gone through in her life, yet I keep trying. But I have learnt, through writing this book, that the people of my childhood were resilient and vital, with enormous courage to face each new day, each new challenge. They may have been scarred, but they were not defeated. They had survived! And now, as I hold my newborn granddaughter in my arms, I begin to understand the true significance of survival.

Acknowledgements

A number of people were very helpful and encouraging to me in the course of this project. Their assistance is greatly appreciated.

I would like to thank Vivienne Ulman, writer and reviewer, for reading an early version of the manuscript and giving me reassurance to further explore and articulate my own responses; Dr George Halasz, child and adolescent psychiatrist and himself a son of Holocaust survivor parents, who encouraged me to continue writing and understood the struggle and significance of what I was trying to do; and Guy Blay, my husband, who has been caring and supportive during the long writing process, and whose insights and suggestions I always value.

My thanks also to Marysia Nick (Sperling) in Tel Aviv and Mila Singer (Braw) in Melbourne for providing valuable information about my aunt's experiences in Płaszów and Auschwitz; and to Maurice Daniels, another survivor of Płaszów, for his readiness to be consulted on particular facts and details.

I wish to express my sincere appreciation to Alex Skovron for his discerning and sensitive editing. His help in structuring the book, clarifying meaning, offering suggestions and refining the text was invaluable. Working together was an enjoyable and enlightening experience.

To all at Hale & Iremonger, thank you for having the faith and vision to see the book through to its completion, and for offering me the opportunity to reach a wide readership.

And finally, with deep gratitude I thank my mother, Hela Rosner, and my late aunt, Janka Gross, for their willingness to confront the pain of the past and share with me their life's experiences.

A guide to Polish pronunciation

Words and names in Polish are pronounced according to consistent rules. The following is a selective and highly simplified guide to the principal sounds. The stress (') in Polish almost always falls on the second-last syllable.

The six basic oral vowel sounds are:

a as in *art*	Janka ('Yan-ka)
e as in *men*	Hela ('Hell-a)
i as in *deep*	Kogutki (Ko-'goot-kee)
o as in *pot*	Zawoja (Za-'vo-ya)
u and **ó** as in *book*	Józek ('Yoo-zek)
y as in *tin*	Maryna (Ma-'ri-na)

There are two other vowel sounds, often nasal or with a nasal consonant added:

ą is close to *o*	trąba ('trom-ba)
ę is close to *e*	Węgierska (Ven-'gier-ska)

Most consonants are pronounced rather as in English, but note the following:

c reads *ts* (as in *blitz*)	Mariacki (Marr-'yats-kee)
j reads *y* (as in *yes*)	Jelenia Góra (Ye-'le-nia 'Goo-ra)
w reads *v* (as in *vat*)	Kraków ('Kra-koov)
ł reads *w* (as in *way*)	Płaszów ('Pwa-shoov)
ń (and **ni**) reads *ñ* (as in *onion*)	nitka ('neet-ka)

sz reads *sh* (as in *shut*)

cz reads *ch* (as in *chop*)

ch reads like Scots *ch* (as in *loch*)

rz and **ż** read *zh* (as in *measure*)

szczur ('shchoor)

Świczarczyk (Shvee-'char-chick)

Częstochowa (Chens-to-'ho-va)

Różyczka (Roo-'zhich-ka)

The following consonant sounds are more difficult to approximate in English:

ś (and **si**) is closest to *sh*

ć (and **ci**) is closest to *ch*

ź (and **zi**) is closest to *zh*

dź (and **dzi**) is closest to *dzh* or *dj*

Joasia (Yo-'a-shia)

rozmawiać (roz-'ma-viach)

Rózia ('Roo-zhia)

Łódź ('Woodzh)

Photograph: Danny Blay

Born in Paris in 1947, Anna emigrated with her parents to Melbourne in 1949. She is married with three grown-up sons and one grandchild. Her love of art, music and painting has been engendered in her three sons. Anna became an English and French teacher in 1985 and is now Head of LOTE (Languages Other Than English) in a private school in Melbourne.

She visited Kraków and Auschwitz on her honeymoon, and is a member of Descendants of the Shoah Inc., a second-generation group that meets regularly in Melbourne to discuss their parents' relationship to the Holocaust, and their relationships with their parents.

Her first book, *If All the Seas were Ink ...* (1993), was about her uncle Jozef Gross, one of the group saved by Schindler.